WORKING WITH SDI 2.0

The complete guide to understanding motives, managing conflict, and coaching strengths at work

TIM SCUDDER

Core Strengths, Inc.
7668 El Camino Real
Suite 104716
Carlsbad, CA 92009 USA

www.corestrengths.com

Cataloging-In-Publication Data

Scudder, Tim.
Working with SDI 2.0: The complete guide to understanding motives, managing conflict, and coaching strengths at work / Tim Scudder
p. cm.
Includes index, notes, and bibliographical references.
ISBN: 978-1-932627-02-2
1. Interpersonal Relations. 2. Psychology. 3. Motivation. 4. Leadership.

Cover design by Josh Webb
Layout by Christine Birch and Josh Webb

Printed in China

3420ENUSV1.0

"Working with SDI 2.0 has been a game-changer for our leadership and development transformation. To understand others, we need to be aware of ourselves – our motives, strengths, how we manage conflict – so that we can optimize relationships to build trust faster and achieve results. The more we invest in our own self-discovery and exploration, the more fulfilled we are, which fuels effective relationships and ultimately leads to purposeful outcomes."

— Rae Kyriazis, Global Vice President Field Transformation & Readiness, SAP

"Working with SDI 2.0 is the ultimate handbook for building mutually rewarding and effective relationships. It's a comprehensive, yet easy-to-understand guide to self-awareness; one that will also boost your understanding and appreciation of the different personalities that surround you."

— Betsy N. Riley, M.A., Organization Development Manager, Disney Consumer Products

"SDI 2.0 is about creating a sense of hyper-awareness of what makes each of us unique – and how we can use understanding of our differences to work more productively with each other every day."

— Pete Baker, Global Head of Learning & Organisation Development, Maersk Line

"To be able to listen to oneself is a prerequisite for the ability to listen to others; to be at home with oneself is the necessary condition for relating oneself to others."

— Erich Fromm

Contents

PART 3: CONFLICT SEQUENCES

PART 4: STRENGTH DEPLOYMENT

PART 5: THEORY AND STATISTICS

How to Use This Book

When used with your SDI 2.0 results, the content of this book will help you make better choices, get better results, and improve relationships, whether they are at work, at home, with friends, or in your community.

It all starts with self-awareness, an understanding of who you are at your core. This leads to a deeper, more accurate understanding of others. That understanding leads to greater acceptance and appreciation of others, which in turn helps you build more effective, mutually rewarding, and sustainable relationships. You can also anticipate and prevent some of the unnecessary conflict that happens all too often in relationships, identify conflict more quickly when it does happen, and do a better job of managing it and bringing it to a productive resolution.

The bottom line? Working with the SDI 2.0 is all about improving your Relationship Intelligence – insight to adjust your perceptions and your approach to others, making interactions more effective and productive.

OVERVIEW

No book about relationships can take the place of learning in real situations, but it can be a useful guide and resource. Your learning is not limited to a classroom or an online platform. Learning happens every single day – if you let it.

This book reinforces and expands concepts from the Strength Deployment Inventory 2.0 (SDI). It is unlikely that you will read it straight through, from cover to cover. Instead, the book is a resource as you continue learning and as you continue to develop your interpersonal skills.

To get started, read Part 1: Introduction. This will help you solidify your understanding of key concepts and how these concepts connect to each other.

DISCOVER YOUR RESULTS

Part 2 describes each MVS in detail. You'll probably want to take a look at your own MVS first, and if your MVS dot is near the border of another MVS region on the triangle, take a look there, too. The first section of each MVS chapter is descriptive; reflect on this to build your self-awareness. The second section of each MVS chapter is advice about how to work with people who have that MVS. Read the advice for your own MVS; imagine that people are working with you as described here. Is this good advice about how to work with you? Follow the same process with your Conflict Sequence in Part 3.

THINKING ABOUT OTHERS

Read the detailed descriptions about other people's MVSs and Conflict Sequences, including suggestions about working more effectively with them and preventing conflict with them. If you want to think about people whose SDI results you don't know, take a look at *SDI 2.0 Results at a Glance;* make educated guesses based on your experiences and perceptions of them. Then read the detailed chapters to see if the fuller descriptions fit and to gain insight about working with them.

UNDERSTANDING STRENGTHS

You have access to many strengths that can help you improve your relationships, and you are not limited to your top strengths. But while it's easy to say, "Choose the right strength at the right time" or "Use the best tool for the job," it can be difficult to do so in real-time. This book helps you learn how to bring the right strength to your situations and relationships.

Part 4, *Strength Deployment,* helps you to make essential connections between strengths and motives. This provides insight into the underlying reasons that people do what they do. It also helps to anchor your strength choices in your core motives. However, strengths can be overdone. Therefore, this part of the book provides tips about recapturing strength from apparent weakness and preventing conflict by assuming productive and positive intent in others.

MAKE IT YOURS

Whenever you find something insightful or useful, make it easy to find later. Add notes and bookmarks. This is a book for you to use. Ideas aren't useful if you can't remember or find them. So make this book yours. For additional resources, videos, and collaboration tools, please go to CoreStrengths.com.

1 INTRODUCTION

Relationship Intelligence

It's been said that "It's not what you know, but who you know" that matters. That might be true for networking, but for sustainable relationships and improving your Relationship Intelligence, it's *what you know* about *who you know* that makes the difference.

Human relationships are connections between people that are built on a foundation of shared experiences, interactions, and expectations. Relationship Intelligence is insight for adjusting one's approach to make interactions more effective. When behavior is authentic and dialogue is open and clear, relationships accumulate positive shared experiences, which sets the stage for meaningful and attractive expectations for the future.

Every relationship has a past, present, and future. If two people don't have sufficient history together, it might be referred to as an acquaintance, not a relationship. And no matter how much history there is, when there is no shared expectation for the future, the relationship is over — although it could be renewed at some point.

Productive relationships typically have positive views of past experiences, productive present interactions, and optimistic expectations about a shared future. Poor relationships are the opposite: negative experiences have accumulated, and there is not much current hope for future improvement. Of course, most relationships have both good times and bad times; when the positive outweighs the negative, the relationship has a positive balance.

Any relationship, however, can be improved if we are clear about what a relationship actually is — an authentic connection between people based on shared experiences, present interactions, and future expectations. To improve relationships, insights from the SDI 2.0 can be applied in one or more of these three domains:

- **Recast the Past:** Perspective, or point of view, is a key element in any relationship. Learning new information or correcting faulty assumptions can change people's opinions about past experiences. SDI results help explain the underlying motives behind past interactions, including why conflict may have occurred and how it transpired. Seeing what people were really trying to do can clarify past experiences and help people to let go of limiting assumptions.
- **Master the Moment:** Being aware of people's motives, values, conflict triggers, and strengths provides essential insight for adjusting communication and behavior. Perhaps even more importantly, insight from the SDI improves the accuracy of interpersonal perception — like a decoding key to see, in real-time, the motives or intent behind people's behaviors. Today's interactions become tomorrow's past shared experiences.
- **Co-create the Future:** When people understand each other's motives, they have insight into what future activities or results will satisfy those motives. Collaboratively creating and communicating about a future that is attractive and rewarding to everyone involved is easier when everyone's motives are clearly shared and understood. When everyone can respond to "what's in it for me?" with an answer that is something they actually want, then their intrinsic motives will help propel them toward that future.

Overview of the SDI 2.0

The SDI 2.0 provides four views of a person. Two describe personality: the motivational traits that are fairly constant for people over time and across situations. The other two are behavioral and situated within the context of work.

1. The Motivational Value System (MVS) is part of core personality when people are at their best and feeling good about themselves. Part 2 of this book describes the MVS in detail.
2. The Conflict Sequence (CS) is also part of core personality, but it describes the way people's motives change when they are faced with conflict. Part 3 of this book describes the Conflict Sequence in detail.
3. The Strengths Portrait (SP) shows a set of 28 strengths, prioritized from most likely to use at work to least likely to use at work. Part 4 of this book describes the SP in detail, as well as how behavioral strengths are connected to people's motives.
4. The Overdone Strengths Portrait (OSP) shows the overdone, or nonproductive, versions of the 28 strengths, ranked from most likely to overdo at work to least likely to overdo at work. Part 4 of this book describes the OSP in detail, as well as how overdone strengths may limit people's effectiveness or trigger conflict in relationships.

For a comprehensive explanation of the SDI 2.0, refer to Section 5, *SDI 2.0 Methodology and Meaning.*

MOTIVES UNDER TWO CONDITIONS

The SDI describes motives under two conditions: 1) when things are going well and people feel good about themselves, and 2) when things are going wrong and people experience conflict. When things are going well, three primary motives work together as a system — the Motivational Value System (MVS). When people experience conflict, three primary motives work in sequence — the Conflict Sequence.

Table 1.1 *Motives and Colors In Two Conditions*[1]

SDI Color	When Things Are Going Well	When There Is Conflict
Blue	People	Accommodate
Red	Performance	Assert
Green	Process	Analyze

The SDI produces a set of three scores for motives under each condition, and these scores are used to determine the MVS and Conflict Sequence results for each person.

SDI 2.0 Results at a Glance

THE SDI TRIANGLE AND THE SDI ARROW

The first two views of a person, the Motivational Value System and Conflict Sequence, are presented together graphically as an arrow on the SDI Triangle. The triangle represents the three motives, and each person's results can be placed on the triangle to show the relative blend of the three motives for each person. The origin, or dot, of the arrow represents the blend of three motives when things are going well — the MVS. The arrowhead represents the progression of three motives during conflict — the Conflict Sequence (CS). A line connects the dot and arrowhead to indicate that they represent the same person.

Figure 1.1 *The SDI Triangle*

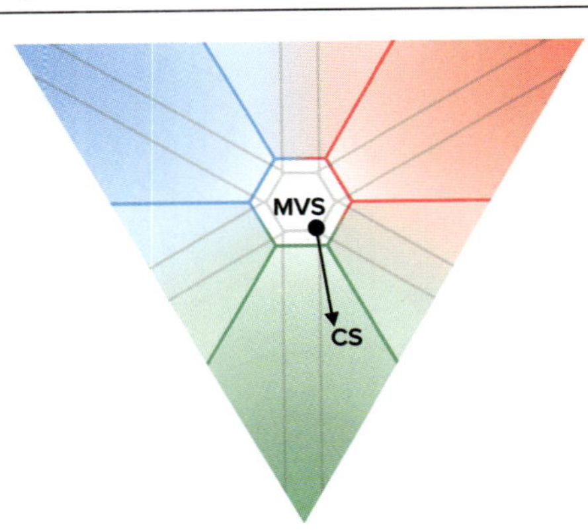

MOTIVATIONAL VALUE SYSTEMS

Each MVS result is displayed in one of seven regions of the SDI Triangle. These regions delineate seven personality types when things are going well. People with the same MVS type have a similar pattern of motives, but that does not mean they are exactly the same. There can be variation within types as shown by the MVS scores, which indicate the relative frequency of all three motives. Variation within types is also revealed by the Strengths Portrait; people with the same MVS may deploy their strengths in entirely different ways.

Figure 1.2 *The 7 Motivational Value Systems*

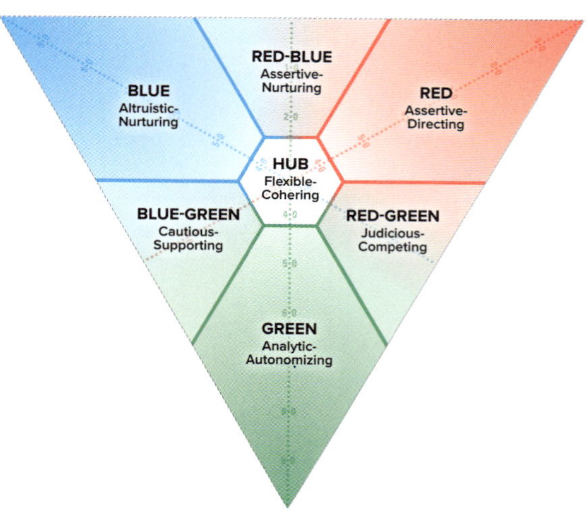

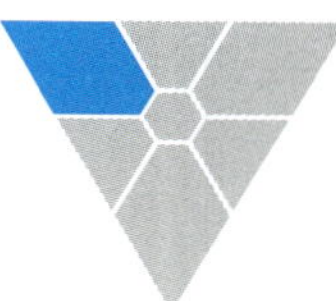

Blue: People who are motivated by the protection, growth, and welfare of others. They have a strong desire to help others who can genuinely benefit.

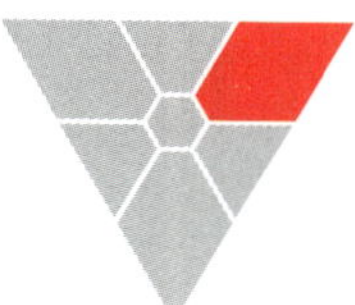

Red: People who are motivated by task accomplishment and achieving results. They have a strong desire to set goals, take decisive action, and claim earned rewards.

Green: People who are motivated by meaningful order and thinking things through. They have a strong desire to pursue independent interests, to be practical, and to be fair.

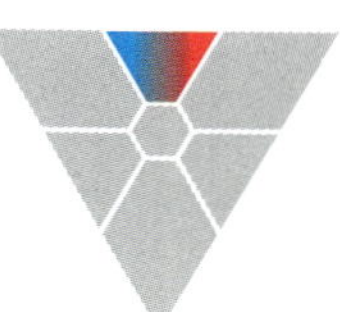

Red-Blue: People who are motivated by the maximum growth and development of others. They have a strong desire to direct, persuade, or lead others for the benefit of others.

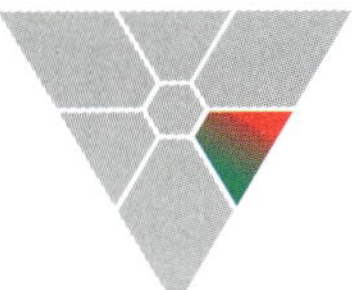

Red-Green: People who are motivated by intelligent assertiveness and fairness in competition. They have a strong desire to develop strategy and assess risks and opportunities.

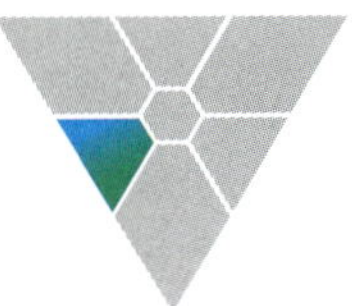

Blue-Green: People who are motivated by developing self-sufficiency in self and others. They have a strong desire to analyze the needs of others and to help others help themselves.

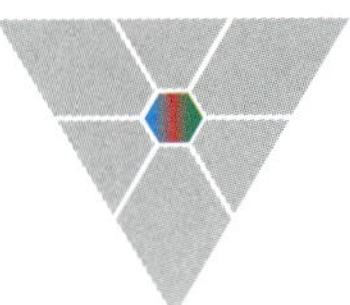

Hub: People who are motivated by flexibility and adapting to others or situations. They have a strong desire to collaborate with others and to remain open to different options and viewpoints.

CONFLICT SEQUENCES

Each Conflict Sequence result is displayed in one of 13 regions of the SDI Triangle. These regions delineate 13 personality types during conflict. People with the same type have a similar pattern of motives during conflict, but that does not mean they are exactly the same. Differences between people with the same Conflict Sequence are often revealed when they have different Motivational Value Systems, because efforts during conflict are directed at returning to the MVS. The Conflict Sequence descriptions in Part 3 present seven different "path-back to MVS" statements for each of the 13 Conflict Sequences.

Figure 1.3 *The 13 Conflict Sequences*

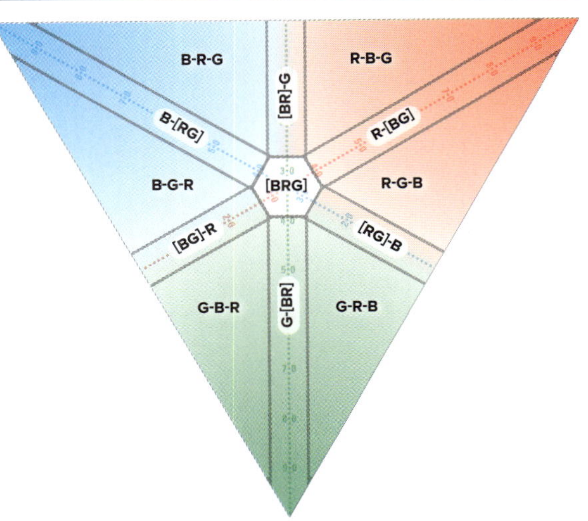

B-R-G: People who want to keep peace and harmony. If that does not work, they want to take a stand for their rights. If that does not work, they may feel compelled to withdraw as a last resort.

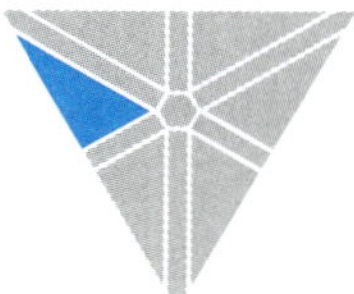

B-G-R: People who want to keep harmony and goodwill. If that does not work, they want to disengage and save what they can. If that does not work, they may feel compelled to fight, possibly in an explosive manner.

B-[RG]: People who want to keep harmony and accommodate the opposition. If that does not work, they want to make a choice based on what's best for everyone: to rely on logic and principle or to employ assertive strategies to prevent defeat.

R-B-G: People who want to challenge conflict directly. If that does not work, they want to restore or preserve harmony. If that does not work, they may feel compelled to withdraw from the situation or end the relationship.

R-G-B: People who want to prevail through competition. If that does not work, they want to use logic, reason, and rules. If that does not work, they may feel compelled to surrender as a last resort.

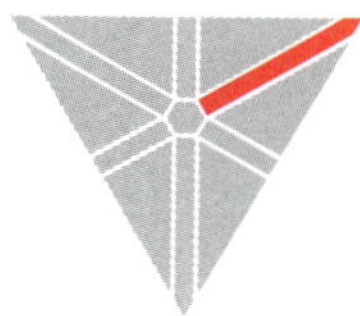

R-[BG]: People who want to assert their rights and win. If that does not work, they want to make a choice depending on what's better in the situation: to give in with conditions or to disengage and save what they can.

G-B-R: People who want to carefully examine the situation. If that does not work, they want to defer to other people in the interest of harmony. If that does not work, they may feel compelled to fight, possibly in an explosive manner.

G-R-B: People who want to analyze the situation logically. If that does not work, they want to forcefully press for a logical resolution. If that does not work and others have more power in the situation, they may surrender.

G-[BR]: People who want to maintain order and principles. If that does not work, they want to make a choice, depending on what's more reasonable in the situation: to give in with conditions or to forcefully engage.

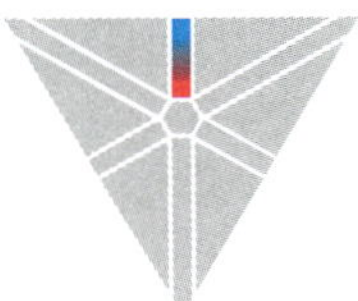

[BR]-G: People who want to press assertively to maintain harmony and goodwill, but they do not want to sacrifice results for harmony. If that does not work, they may decide to withdraw from the situation.

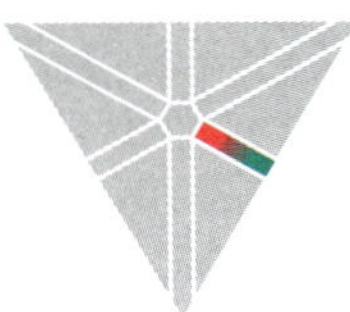

[RG]-B: People who want to engage conflict quickly, but indirectly, with thoughtful strategies. If that does not work and others have more power in the situation, they may surrender.

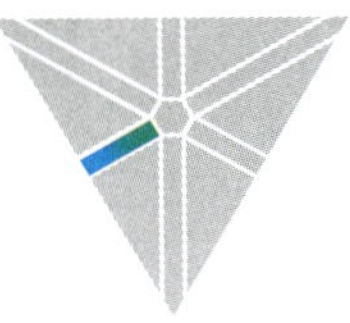

[BG]-R: People who want to maintain peace and harmony with caution regarding the personal costs of doing so. If that does not work, they may feel compelled to fight, possibly in an explosive manner.

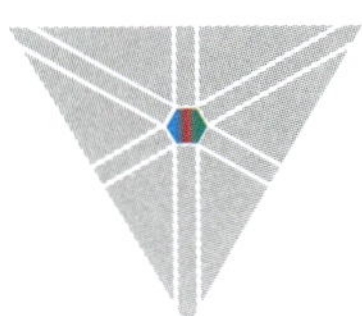

[BRG]: People who want to determine the most appropriate response to each situation and choose an accommodating, assertive, or analytical approach. Their approach differs according to the situation, rather than following a fixed sequence.

THE LENGTH OF ARROWS

The length of the line connecting the dot to the arrowhead offers insight into the transition from the going well state into conflict. Generally, the longer the line is, the greater the change people experience as they move from feeling good about themselves to feelings of conflict in the first stage. Since behavior arises from motives, the change in behavior tends to be more noticeable for people with long lines than for people with short lines.

Table 1.2 *Arrow Lengths*

Arrow	Length	MVS	1st Stage of Conflict
1	Short	**Red**	R: Red
2	Medium	**Red**	[RG]: Red/Green
3	Long	**Red**	G: Green

The length of the line offers an easy way to think about changes between the MVS and the Conflict Sequence. It also raises a different question: Is the first stage of conflict the same color as the MVS, or is it a different color?

With a short arrow (10 points or less), the dot and arrowhead are close together. The MVS and the first stage of conflict are likely to be the same color. Therefore, the behaviors arising from these two conditions are likely to appear similar. This is why people often say that it is hard to identify conflict in people who have a short arrow. A person with a short arrow may also experience a significant change in motives between the MVS and the first stage of conflict, but the most noticeable change in behavior is likely to be between stages one and two, when the color of the motive is more likely to change.

With a long arrow (25 points or more), the dot and arrowhead are far apart. The MVS and the first stage of conflict are likely to be different colors. Therefore, the behaviors arising from these two conditions are likely to be different. This is why people often say that it is easy to identify conflict in people who have a long arrow.

With a medium-length arrow (10 to 25 points), the MVS and the first stage of conflict may be the same color or different colors—depending on where the arrow is. Therefore, a general statement about medium-length arrows is not practical.

STRENGTHS AND OVERDONE STRENGTHS

The Strengths Portrait and Overdone Strengths Portrait do not show personality types; instead, they report the way strengths are deployed and prioritized in the context of working relationships. Personality and context both influence the behavioral expression of strengths, just as the movement of a buoy is influenced by the environment and the anchor to which it is connected.

Figure 1.4
The Anchor and Buoy Metaphor

A buoy moves in response to currents, tides, wind, waves, and other environmental factors. People's use of Strengths and Overdone Strengths at work are influenced by environmental factors such as opportunities, obligations, deadlines, workload, culture, and role responsibilities.

Just as the buoy is connected to an anchor below the surface, people's behaviors are connected to underlying motives. Unlike a buoy, however, people have free will and choose how to respond to any situation[2], how to behave, and how to communicate. To better understand those choices and offer insights to make better choices, the SDI 2.0 connects strengths at work to the MVS reasons for deploying those strengths.

Figure 1.5
Format for Strengths Portrait and Overdone Strengths Portrait

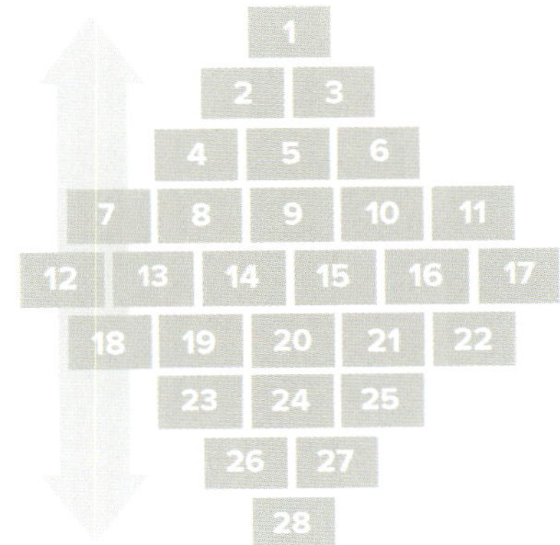

The Strengths Portrait section of the SDI 2.0 shows a pattern of strength deployment at work in a diamond-shaped format with the strengths the person is most likely to use at work at the top. In the Overdone Strengths Portrait, those most likely to be overdone at work are at the top. Section 4 of this book explains the portraits in more detail.

There are 28 strengths in four categories, Blue (People), Red (Performance), Green (Process), and Hub (Perspective). While there are three motives, there are four categories of behavior. For a full explanation of this, refer to Section 5, *SDI 2.0 Methodology and Meaning.*

Table 1.3 *Strengths and Overdone Strengths*

	Strength	If Overdone Becomes
BLUE STRENGTHS	Supportive	Self-Sacrificing
	Caring	Submissive
	Devoted	Subservient
	Modest	Self-Effacing
	Helpful	Smothering
	Loyal	Blind
	Trusting	Gullible
RED STRENGTHS	Risk-Taking	Reckless
	Competitive	Aggressive
	Quick-to-Act	Rash
	Forceful	Domineering
	Persuasive	Abrasive
	Ambitious	Ruthless
	Self-Confident	Arrogant
GREEN STRENGTHS	Persevering	Stubborn
	Fair	Cold
	Principled	Unbending
	Analytical	Obsessed
	Methodical	Rigid
	Reserved	Distant
	Cautious	Suspicious
HUB STRENGTHS	Option-Oriented	Indecisive
	Tolerant	Indifferent
	Adaptable	Compliant
	Inclusive	Indiscriminate
	Sociable	Intrusive
	Open-to-Change	Inconsistent
	Flexible	Unpredictable

A Brief History of the SDI 2.0

The SDI was first published in 1971 by Elias Porter, a consultant, professor, and psychologist. Porter was a student of Carl Rogers at The Ohio State University where Rogers was an advisor for Porter's doctoral dissertation. Porter joined Rogers as a peer at the University of Chicago's Counseling Center in the late 1940s and was part of the team that created encounter groups. Porter had an experimental and measurement-oriented background and was the first to measure the effectiveness of non-directive techniques used by therapists. Porter's further developments of therapeutic methods were later included in Rogers' landmark book, *Client Centered Therapy.*

While at Chicago, Porter began creating personality assessments based on Erich Fromm's descriptions of personality types, which were an advancement of Sigmund Freud's ideas. Porter, however, had a severe disagreement with Carl Rogers over the ethical use of personality assessments. Rogers believed that personality assessments would lead people to accept statements about themselves that were not true. He believed that test administrators would have too much power and authority, because the test administrators would choose the questions and hold the key to the answers.

"The more a personality theory can be for a person, rather than about a person, the better it will serve that person," Porter said. He wanted to create something that would be useful for people, not a diagnostic tool.

Ironically, the conflict with Rogers may have contributed to Porter's development of his theory of personality by helping him recognize the two conditions in which personality may be experienced and expressed. The first is when things are going well, and the second is when there is conflict.

As he continued his developmental, academic, and consulting work, Porter created several versions of the assessment, incorporating features such as a primary drive for self-worth, a focus on strengths, the descriptions of the Conflict Sequences (his most original contribution to the field of psychology), and the use of colors to promote a simple, common language. The SDI was the first personality assessment to use colors in this way.

The SDI 2.0 goes beyond Porter's original SDI in both methodology and content by integrating all four views of a person (the original SDI focused on the Motivational Value System).

For a more complete version of the SDI story with academic references, please refer to Section 5, *History and Development of the SDI 2.0.*

Key Concepts and Definitions

The SDI 2.0 is based on a theory of relationships.[3] When people complete the SDI, the items require them to consider the way they relate to others. The insight from the SDI helps to improve the quality of relationships.

- **Relationship:** a connection between two or more people built on a foundation of shared experiences, interactions, and expectations. Human relationships have a time dimension, they have a past, present, and future.
- **Relationship Intelligence:** insight for adjusting one's approach to make interactions more effective. Insights from the SDI 2.0, help people to:
    - better understand **past** experiences, enabling a deeper understanding and appreciation of self and others
    - manage choices and perceptions in the **present,** enabling more effective interactions and communication
    - anticipate the thoughts, feelings, and expectations of others, giving greater control over the **future** outcomes of relationships.

Relationship Intelligence (RQ) can improve Emotional Intelligence (EQ), but they are not the same thing. Emotional Intelligence is a competency framework. As Daniel Goleman said: lumping relationships in with emotional intelligence stunts fresh thinking about the human aptitude for relationships, ignoring what transpires as we interact.[4] Relationship Intelligence goes beyond EQ by focusing on motives (not just emotions) that drive interactions between people with different personality types. Measures of EQ are based on competencies; individuals are measured against a standard — high EQ or low EQ. The effectiveness of relationships is determined by the people in the relationships. And people with different personalities measure relationship effectiveness by different standards.

The SDI 2.0 is about both personality and behavior. The arrow on the triangle represents the MVS and Conflict Sequence, which are two elements of personality. Behaviors at work are shown by the Strengths Portrait and Overdone Strengths Portrait.

This enables insightful exploration of questions such as: What matters most to you and how do you express that at work? What do you do at work that contributes to you feeling good about yourself — or that causes conflict for you? How can you connect with what needs to be done at work so you can engage your core motives and values?

Behavior is more easily observed than personality, because it is easier to see what someone does than it is to know why they do it. In other words, strengths are easier to see than motives. Think of every person sort of like an iceberg with some things above the surface of the water and some things below it.

WHAT'S ABOVE THE SURFACE?

The following terms[5] describe things people can observe in others:

- **Behavior:** the way a person acts or communicates.
- **Trait:** a behavior (or pattern of behaviors) that occurs frequently enough that it becomes a defining quality or characteristic of a person.
- **Type:** a category of people with similar characteristics. No individual person is a type. People in a type are more similar to others in that type than they are to people of different types, but each person in a type is still a unique individual. People of the same personality type share a common pattern of motives, but they may express their motives with different strengths. Consider a non-personality example: All palm trees share some defining characteristics and are easily distinguishable from other types of trees, but there are many differences in individual palm trees.

Figure 1.6 *Iceberg Model*

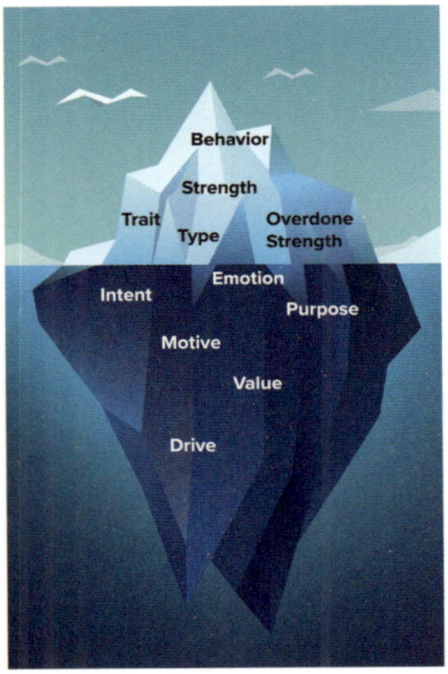

- **Strength:** a behavior deployed in an effective interaction between people. A behavior that produces results for one person at the expense of another is not a considered strength; it is classified as an overdone strength.[6] Strengths are different than talents.[7] Talents are the skills of individuals, while strengths are relational.
- **Overdone Strength:** a behavior that may be intended to produce results in relationships but does not do so, because it is perceived negatively by oneself or others. Strengths may be overdone (or perceived as overdone) in frequency, duration, or intensity.[8] They may also be misapplied (or perceived as misapplied) depending on the context.

WHAT'S BELOW THE SURFACE?

These terms describe things people cannot easily observe in others:

- **Drive:** an innate energizing force. People have both physical drives (hunger, sex, etc.) and psychological drives; this book's emphasis is on psychological drives.

- **Value:** a principle or standard, a belief about what is important in life. Psychological drives can be a basis for values as people develop. Sometimes, people consider their top strengths to be values.
- **Motive:** the underlying reason why something is done. Motives can be conscious or unconscious. The word motivation can refer to having or giving energy for a task — rewards and punishments, for instance. This book's focus is on the purposive meaning of motive — the reason for doing things.
- **Emotion:** a state of mind or feeling deriving from one's situation or relationships. Common emotions include: joy, rage, contentment, and sorrow. The SDI describes personality under two emotional (or affective) states: when people feel that things are going well, and when they are experiencing conflict.
- **Purpose:** the conscious reason why something is chosen or done. Motives, purposes, and values can be closely aligned. The consideration of purpose sometimes helps to discover a person's motives and values.
- **Intent:** a conscious choice of behavior that is targeted to create a desired outcome or effect. Motives and purposes can give rise to intentions. While intentions sometimes sound similar to motives or purposes, intentions tend to be more closely aligned with specific outcomes, while motives explain the importance of the intended outcome.

HOW DOES IT ALL FIT TOGETHER?

People are more complex than can be described by lists of traits or categories. The following terms[9] describe the parts of personality that fit together to form systems that give rise to different behaviors in different circumstances:

- **Motivational Value System (MVS):** a fairly constant set of motives and values that serve as a basis for:
    - choosing and giving purpose to behavior.
    - focusing attention on certain things while ignoring others.
    - perceiving and judging self and others.

  Every MVS is a blend or combination of three color coded primary motives: Blue (concern for people), Red (concern for performance), and Green (concern for process). When SDI results are charted on the SDI Triangle, the dot represents the MVS. There are more than 5,000 unique points on the SDI Triangle, which is divided into seven regions to show seven different Motivational Value Systems.

- **Conflict Sequence:** a series of changes in motives during conflict that typically results in a related series of changes in behavior. The three stages in a Conflict Sequence are characterized by a concentration of energy and a diminishing focus as follows:

    - Stage 1: focus on self, problem, and other
    - Stage 2: focus on self and problem
    - Stage 3: focus on self

  Conflict can be resolved or left unresolved in any stage. When SDI results are charted on the SDI Triangle, the arrowhead represents the Conflict Sequence. There are more than 5,000 unique points on the SDI Triangle, which is divided into 13 regions to show 13 different Conflict Sequences.

- **Filter:** a method of selective perception and evaluation of a situation. People's Motivational Value Systems and Conflict Sequences act as filters that influence the way they see situations, other people, and themselves. Filters may also result from a number of other factors such as past experiences, education and training, expectations, and belief systems.

A FEW MORE TERMS TO HELP WITH CONFLICT

The word conflict is sometimes used in everyday language to describe opposition; however, this book separates the two ideas. These terms[10] describe different aspects of opposition and conflict that are important to know when building Relationship Intelligence:

- **Opposition:** disagreement, contrast, difference, resistance, or dissent. Opposition is not necessarily conflict, but it can grow into conflict when it gets personal. Most conflicts have elements of opposition in them. Opposition can be productively engaged when things are going well.
- **Conflict:** the experience or perception of a threat to self-worth. Conflict is generally more personal and emotional than opposition. Most conflicts also have an element of opposition, but conflict can make it difficult to deal objectively with opposition.
- **Conflict Trigger:** an event, behavior, situation, or perception that threatens, or has the potential to threaten, a person's self-worth. People only experience conflict about things that are important to them. Therefore, conflict triggers include the opportunity to learn about what matters to people. Conflict triggers also present an implied choice:
    - to enter conflict based on the perceived trigger.
    - to re-frame the situation so that a threat is no longer perceived.
- **Preventable Conflict:** a threat to a person's sense of self-worth that could have been prevented. Sometimes issues or disagreements are so important to someone's sense of self-worth that it is difficult to prevent conflict. However, many conflicts, especially those that develop from the perception of overdone strengths, are preventable.

- **Conflict Management:** managing the emotional experience and content of conflict and making decisions about whether to:
    - attempt to resolve conflict.
    - go deeper into conflict.
    - leave conflict unresolved.
- **Conflict Resolution:** resolving conflict in such a way that the elements of opposition are addressed and the threats to self-worth are removed. This suggests that people follow a path from their Conflict Sequence back to their Motivational Value System, where they feel good about themselves again.
- **Unresolved Conflict:** a conflict that has been avoided, without addressing the elements of opposition or removing the threats to self-worth. Unresolved conflict can be re-engaged where it was left. It can repeat and turn into habitual conflict. It can also complicate future conflicts, because new issues can get added to unresolved issues.
- **Reconciliation:** the restoration of productive relations. Reconciliation is a step further than conflict resolution. Reconciliation often includes forgiveness for the past, a closer present connection between people, and a commitment to work together in future.

SDI 2.0 Applications

The insights of the SDI 2.0 can be used with individuals, teams, and organizations to improve Relationship Intelligence wherever people interact. Productive relationships are essential to success and work is more enjoyable when people on teams get along well with each other. There always exists, however, the potential for interpersonal conflict, which can actually become a source of productivity if well-managed. SDI results can also be used to develop leaders and to help managers more effectively coach people to use their strengths effectively. Following are six applications of the SDI 2.0 that improve Productivity, Emotional Intelligence, Team Performance, Conflict Management, Leadership Development, and Coaching.

PRODUCTIVITY

Part of the purpose of working with the SDI is to become more effective in relationships. Knowing what to do in relationships requires self-awareness and awareness of others. That's why structured, SDI-based learning experiences begin with self-awareness and then move into interpersonal awareness. With that awareness, it's easier to make more informed and effective choices about behavior.

Perception comes before choice. The Motivational Value System acts as a filter that influences what people perceive and that judgments or decisions based on these filtered perceptions may be limited. Therefore, changing perceptions can be an effective way to be open to new ideas, to make better decisions, and to choose more effective strengths.

Being more productive[11] and getting better results through relationships can be as simple as ABC. A is for Assess motives—knowing the MVS and Conflict Sequence of people in relationships. B is for Bring the right strengths—choosing strengths that are most likely to be productive with others, finding authentic reasons to use those strengths, and guarding against the actual or perceived overdone forms of those strengths. C is for Communicate in the right style—knowing your audience and sharing what's important to you in a way that they can hear it.

Figure 1.7 *The ABCs of Results through Relationships*

EMOTIONAL INTELLIGENCE

Most emotional intelligence competency frameworks[12] include self-awareness and interpersonal awareness. Measures of emotional intelligence indicate how aware people are of themselves and others. The SDI 2.0 provides a personality typology that both accelerates self-awareness and improves the accuracy of interpersonal perception. Where emotional intelligence assessments measure the level of competency, insights from the SDI help to develop these critical competencies.

Emotional intelligence frameworks generally also include competencies in the arenas of self-control and relationship management, such as regulating emotions, communication, and conflict management. The SDI helps improve competencies in all those areas, especially conflict management.[13] Emotional Intelligence, despite its significant value, has a few practical shortcomings or missing links that can be addressed with Relationship Intelligence insights from the SDI.

Emotional intelligence does not account for the role of context or for individual differences in personality, it does not adequately define a relationship, and it does not distinguish relationships from interactions. Emotional intelligence is largely transactional, focused on the emotions that influence interactions in the moment. Relationship Intelligence is focused on the underlying motives that govern relationships. The SDI 2.0 advances Emotional Intelligence by providing a practical framework to understand oneself and others, and to improve the quality of relationships over time.

TEAM PERFORMANCE

Most teams have people with diverse skills, talents, knowledge, and life experiences. The SDI 2.0 adds an element of cognitive diversity, showing what drives people at their cores and how they choose to use their strengths as they work together.

Figure 1.8 *SDI Team Triangle*

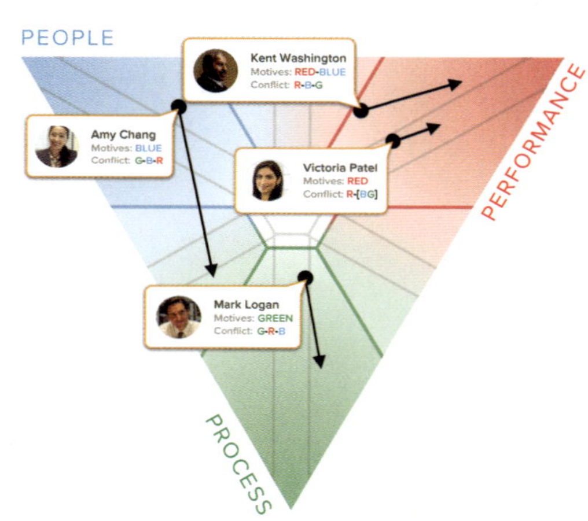

Showing the personalities of the whole team on the SDI Triangle provides insight into the team's dynamics. At a glance, team members can see what drives everyone when things are going well, how the team members experience conflict, and how noticeable the change from MVS to Stage 1 conflict is for each person. The team triangle offers a shared frame of reference for important conversations about the team's purpose, goals, and each member's contributions.

Figure 1.9 *Team Strengths Portrait*

Teams also benefit from seeing the composite view of their strengths. These views, which rank the entire team's strengths from most likely to deploy at work to least likely, provide a window into the team's culture and norms. They show which strengths are most characteristic of the team, as well as which strengths are potentially overlooked or not otherwise valued by the team. Comparing the Team Strengths Portrait to the organization's values, mission, or other key documents can shed light on exactly how the team fits within the broader organization.

CONFLICT MANAGEMENT

Opposition, or objective disagreement, is usually a very powerful factor in collaboration, innovation, and all manner of conversation. But if people are afraid the opposition will degenerate into conflict, the benefits of constructive opposition can be lost.

Interpersonal conflict represents a significant cost for many organizations. Conflict contributes to errors and inefficiencies, employee's intentions to leave the organization, bad decisions, missed opportunities, and even increased healthcare and legal costs.

Insights from SDI results help leaders and their teams engage in more productive opposition, which is a source of creativity and innovation. Individuals and teams can build trust and manage conflict with more Relationship Intelligence by applying five keys[14] to conflict management:

1. **Anticipate:** The SDI describes conflict triggers for different personalities so that potential conflict can be anticipated, which is the prerequisite to preventing it.
2. **Prevent:** Preventing conflict is different than avoiding conflict. Prevention takes advance thought and effort to stop something from happening, whereas avoiding conflict is an attempt to not get involved with something that has already happened. Conflict can be triggered when something goes against a person's values or stops them from satisfying their motives. Therefore, knowing a person's Motivational Value System is essential to preventing conflict. Similarly, being aware of one's own conflict triggers, such as other people's overdone strengths, can help to manage perceptions and prevent negative judgments that can lead to conflict.
3. **Identify:** Despite our best efforts to prevent it, interpersonal conflict sometimes still happens. SDI results provide insight to identify conflict more quickly so it can be addressed in the first stage. If conflict is not identified in the first stage, when people's focus includes themselves, the problem, and each other, it becomes more difficult to manage. Understanding the Conflict Sequence facilitates accurate perception of the motives of people who are experiencing conflict.

4. **Manage:** Accurately identifying conflict (by color and stage) is essential to successful conflict management. When people are in stages 2 or 3 of their Conflict Sequence, the strategy for conflict management is to engage in conversation that will help them move back to Stage 1, where resolution is more likely. Generally, this involves a conversation focused on the person who is experiencing conflict and feeling threatened: what is most important to them? What is their view of the problem? What is their ideal solution? Once people in conflict are clear about their views and desires, they are more readily able to return to Stage 1, where they can expand their focus and include the views and desires of others.
5. **Resolve:** Conflict resolution, as opposed to conflict deferral, means that the elements of opposition are addressed, the feelings of conflict have been managed, and people feel good about themselves again. In short, they are not acting based on motives related to their Conflict Sequence, but are now acting from their Motivational Value System. Unresolved conflicts can resurface with the same intensity, which can create a difficult pattern in any relationship.

Conflict management techniques are generally applied to specific situations. But Relationship Intelligence can go a step further, to reconciliation. Reconciliation often involves forgiveness for the past or a deeper understanding and appreciation of past events, a closer present connection between people that is more authentic and genuine, and a commitment to work together in future toward mutually meaningful goals.

LEADERSHIP DEVELOPMENT

Leadership is a relationship in a context.[15] SDI 2.0 results offer insight to leader-follower dynamics when things are going well and during conflict or crisis, because personality influences behavior and communication in all situations.

Leaders often project their personalities onto their positions, or even the entire organization. They lead in a way that reflects their personal drives and motives — or they interpret the organization's purpose in a way that connects with their MVS. Leaders' MVS and Conflict Sequences offer insights into what they will perceive as threats to the organization and how they will respond to those threats. The Overdone Strengths Portrait offers leaders insight into the way their well-intended strengths can become non-productive or self-limiting. Leadership development efforts often result in actionable insight to reduce the undesirable effects of overdone strengths.

For leaders, awareness of personality type goes beyond self-management or leadership team dynamics. Leaders also need to communicate in a way that engages the diverse personalities of followers and connects with their core motives. Simply stated, these motives are concerns for people, performance, and process. Leaders who overemphasize their own primary concerns are likely to alienate people with different personalities. Overcommunication about performance can leave people feeling overlooked or neglected – or wondering exactly how the desired performance can be produced. Similarly, overcommunication about process can leave people feeling stuck in an impersonal, slow-moving bureaucratic environment. A more effective technique for leaders to communicate purpose, values, and goals is to give about equal time and emphasis to the people, performance, and process elements of any strategy or plan. These three pillars align with the three primary motives that blend to create every personality.

COACHING

Managers can use the SDI 2.0 to coach for both performance and development. Openly sharing SDI results promotes rich learning in the coaching relationship that is based on what motivates people to want to do their best work and how they hold themselves accountable.

Figure 1.10 *Personal Accountability at Work*

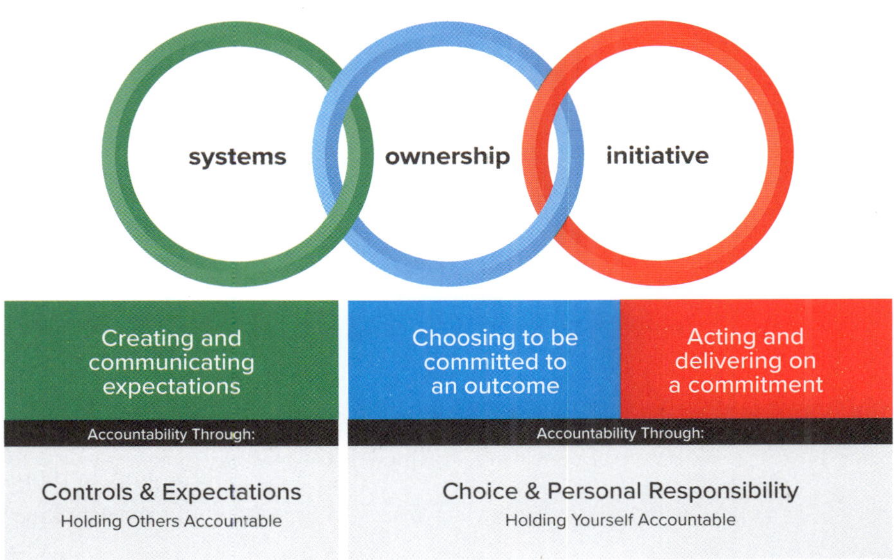

Discussions about accountability often start with organizational structures or systems. They lead to questions such as: "What are the goals, roles, and reporting relationships?" "What positive and negative consequences are available?" and "How do we get people to want to do what they are supposed to do?" While these are valid and important questions, they do not lead to a full understanding of accountability. Techniques designed to answer these questions often fail to account for the human experience of becoming accountable and for individual differences in motives and values. That's where coaching with the SDI comes in.

Accountability cannot be sustainably demanded or imposed; taking ownership for an outcome is a free act.[16] Accountability flows naturally from choice. When people make choices that are intended to produce results that are important to them, they become more accountable for their actions. When coaches guide people to make free choices, they tap into their Motivational Value System. This energizes people, propels them toward goal accomplishment, and inspires maximum, motivated effort. Choice increases accountability. This insight is at the heart of coaching with the SDI. When coaches guide people to make better choices, it helps them both develop and perform.

2 MOTIVATIONAL VALUE SYSTEMS

What is a Motivational Value System?

A Motivational Value System (MVS), as its name suggests, is a system of motives and values. Systems are groups of things that work together to create something that is not just greater than the sum of its parts, but different than the sum of its parts. Motives and values work together to direct energy toward things that are important to people; they give purpose and meaning to activities and relationships.

Figure 2.1 *The 7 Motivational Value Systems*

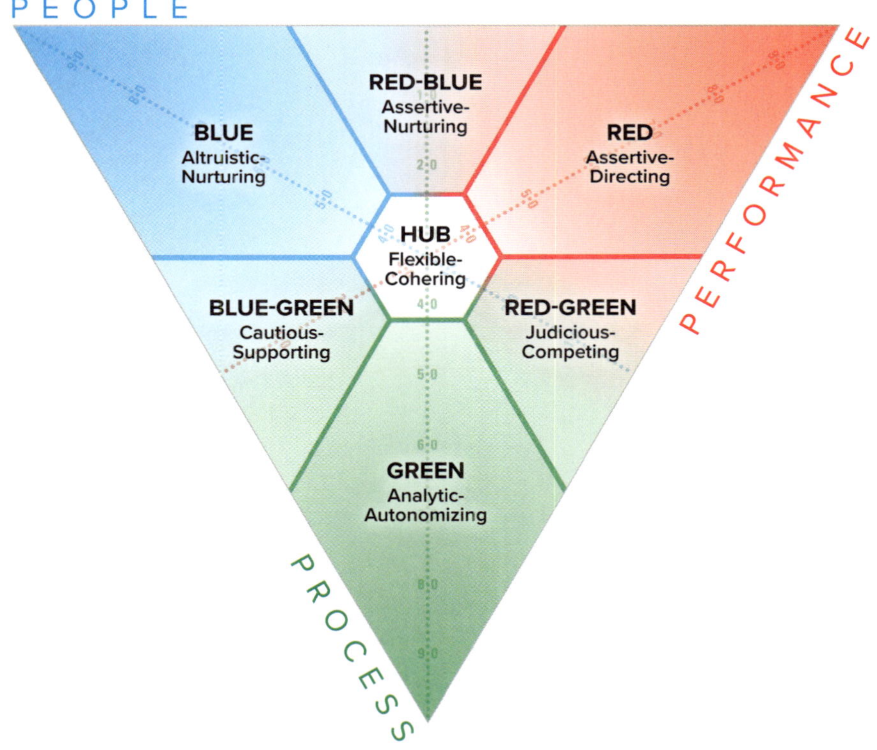

A Motivational Value System is a simple and practical way of thinking about people from the perspective of motives. The MVS helps to explain the complex reasons that people do the things they do.

In SDI terms, a Motivational Value System is a person's unique blend of Blue (People), Red (Performance), and Green (Process) motives.

All people share a desire to feel good about themselves. It feels good to fulfill a motive by doing what they intended to do. The SDI shows how everyone has the same three core motives, but those motives are present in different frequencies. The three MVS scores on the SDI, which together must equal 100 points, represent these frequencies. Therefore the SDI scores are an indication of what makes each person feel best about themselves.

Different combinations of motives produce seven distinct Motivational Value Systems, which are described in detail in the following pages. Three have a single color motive occurring most frequently; three have two colors of motives occurring about equally; one (the Hub) has all three colors of motives occurring about equally.

Figure 2.2 *Example of Test/Retest Reliability*

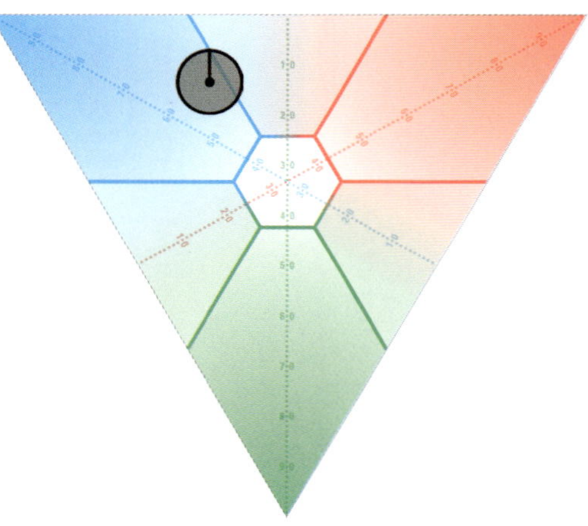

The scores from the "going well" portion of the SDI are charted as a dot on the SDI triangle to represent a person's MVS. The location of the dot suggests one of the seven Motivational Value Systems. When a dot is close to another MVS region (within six points[1] as illustrated in Figure 2.2), however, the person may identify with portions of the descriptions of more than one MVS. Unlike a typecasting exercise, the goal here is not to force a person to choose only one of the descriptions. Instead, the goal is to allow the individual flexibility to identify the most characteristic portions of each description.

WHAT DOES THE MVS DO?

Behavior is driven by motives, so the MVS activates and motivates behavior. When people feel free to choose behavior that makes them feel good about themselves, they can engage their strengths and act in ways that feel consistent with their motives. These consistent and congruent[2] experiences affirm people's sense of self-worth.

The MVS gives meaning to behavior, relationships, and situations. It acts as a filter through which life is perceived, interpreted, and understood. Filters stop some things and allow other things through. The MVS filters and influences perception; information deemed important is readily received, but information deemed irrelevant is actively or even subconsciously screened out of awareness. Differences in personal filters can help to explain why two people can have entirely different memories of a shared experience.

Behavior is a choice, and choices are limited by perceived options. The MVS, acting as a filter, can constrain or expand the range of choices people believe they have.

The MVS also gives clues to sources of conflict. Because conflict is a threat to self-worth, and the MVS generates feelings of self-worth, anything that restricts the fulfillment of motives can be a conflict trigger. People may experience conflict when they are cut off or restricted from acting in accordance with their values. They may also experience conflict when acting in accordance with their values is discounted or disregarded by others.

Similarly, the MVS gives clues about how to resolve conflict. When people experience conflict, the ideal resolution allows them to feel good about themselves again. Therefore, resolving conflict requires more than dealing with people's feelings in conflict; it also requires awareness of what brings self-worth to those people. The MVS is the destination on the path back from conflict. For example, a person with a Blue MVS who is in Stage 1 Green conflict will want to analyze (Stage 1 Green) the situation in order to find a way to restore harmony and be helpful to other people (Blue MVS).

The MVS does not indicate skills, though people may want to develop skills in areas that interest them. The MVS also is not an indicator of effectiveness. It shows why people want to do things, not how effective they are at doing them. For example, people may want to help others, but the things they do may not be helpful to others. The MVS is not a diagnosis. Just as it does not indicate skills, it does not indicate problems. While every person has imperfections and development opportunities, and some of these may be common for people with the same MVS, every person is also unique.

ARE THERE REALLY ONLY SEVEN KINDS OF PEOPLE?

There are seven Motivational Value Systems.[3] People with the same MVS generally agree about why they do things, but they may not necessarily agree about what to do in a given situation.

Each MVS covers a region of the SDI triangle that includes many possible SDI scores. Within each region, many differences are possible for scores and also for people. The MVS scores show the relative frequency and priority of each of the three primary motives. For example, everyone with a Hub MVS shares some common motives of wanting to be flexible and bring people together. However, there may be subtle but important differences in the frequency of motives between people on the Blue, Red, and Green sides of the Hub.[4] Within their shared flexibility, these people may place different emphasis on people, performance, and process.

The MVS is not the whole story. While the personality types described by the SDI include everyone, they do not explain everything about everyone. The SDI's personality types are based on people's motives—their sense of purpose and intentions. There are other valid ways to describe categories of people, and these ways can usually complement the SDI. For example, personalities may be sorted into learning style groups.[5] Some learn best by seeing, others by hearing, and others by doing. Personalities may be sorted into groups based on levels of extraversion, conscientiousness, agreeableness, or other factors.[6] Personalities may also be sorted into groups based on mental processes, such as collecting information and making decisions.[7]

When coupled with motives, these different views of personality can offer greater self-insight and interpersonal understanding. For example, two people with a Red MVS may share similar motives but have different styles of learning and making decisions. These differences don't contradict or negate the shared motives; they help to explain how two people express similar motives differently.

WHAT NEXT?

As you read the MVS descriptions, start with your own MVS. When you find something useful, make it easy to find again. Remember that each section is written with an MVS type in mind and that you are not a type. You are an individual. You will probably not agree with everything as presented, especially if your MVS dot is close to the border of another MVS region on the triangle.

Your MVS is one point of an arrow on the SDI triangle. The Conflict Sequence is the other, and these points are related. We experience conflict only about things that are important to us. The things that trigger conflict affect the way we experience conflict, so whatever gets us into conflict provides important clues about getting us out.

Don't stop with the MVS. You will understand more about yourself by considering your Conflict Sequence. Then do the same for other people, and you will build your Relationship Intelligence. While your SDI results are about you, you'll get more value when you consider yourself in the context of your relationships.

BLUE MVS

ALTRUISTIC-NURTURING

Al•tru•is•tic—unselfish concern for the welfare of others
Nur•tur•ing—protecting, supporting, and encouraging others

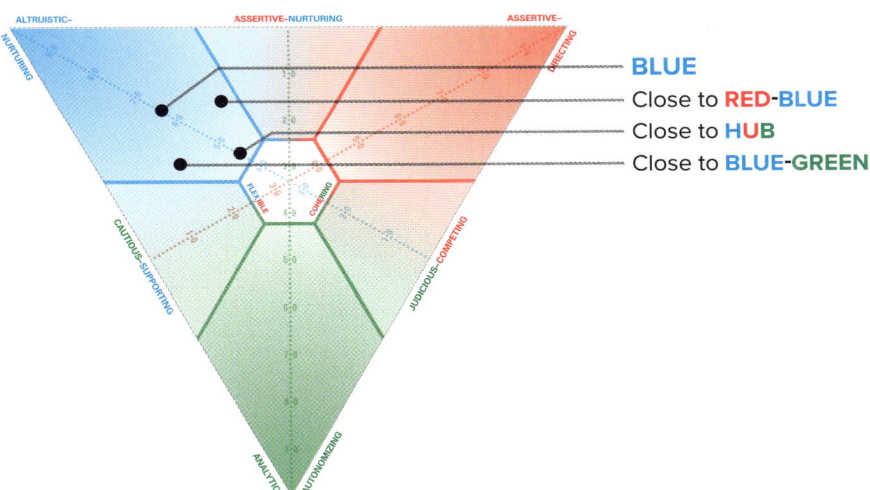

This descriptive text is written about an MVS dot in the center of the Blue MVS region. Individuals with MVS dots close to the borders (within 6 points) of other MVS regions may differ slightly from this description. They will likely find that the descriptions of the neighboring region(s) also influence their understanding of themselves and the way they are perceived by others.

BLUE MOTIVES AND VALUES

The motivation of people with an Altruistic-Nurturing Motivational Value System (hereafter referred to as Blues) is to achieve feelings of self-worth by being genuinely helpful to others, with little or no concern for what they receive in return.

Blues tend to find satisfaction in life by helping others in ways that enhance their happiness and genuinely meet their needs. Blues understand the productivity behind expressing concern for the welfare of others. Blues understand and value the forgiveness of others, placing their faith in others, and offering others the benefit of the doubt. Blues believe that giving others praise and rewards creates happiness and gratefulness in the hearts and minds of those who receive the praise and rewards. Blues value the power of helping people grow.

Blues' sense of personal integrity comes from meeting the opportunities life affords to provide help to others, and the real reward for Blues is the evidence that the help was received and valued. For Blues, the effort and intent to help are most important. Blues tend to discount any thanks for these helping efforts, believing that the true reward is in the act of helping. Blues value recognition but tend to believe that any external reward for their efforts will be offered without having to ask for it.

For Blues, the act of helping is not always enough. The greatest enjoyment in the act of helping comes from seeing the other person's benefit. For Blues to experience maximum feelings of self-worth, the help must be accepted, valued, and appreciated.

OBSERVING BLUE BEHAVIORS

While motives cannot be directly observed, consistencies in behavior can offer insight into a person's underlying motives. Blues are motivated by the protection, growth, and welfare of others. They have a strong desire to help others who can genuinely benefit. They express their motives through behavior and tend to:

- Be open and responsive to the needs of others.
- Seek ways to bring help to others, trying to make life easier for others.
- Defend the rights of others with courage and conviction, sometimes without claiming their own rights in the process.
- Be idealistic and admire the accomplishments of others, often playing down their own personal achievements out of a desire to remain modest.
- Be humble, rarely asking for recognition, simultaneously putting great trust in others.
- Respond when asked for help.
- Believe that conscientious involvement will demonstrate individual worth—*and* inspire reward without request.
- Ensure that others reach their potential and are fully valued.
- Try never to be a burden to others, preferring to give help rather than receive it.

Blue strengths confirm the self-worth of both people in a relationship. When Blue strengths are overdone, they may threaten the self-worth of Blues or the other people who perceive these strengths as overdone. Table 2.1 illustrates two examples.

Table 2.1 *Examples of Blue Overdone Strengths*

Productive Strength	Effect of Overdone Strength
When Blues help others in ways that genuinely benefit others, Blues and others are affirmed.	When Blues help people who do not need or want help, the help may be seen as smothering or a violation of personal space.
When Blues trust others who are worthy of and value that trust, the relationship is enhanced.	When Blues trust too much or trust inappropriately, they may be taken advantage of or perceived as gullible.

REASONS THAT BLUES ENTER CONFLICT

Blues tend to go into conflict about things that negatively affect the welfare of other people or things that restrict or discount their ability to bring help and support to others. They have difficulty with people who are overly competitive and take advantage of others. Awareness of the potential causes of conflict can help Blues to manage their own reactions to conflict triggers and can help others to adjust their behavior in an attempt to prevent conflict.

Blues may experience conflict when they perceive any of the following conflict triggers:

- Others won't accept help.
- Others change loyalties "for the moment."
- Other people are taken advantage of.
- People are selfish or unconcerned about others.
- Others are insincere about helping.
- Competition results in people being hurt.
- Behavior appears rude or unkind.
- Display of emotion is disregarded, ignored, or punished.
- Relationships are not regularly maintained.
- Issues are personalized.

When in conflict, Blues want to defend their values, so they can get back to relating to others productively. The ways they defend their MVS in an effort to return to feeling good about themselves will vary, depending on their Conflict Sequence.

PRODUCTIVE RESULTS OF CONFLICT FOR BLUES

When in conflict, regardless of their individual Conflict Sequences, Blues share a desire to return to feelings of self-worth and activities that support others. They are more likely to resolve conflict when they see the potential for some of these outcomes:

- Restored, renewed, or improved relationships.
- A peaceful and harmonious environment.
- Increased understanding between people.
- They will be included, needed, and appreciated.
- Greater interpersonal commitment and participation.

HOW BLUES CAN IMPROVE INTERACTIONS

Blues' preferred approach to situations and other people may not always result in outcomes that are valuable to Blues or to others. Sometimes, nurturing strengths may not fit the situation, or they may be perceived as overdone, possibly triggering conflict in others. Adjusting behavior is most effective when considering the MVS of others, and advice about how to approach people with different Motivational Value Systems can be found in the other MVS sections of this book.

Blues may bear the burden of guilt. They want to help others, believe they can help others, and feel most rewarded when they do. When the help they offer is accepted but their efforts do not make things better for others, Blues may feel guilty that they could not find a way to make a difference for that person. They may put others' needs above their own. Blues' desire to help may make it difficult to refuse when others ask for help. Even when it is in Blues' best interest not to offer help or to refuse to help when asked, failing to be of help may result in an equally strong sense of guilt.

In general, Blues may be able to improve the quality of their interactions, and the results they produce, by deploying some behaviors that are not typical of their MVS. Some examples include:

- Firmly saying "no" in situations where they don't have the capacity to help.
- Clearly stating individual desires and expectations.

- Being objective and analytical in the judgment of others.
- Clarifying the urgency and priority of tasks before committing to help.
- Confidently sharing thoughts, feelings, and ideas with others.
- Accepting compliments without making dismissive remarks.

THE BLUE STYLE OF PERSONAL LEADERSHIP

When leading others, Blues tend to focus on the needs of the people they lead, believing that people who feel supported, trusted, and cared for will be more productive. Blues view the purpose of leadership as helping others to grow and develop in their work. The Blue style of leadership is supportive and enabling, ensuring that the people they lead have the tools, resources, and knowledge necessary to succeed and to maximize their potential. Blue leadership is often characterized by:

- Efforts to maintain harmony, goodwill, and a friendly culture.
- Keeping channels of communication open, so people can build and maintain fulfilling working relationships.
- Protecting the people they lead.
- Placing their faith in the people they lead.

Working with BLUES

LISTENING TO BLUES

Working effectively with Blues means you will need to understand what they are saying. Listening well to Blues will ensure that they feel heard, and know that you appreciate them and their intent to help. When you are listening, and engaging in dialogue, keep these points in mind:

- When listening, interpret through the lens of who they are trying to support.
- Don't mistake kindness for weakness; they are really trying to help.
- Be receptive, open, and genuine. Thank them for their help or contributions.
- Don't be abrupt. Don't discount others feelings about things.
- Take the time to ask how they feel about things.

REWARDING AND RECOGNIZING BLUES

Blues like to feel that they are needed and appreciated and that the help they provided was genuinely useful to another person and made a difference. Blues may be uncomfortable asking for or accepting rewards; they generally prefer that rewards and praise be given personally, in private settings or small groups.

The best compliments are specific about the help provided and the benefits experienced. Some compliments might include:

- "Thank you. I couldn't have done it without your help."
- "Your support made my life easier."
- "You really did your job well, and everyone benefitted from your efforts."
- "You made our customers happy by sensing their needs and serving them beyond anyone's expectations."

HOW TO APPROACH BLUES

- Be open, honest, one-to-one, personal, sincere, trusting, and inclusive.
- Genuinely express feelings or concerns.
- Show regard for people and appreciation for others.
- Link benefits to their effect on others.
- Listen fully and attentively; ask for their ideas, reactions, and feelings.

THINGS TO AVOID WHEN APPROACHING BLUES

- Open or public competition, hostility, confrontation, negativity, or arrogance.
- Being aloof or distant, or appearing disinterested.
- Dismissing or devaluing their helpfulness.
- Appearing to take advantage of people.
- Assuming that silence or tentative responses equate to agreement or acceptance.

PREVENTING CONFLICT WITH BLUES

Much conflict with Blues can be prevented by acting or communicating in ways that recognize and respect the Blue MVS and that do not introduce conflict triggers. Proactive conflict prevention strategies can be employed to reduce the chance that the self-worth of Blues will be threatened.

- Be sincere, genuine, and authentic.
- Allow time to discuss the feelings and emotional aspects of the issue or situation.
- Affirm the relationship before addressing the issue.

- Verbally acknowledge the potential threat to self-worth.
- Do not appear to patronize Blues or diminish the importance of their emotions.
- Consider the impact on other people involved.
- Check in regularly, not just when there is a specific need.

INFLUENCING BLUES

The key to influencing Blues is to create or communicate conditions that are intrinsically rewarding to them. The more that what you want them to do is clearly linked to the protection, growth, or welfare of others, the more willing Blues will generally be to engage their strengths in those activities.

Blues will tend to feel more motivated in open, friendly, and socially supportive environments. They are likely to follow people who are strong, know exactly what they want to do, and work hard to include Blues in their activities.

To influence Blues, engage them in a conversation about how a desired action will:

- Benefit another person who is in need.
- Make life easier for others.
- Help others reach their potential.
- Ensure that others are valued and recognized.

RED MVS

ASSERTIVE-DIRECTING

As•ser•tive—confidently self-assured and forceful
Di•rec•ting—giving authoritative instruction or guidance

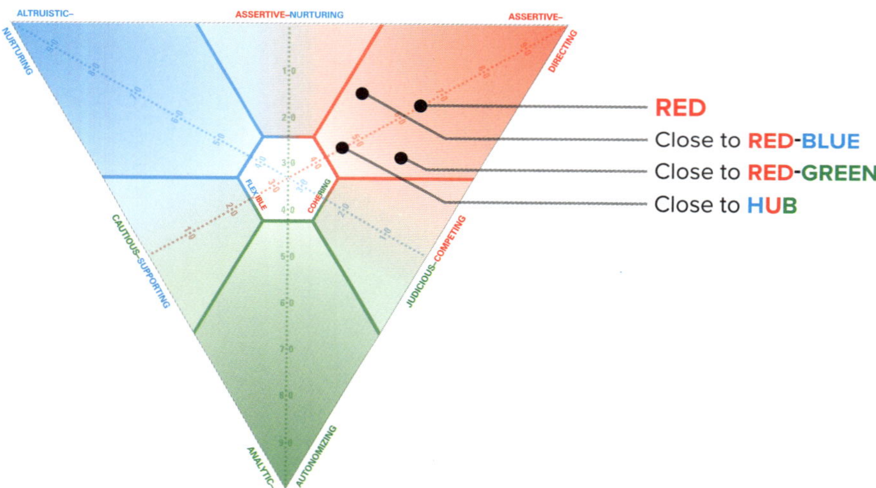

This descriptive text is written about an MVS dot in the center of the Red MVS region. Individuals with MVS dots close to the borders (within 6 points) of other MVS regions may differ slightly from this description. They will likely find that the descriptions of the neighboring region(s) also influence their understanding of themselves and the way they are perceived by others.

RED MOTIVES AND VALUES

The motivation of people with an Assertive-Directing Motivational Value System (hereafter referred to as Reds) is to achieve feelings of self-worth by being a successful, winning leader of others and by providing the direction needed to achieve results.

Reds tend to find satisfaction in life by being an achiever in the face of competition. They understand that in order to achieve, they must be clear about their goals and capable of giving the direction required to achieve those goals. Reds value the exercise of power and control, the setting of high performance standards, and decisive action. Reds tend to believe that the bigger the game, the greater the need to rally support to achieve success. Reds value the power of directing others productively.

Reds' sense of personal integrity comes from succeeding in a world where opportunities are constantly being discovered and where challenges are revealed so they can be overcome. For Reds, a missed opportunity equals failure. Reds want to rise to positions of ever-increasing authority, thereby creating platforms for ever-widening spheres of influence, direction, and responsibility.

For Reds, there is a desire to accomplish things and direct others—but not at the expense of others. Reds believe that competition is the "name of the game" and that winning—both the goals that they seek and the loyalty of others—is the real measure of success.

OBSERVING RED BEHAVIORS

While motives cannot be directly observed, consistencies in behavior can offer insight into a person's underlying motives. Reds are motivated by task accomplishment and achieving results. They have a strong desire to set goals, take decisive action, and claim earned rewards. They express their motives through behavior and tend to:

- Compete for authority, responsibility, and positions of leadership.
- Exert power and control to achieve results.
- Challenge the opposition, actively engaging to overcome resistance.
- Exercise persuasion, using arguments to convince and direct.
- Set goals and deadlines, allocate tasks, and monitor progress.
- Seek out opportunities that others miss.
- Take quick action, seeking immediate results.
- Claim the right to earned rewards when the results are delivered.
- Expect recognition if they've steered things to a successful conclusion.
- Accept risk-taking as necessary and desirable.

Red strengths confirm the self-worth of both people in a relationship. When Red strengths are overdone, they may threaten the self-worth of Reds or other people who perceive these strengths as overdone. Table 2.2 illustrates two examples.

Table 2.2 *Examples of Red Overdone Strengths*

Productive Strength	Effect of Overdone Strength
When Reds speak or act directly in order to get to the bottom line, results in the relationship can be achieved more quickly.	When Reds are overly direct, they may be viewed as tactless or abrasive, which can generate resistance to action and hard feelings in the relationship.
When Reds are confident in their beliefs and capabilities, it can raise the confidence of others and encourage them to follow.	When Reds are overly confident, they may attempt to do more than is realistic, and they may be viewed as arrogant.

REASONS THAT REDS ENTER CONFLICT

Reds tend to go into conflict about things that block their ability to get things done, to provide leadership, to achieve goals, and to take necessary risks. They have difficulty with people who don't stand up for themselves or withhold their opinions or ideas. Awareness of the potential causes of conflict can help Reds manage their own reactions to conflict triggers and can help others adjust their behaviors in an attempt to prevent conflict.

Reds may experience conflict when they perceive any of the following conflict triggers:

- Others do not view them as strong, ambitious people, deserving of the opportunity to provide leadership and direction.
- Others do not clearly understand the productivity behind the exercise of power and control.
- Other people view Reds' love of competition as unhealthy rivalry.
- People appear gullible, indecisive, or incapable of action.
- Others lose out because they are unwilling to stand up for themselves.
- Others keep a shell of reserve around themselves that Reds cannot penetrate.
- Behaviors directed at making everyone winners are viewed as unfeeling and/or dictatorial.
- The desire to get an immediate outcome is viewed as irrational and uncaring.
- Relationships are clouded with emotions that confuse issues and make the right choice of action difficult.
- Pursuit of the desired goal is lost through unnecessary, time-consuming collaboration or emotional considerations.

When in conflict, Reds want to defend their values, so they can get back to relating to others productively. The ways they defend their MVS in an effort to return to feeling good about themselves will vary, depending on their Conflict Sequences.

PRODUCTIVE RESULTS OF CONFLICT FOR REDS

When in conflict, regardless of their individual different Conflict Sequences, Reds share a desire to return to feelings of self-worth and activities that lead to results. They are more likely to resolve conflict when they see the potential for some of these outcomes:

- Renewed focus on task accomplishment with a clarified direction.
- New opportunities that are innovative and creative.
- Increased energy that allows a robust exchange of ideas.
- Renewed effort for personal and team advancement.
- Willingness on the part of others to take a chance.

HOW REDS CAN IMPROVE INTERACTIONS

Reds' preferred approaches to situations and other people may not always result in outcomes that are valuable to Reds or to others. Assertive strengths may not fit certain situations, or they may be perceived as overdone, possibly triggering conflict in others. Adjusting behavior is most effective when considering the MVS of others, and advice about how to approach people with different Motivational Value Systems can be found in the other MVS sections of this book.

Reds may bear the burden of pride. Reds like to be the best at what they do, but no person can be the best at everything. In classic literature, the tragic flaw of *hubris* or pride makes every hero fail. When Reds are so proud they fail to assess their weaknesses adequately, they risk failure. Pride may keep Reds from hearing an opposite argument that will achieve better results or seeing the flaws in their own plans.

In general, Reds may be able to improve the quality of their interactions, and the results they produce, by deploying some behaviors that are not typical of their MVS. Some examples include:

- Regulating their natural energy around issues that are important to them, acknowledging that their passion may sometimes intimidate others.
- Attending to relationships on a daily basis—not just when something is needed.

- Slowing down and thinking things through before attempting to persuade others of their position.
- Being more considerate of other people's feelings and wishes.
- Soliciting input from others, even when the right course of action seems obvious.
- Being more tolerant of people who have difficulty standing up for themselves.

THE RED STYLE OF PERSONAL LEADERSHIP

When leading others, Reds tend to focus on the vision, goal, or other results, believing that competition strengthens everyone involved. Reds view the purpose of leadership as setting goals and targets, defining success, and inspiring people to take on challenges. The Red style of leadership is by direction and example, initiating ambitious tasks and projects and expecting others to do the same. Red leadership is often characterized by:

- Striving for results quickly and efficiently.
- Providing rewards for innovation and performance.
- Being generous and responsive to those who are loyal and committed.
- Being willing to take risks and absorb small defeats in pursuit of long-term gains.

Working with REDS

LISTENING TO REDS

Working effectively with Reds means you will need to understand what they are saying. Listening well to Reds will ensure that they feel heard, and know that you understand what they are trying to do. When you are listening, and engaging in dialogue, keep these points in mind:

- When listening, interpret through the lens of their ultimate goal or objective.
- Don't mistake directiveness for being controlling; they just want to make something happen.
- Be energetic, direct, and focused on results.
- Don't waste time. Don't revisit past decisions unless absolutely necessary.
- Keep a brisk pace. Always look ahead to what might be coming up next.

REWARDING AND RECOGNIZING REDS

Reds like to be recognized and respected for their ability to get things done and told that their accomplishments made a significant difference in the organizational "big picture." Reds will generally claim earned rewards and will compete vigorously for the right to do so.

The best compliments are specific about the effectiveness of the direction provided and to the success of the outcomes. Some compliments might include:

- "That project would never have happened without your focus, passion, and ability to get things done."
- "Your direction and extra push made it possible for me to achieve my goals."
- "You have set a new standard that others will have to measure up to."
- "You have achieved the best results possible for this company—and for your customers."

HOW TO APPROACH REDS

- Be clear, direct, positive, challenging, and brief.
- Start with a goal or result, and get to the point quickly.
- Identify opportunities, and show confidence.
- Have clear time frames, end results, benefits, and relevant facts.
- Hear them out fully.

THINGS TO AVOID WHEN APPROACHING REDS

- Interrupting, indecisiveness, giving in too quickly.
- Wasting time, not getting to the point.
- Focusing overly on social matters, details, or emotions.
- Taking undeserved credit or denying appropriate credit to them.
- Withholding information that could affect goals or task accomplishment.

PREVENTING CONFLICT WITH REDS

Much conflict with Reds can be prevented by acting or communicating in ways that recognize and respect Reds' MVS and that do not introduce conflict triggers. Proactive conflict prevention strategies can be employed to reduce the chance that the self-worth of Reds will be threatened.

- Deliver important and appropriate data directly, using a point-by-point approach.
- Demonstrate an understanding of the issue's importance, and respond with an appropriate sense of urgency.
- Stand and engage with passion and energy.
- When expressing an opinion or idea, get to the point quickly.
- Deliver your ideas with confidence, as a subdued approach may be perceived as weakness or uncertainty.
- Match the Red intensity whenever possible, indicating a clear understanding of the urgency of the issue.
- Use phrases like, "This is priority number one," "We need a solution now," and, "What do you want me to do?"
- Focus on resolving the issue and on taking action.
- Intensify language and word choices.
- De-personalize the issue by keeping the interaction free from unnecessary emotions.

INFLUENCING REDS

The key to influencing Reds is to create or communicate conditions that are intrinsically rewarding to them. The more that what you want them to do is clearly linked to accomplishment and the direction of people and resources toward results, the more willing Reds will generally be to engage their strengths in those activities.

Reds will tend to feel more motivated in challenging, fast-moving, and opportunity-rich environments. They are likely to follow people who are generous and responsive and who want to include Reds in their success.

To influence Reds, engage them in a conversation about how a desired action will:

- Allow them to compete fairly and be rewarded for winning.
- Quickly seize an opportunity.
- Provide opportunities to lead and direct others productively.
- Engage them in a challenging venture.

GREEN MVS

ANALYTIC-AUTONOMIZING

An•a•lyt•ic—methodical examination of structures or information
Au•ton•o•mi•zing—maintaining objective independence, self-governing

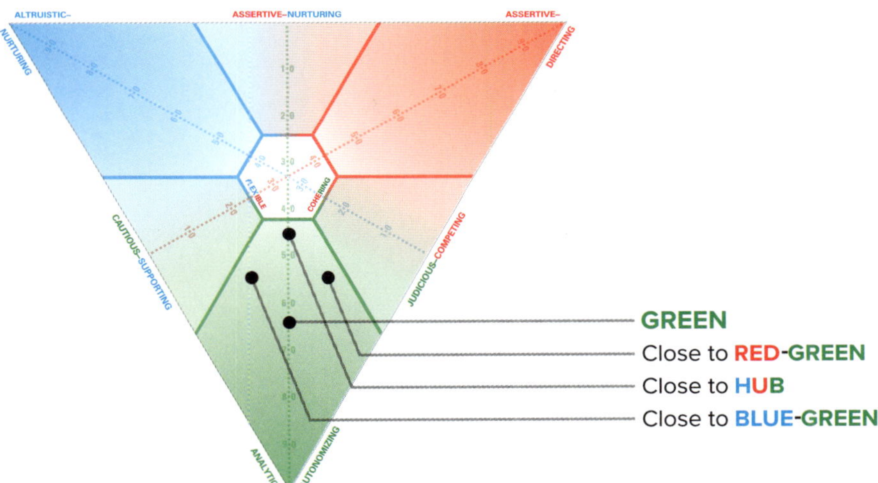

This descriptive text is written about an MVS dot in the center of the Green MVS region. Individuals with MVS dots close to the borders (within 6 points) of other MVS regions may differ slightly from this description. They will likely find that the descriptions of the neighboring region(s) also influence their understanding of themselves and the way they are perceived by others.

GREEN MOTIVES AND VALUES

The motivation of people with an Analytic-Autonomizing Motivational Value System (hereafter referred to as Greens) is to achieve feelings of self-worth by creating self-direction and autonomy through logical analysis and thoughtful planning.

Greens tend to find satisfaction in life through independent discovery, interpreting and explaining things based on analysis. They value the pursuit of excellence and the principled application of policies, procedures, and services. Greens understand and value the productivity behind exercising foresight, planning carefully, and attaining certainty before commitment. Greens tend to believe in the full, careful consideration of any potential action. Greens value the power of shaping order out of chaos.

Greens' sense of personal integrity comes from establishing and maintaining a sense of order, objectivity, and independence. For Greens, the real measure of success is achieving control over their own lives and emotions. Greens believe in fairness over feelings and in principles over power. Greens tend to feel a sense of self-worth when others respect them for their logic and fairness and when their right to privacy is valued and honored. Greens tend to view the preservation of resources as a means to ensure self-dependence.

For Greens, life is often about thinking things through and creating structure in whatever they do. Greens tend to want systems that minimize risks by always planning ahead. Greens prefer to rely on the use of logic, facts, and rationale, carefully weighing alternatives to ensure predictability and order.

OBSERVING GREEN BEHAVIORS

While motives cannot be directly observed, consistencies in behavior can offer insight into a person's underlying motives. Greens are motivated by meaningful order and thinking things through. They have a strong desire to pursue independent interests, to be practical, and to be fair. They express their motives through behavior and tend to:

- Be objective and logical, practically thinking things through before taking action.
- Be cautious and thorough, documenting details to ensure accuracy.
- Weigh alternatives, seeking solutions that are practical and fair.
- Give careful consideration to all costs of any plan or action.
- Maintain their self-dependence, working alone when possible.
- Create meaningful order from chaos, building systems to maintain ongoing effectiveness.
- Plan carefully, double-checking facts and preparing alternative and/or "fall back" plans.
- Approach life seriously, providing thoughtful consideration of all aspects of a situation.

- Manage their emotions, diminishing the impact of feelings on outcomes and relying on logical interaction as the primary communication style.
- Act with resolution and perseverance to implement a carefully considered, logically developed plan.

Green strengths confirm the self-worth of both people in a relationship. When Green strengths are overdone, they may threaten the self-worth of Greens or other people who perceive these strengths as overdone. Table 2.3 illustrates two examples:

Table 2.3 *Examples of Green Overdone Strengths*

Productive Strength	Effect of Overdone Strength
When Greens analyze situations in ways that enable more effective decisions, everyone involved can benefit.	When Greens over-analyze situations, they may be slow to decide; in response, others may make decisions without Greens' input.
When Greens are cautious, they identify risks and thereby enable everyone to avoid negative outcomes.	When Greens are overly cautious, they may become suspicious and disregard the input of other people.

REASONS THAT GREENS ENTER CONFLICT

Greens tend to go into conflict about things that restrict or limit their self-reliance, things that are disorderly, chaotic, irrational, or things that seem to be the result of biased or emotional decision making. They have difficulty with people who don't take things seriously or violate rules or principles. Awareness of the potential causes of conflict can help Greens to manage their own reactions to conflict triggers and can help others adjust their behavior in an attempt to prevent conflict.

Greens may experience conflict when they perceive any of the following conflict triggers:

- Others force them to rush decisions and to make plans without time for the consideration of details.
- Those around them continually minimize the need for organized plans that are based on logic and careful analysis.
- Others are using broad, unsubstantiated statements as justification for their choices.

- The opposition or conflict is based in emotion.
- They are feeling pressured to accept the opinions of others, forcing unjustifiable compliance.
- They are required to jump to conclusions, making guesses or estimates without adequate time or information.
- Others imply that they are not fair and principled—just fearful.
- The people around them are overly helpful, unaware that the desire to help can be perceived as an invasion of personal rights.
- They are forced to do things someone else's way without adequate explanation.
- They think that others do not take things seriously, lose focus, or trivialize the importance of a calm, orderly world in which to live and work.

When in conflict, Greens want to defend their values, so they can get back to relating to others productively. The way they defend their MVS in an effort to return to feeling good about themselves will vary, depending on their Conflict Sequence.

PRODUCTIVE RESULTS OF CONFLICT FOR GREENS

When in conflict, regardless of their individual different Conflict Sequences, Greens share a desire to return to feelings of self-worth and to activities that are logical and orderly. They are more likely to resolve conflict when they see the potential for some of these outcomes:

- Re-establishing meaningful order, which eliminates the irrational chaos.
- Re-focusing on tasks because predictable systems are working again.
- Creating more effective relationships because expectations are clear.
- Feeling a sense of independence and efficiency when all of the pieces are working together properly.
- Creating greater interpersonal commitment and participation in an improved and clarified plan.

HOW GREENS CAN IMPROVE INTERACTIONS

Greens' preferred approach to situations and other people may not always result in outcomes that are valuable to Greens or to others. Analytical strengths may not fit certain situations, or they may be perceived as overdone, possibly triggering conflict in others. Adjusting behavior is most effective when considering the MVS of others, and advice about how to approach people with different Motivational Value Systems can be found in the other MVS sections of this book.

Greens may bear the burden of certainty. Grounded in facts, systems, and logic, Greens approach the world in a thoughtful way. Because they have thought things through before they present their ideas, they tend to be certain of their correctness, and they have the facts to support that claim. Yet, the selection of data is a subjective process. The hard truth for Greens is that no one, no matter how analytical and rational they are, can be right all of the time.

In general, Greens may be able to improve the quality of their interactions, and the results they produce, by deploying some behaviors that are not typical of their MVS. Some examples include:

- Being open to uncertainty and ambiguity.
- Expressing feelings and reactions so that others will know what they are thinking.
- Accepting help from others when it could be useful.
- Ranking the urgency and importance of completion of some tasks over having all the information desired.
- Moving forward quickly and viewing activity as an experiment with an inherent learning opportunity.
- Considering emotions as additional data, becoming more familiar with what they mean to others.

THE GREEN STYLE OF PERSONAL LEADERSHIP

When leading others, Greens tend to focus on planning that requires logical analysis and rational consistency, believing that great systems will produce great results. Greens view the purpose of leadership as the creation of systems and structures that ensure predictable activity and use unplanned events as opportunities to improve the system. The Green leadership style is principle-centered and process-based, methodically managing people and situations. Their leadership is often characterized by:

- Establishing policies and procedures that govern organizational and individual activity.
- Developing contingency plans to reduce risk.
- Requiring individual self-reliance and rational interactions.
- Conservative use of resources with an emphasis on sustainability.

Working with GREENS

LISTENING TO GREENS

Working effectively with Greens means you will need to understand what they are saying. Listening well to Greens will ensure that they feel heard, and know that you understand the reasoning behind their statements. When you are listening, and engaging in dialogue, keep these points in mind:

- When listening, interpret through the lens of underlying principles or logic.
- Don't mistake silence for disinterest; they are waiting to understand completely before offering input.
- Be calm, clear, complete, and correct.
- Don't push for estimates, guesses, or quick decisions. Don't bend the rules.
- Allow plenty of time for consideration. Be comfortable with periods of silence.

REWARDING AND RECOGNIZING GREENS

Greens like to be respected for their expertise, reliability, and judgment; they like to know that any structure or system they create is useful to others. Greens generally prefer that rewards and praise be given personally, in private settings or small groups. They may appear to be somewhat independent of the reward structure within which they operate.

The best compliments are specific about being rational and reliable, conserving resources, or preventing difficulties by planning ahead. Some compliments might include:

- "Your careful, well-thought-out plan resulted in our completing the project on time and on budget."
- "Your analysis and recommendations significantly improved the system."
- "Your research saved us from making a serious mistake."
- "Your cool, level-headed approach restored objectivity and saved hours of confusion."

HOW TO APPROACH GREENS

- Remain objective, logical, fair, and in control of emotions.
- Respect principles and procedures.

- Be prepared to present supportable facts calmly and methodically.
- Ask questions for added clarification, and allow time for considered responses.
- Analyze the impact of potential decisions.

THINGS TO AVOID WHEN APPROACHING GREENS

- Using broad, unsubstantiated statements or arguments based on emotion.
- Forcing opinions on them, jumping to conclusions, demanding guesses or estimates.
- Rushing discussions and leaving out details.
- Trivializing the need for structure and plans.
- Prying, small talk, inappropriate humor, or forcing help on them.

PREVENTING CONFLICT WITH GREENS

Much conflict with Greens can be prevented by acting or communicating in ways that recognize and respect Greens' MVS and do not introduce conflict triggers. Proactive conflict prevention strategies can be employed to reduce the chance that the self-worth of Greens will be threatened.

- Avoid using broad, unsubstantiated statements or arguments based on emotion.
- Resist making assumptions or jumping to conclusions.
- Be logical and substantive in support of your opinions.
- Allow time for thoughtful consideration without rushing discussions or leaving out details.
- Be conversationally appropriate, avoiding small talk or humor that might be misunderstood.
- Consider the logic of your request or approach, asking questions for clarification.
- Be prepared to present supportable facts calmly, methodically, and unemotionally.

INFLUENCING GREENS

The key to influencing Greens is to create or communicate conditions that are intrinsically rewarding to Greens. The more that what you want them to do is clearly linked to the establishment and maintenance of meaningful order, the more willing Greens will generally be to engage their strengths in those activities.

Greens will tend to feel more motivated in organized and predictable environments that allow sufficient time for decision-making. They are likely to follow people who are open and clear about what they want, without imposing their wants or feelings on Greens.

To influence Greens, engage them in a conversation about how a desired action will:

- Permit them to pursue their interests without undue outside direction.
- Be fair, practical, and adhere to principles.
- Increase the predictability or reliability of a system or environment.
- Enable the testing of a hypothesis or create a learning experience.

RED-BLUE MVS

ASSERTIVE-NURTURING

As•ser•tive—confidently self-assured and forceful
Nur•tur•ing—protecting, supporting, and encouraging others

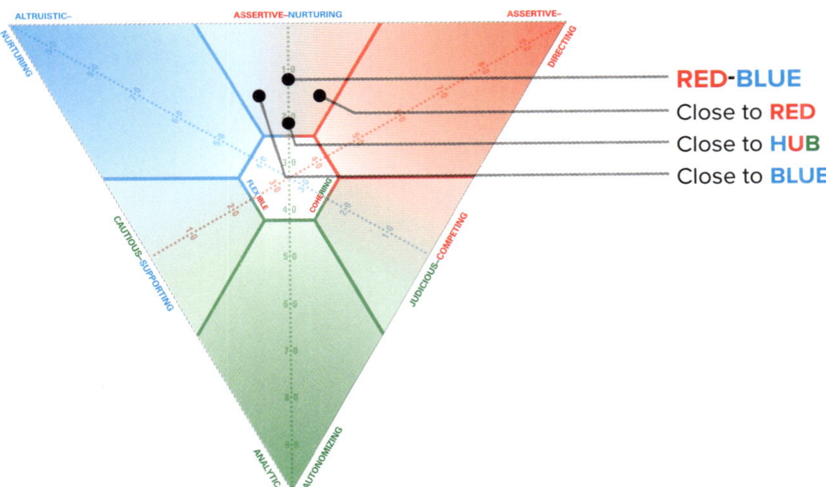

This descriptive text is written about an MVS dot in the center of the Red-Blue MVS region. Individuals with MVS dots close to the borders (within 6 points) of other MVS regions may differ slightly from this description. They will likely find that the descriptions of the neighboring region(s) also influence their understanding of themselves and the way they are perceived by others.

RED-BLUE MOTIVES AND VALUES

The motivation of people with an Assertive-Nurturing Motivational Value System (hereafter referred to as Red-Blues) is to achieve feelings of self-worth by actively encouraging others to grow, succeed, and accomplish results together.

Red-Blues tend to find satisfaction in life by identifying needs quickly, then moving swiftly toward bringing assistance to those in need. They feel drawn to mentoring relationships and often defend those perceived as being vulnerable. Red-Blues are focused on the achievement of their goals, while also actively encouraging others to grow and succeed through their guidance. Red-Blues value the power of recognizing and rapidly developing the potential of others.

Red-Blues' sense of personal integrity comes from advocating for the protection, growth, and welfare of others through task accomplishment and leadership. They tend to combine a friendly and direct approach, gaining satisfaction from seeing others move forward and benefit from their coaching. They value decisiveness and are often quick to know what they should do and what others should do. Red-Blues view advice to others as an expression of their concern for others and belief in others' potential.

For Red-Blues, there is a clear understanding of the compassionate use of power and the need to act promptly in matters affecting others' welfare. Red-Blues work hard to earn recognition and appreciation. They tend to be open, enthusiastic, and friendly, demonstrating sincere compassion for others. They are positive and usually want to support initiatives that facilitate the growth and development of others.

OBSERVING RED-BLUE BEHAVIORS

While motives cannot be directly observed, consistencies in behavior can offer insight into a person's underlying motives. Red-Blues are motivated by the maximum growth and development of others. That have a strong desire to direct, persuade, or lead others for the benefit of others. They express their motives through behavior and tend to:

- Actively seek opportunities to support others.
- Persuade and energize others, often resulting in the growth and development of others.
- Be open to proposals for creating welfare and security for others.
- Create enthusiasm and support in tackling obstacles to success.
- Be positive, enthusiastic, and forward-thinking.
- Demonstrate sincerity, compassion, and decisiveness.
- Clearly state how goals will benefit others, and make decisions on their behalf.
- Recognize the importance of results and the needs of others.
- Be direct, friendly, and action-oriented.

Red-Blue strengths confirm the self-worth of both people in a relationship. When Red-Blue strengths are overdone, they may threaten the self-worth of Red-Blues or other people who perceive these strengths as overdone. Table 2.4 illustrates two examples:

Table 2.4 *Examples of Red-Blue Overdone Strengths*

Productive Strength	Effect of Overdone Strength
When Red-Blues are enthusiastic, they can inspire others to overcome obstacles and become more successful.	When Red-Blues are overly enthusiastic, they may disregard information or push people to act before they are ready.
When Red-Blues are compassionate, they accurately assess and meet the needs of others.	When the compassion of Red-Blues is focused on people before they are ready, it can be viewed as pressuring and intrusive.

REASONS THAT RED-BLUES ENTER CONFLICT

Red-Blues tend to go into conflict about things that impede or delay progress, especially when rules or processes get in the way of doing the right thing for others. They have difficulty with people who are self-serving or stand by idly when others are in need. Awareness of the potential causes of conflict can help Red-Blues to manage their own reactions to conflict triggers and can help others adjust their behavior in an attempt to prevent conflict.

Red-Blues may experience conflict when they perceive any of the following conflict triggers:

- Other people are negative about options and possibilities, refusing to get involved.
- Too much time or detail is required before a decision can be made.
- Others are being taken advantage of, disregarded, blamed, or excluded.
- Their involvement and/or contributions are asked for and then ignored.
- Others refuse to get involved, withholding support for people who could truly benefit.
- Others behave indifferently, seeming to ignore or take for granted the hard work and dedication of Red-Blues.
- The people around them perceive Red-Blue assertiveness as aggression, making accusations that Red-Blues are exploiting others for their own means.

- They feel isolated or left out of what is happening.
- The guidance they offer is not accepted, but instead challenged or even rejected.
- Plans that could lead to others' success are overruled, and the human cost of decisions is ignored.

When in conflict, Red-Blues want to defend their values, so they can get back to relating to others productively. The way they defend their MVS in an effort to return to feeling good about themselves will vary, depending on their Conflict Sequence.

PRODUCTIVE RESULTS OF CONFLICT FOR RED-BLUES

When in conflict, regardless of their individual different Conflict Sequences, Red-Blues share a desire to return to feelings of self-worth and activities that develop others. They are more likely to resolve conflict when they see the potential for some of these outcomes:

- Harmony, openness, and straight-talk in the relationship will be quickly restored.
- Barriers to development will be overcome or removed.
- Others will feel valued because their needs were clearly considered during conflict resolution.
- People who have been disadvantaged will be given equal access to resources or opportunities.
- A renewed and blame-free commitment to each other is established, even in the face of future adversity.

HOW RED-BLUES CAN IMPROVE INTERACTIONS

Red-Blues' preferred approach to situations and other people may not always result in outcomes that are valuable to Red-Blues or to others. Mentoring strengths may not fit certain situations, or they may be perceived as overdone, possibly triggering conflict in others. Adjusting behavior is most effective when considering the MVS of others, and advice about how to approach people with different Motivational Value Systems can be found in the other MVS sections of this book.

Red-Blues may carry the burdens of pride from Red and guilt from Blue. Red-Blues are driven by leading others to get the best results in their lives. Red-Blues take great satisfaction in quickly being able to feel what "the best" is. If that help should fail or be perceived as meddling, Red-Blues may feel guilty because the right result was not achieved. In addition, they may feel discouraged because they should have known how to best advise others.

In general, Red-Blues may be able to improve the quality of their interactions, and the results they produce, by deploying some behaviors that are not typical of their MVS. Some examples include:

- Taking time to assess whether others actually require input or advice before offering advice or help.
- Softening the intensity and directness of communication to ensure that an assertive style does not hide the nurturing intent.
- Pausing, giving others time to think, and listening fully to others before responding.
- Methodically considering the steps required to achieve a goal, without offering too many ideas too quickly.
- Setting opinions about others' best interest aside momentarily and listening carefully to what others desire.
- Calculating the risks inherent in a course of action and becoming more cautious about when to offer support.

THE RED-BLUE STYLE OF PERSONAL LEADERSHIP

When leading others, Red-Blues tend to focus on coaching or mentoring others, believing that by providing assistance, encouragement, and challenges, others will rise to higher levels of engagement and performance. Red-Blues view the purpose of leadership as directing others for the benefit of those others. The Red-Blue leadership style is energetic and charismatic, inspiring people to create a better future that meets the needs of people. Their leadership is often characterized by:

- Seeking opportunities to mentor and coach others.
- Celebrating accomplishments and successes.
- Advising others on how to be their best by actively providing feedback to improve their lives, professionally and personally.
- Focusing others on finding and seizing opportunities.
- Giving extra support to the disadvantaged or overlooked.

Working with RED-BLUES

LISTENING TO RED-BLUES

Working effectively with Red-Blues means you will need to understand what they are saying. Listening well to Red-Blues will ensure that they feel heard, and know that you appreciate their efforts on behalf of others. When you are listening, and engaging in dialogue, keep these points in mind:

- When listening, interpret through the lens of how they are trying to build up other people.
- Don't mistake their advice as commands; they are enthusiastic about what they think you should do.
- Be enthusiastic, considerate of others, and focused on action.
- Don't overwhelm with details. Avoid extensive analysis or explanations.
- Show a sense of urgency when others are in need. Quickly do what seems best.

REWARDING AND RECOGNIZING RED-BLUES

Red-Blues like to be known for their compassion and their ability to improve the lives of others through advice, coaching, or direct intervention. Red-Blues tend to like both public and private recognition and also enjoy seeing the people they helped earn rewards and recognition.

The best compliments are specific about the advice, challenge, or support that led a person or a group to improve. Some compliments might include:

- "We would have never overcome those obstacles without your enthusiasm, hard work, and support."
- "You always know exactly what I need."
- "I admire the way you build other people up; it really makes a difference here."
- "It's so inspiring, the way you recognize talent in people that others miss."
- "You really encouraged people to do their best."
- "It was great to see how people worked so well together under your direction."
- "People will really benefit from your efforts."

HOW TO APPROACH RED-BLUES

- Be positive, enthusiastic, open, and forward-thinking.
- Demonstrate sincerity, compassion, and decisiveness.
- Clearly state how goals will benefit others.
- Recognize the importance of results and the needs of others.
- Keep it direct, simple, friendly, and action-oriented.

THINGS TO AVOID WHEN APPROACHING RED-BLUES

- Being negative, indecisive, apathetic, or refusing to get involved.
- Over-emphasizing process, details, or rules.

- Lacking enthusiasm or focus.
- Disregarding the needs of others, taking advantage of others, or putting self-interest first.
- Ignoring or diminishing their involvement or contributions.

PREVENTING CONFLICT WITH RED-BLUES

Much conflict with Red-Blues can be prevented by acting or communicating in ways that recognize and respect Red-Blues' MVS and do not introduce conflict triggers. Proactive conflict prevention strategies can be employed to reduce the chance that the self-worth of Red-Blues will be threatened.

- Emphasize that you understand how important the issue is to them and that you are committed to solving the problem.
- Demonstrate an understanding of their intent to benefit others through action.
- Clarify that maintaining the relationship is just as important as solving any problem.
- Use energy in your response, reflecting back an understanding of the urgency around finding solutions.
- Don't make commitments lightly or change an agreed-upon course of action.

INFLUENCING RED-BLUES

The key to influencing Red-Blues is to create or communicate conditions that are intrinsically rewarding to Red-Blues. The more what you want them to do is clearly linked to the protection, growth, and welfare of others through task accomplishment, the more willing Red-Blues will be to engage their strengths in those activities.

Red-Blues will tend to feel more motivated in enthusiastic, open, compassionate, and growth-oriented environments. They are likely to follow people who share their power with others, rather than exercise their power over others.

To influence Red-Blues, engage them in a conversation about how a desired action will:

- Create security and well-being for others.
- Generate enthusiasm and buy-in for others to overcome obstacles.
- Result in appreciation and respect from people who benefit from their actions.
- Give an advantage to people who deserve it.

RED-GREEN MVS

JUDICIOUS-COMPETING

Ju•di•cious—having, showing, or being done with good judgment or sense
Com•pet•ing—striving to gain or win by doing something better than others

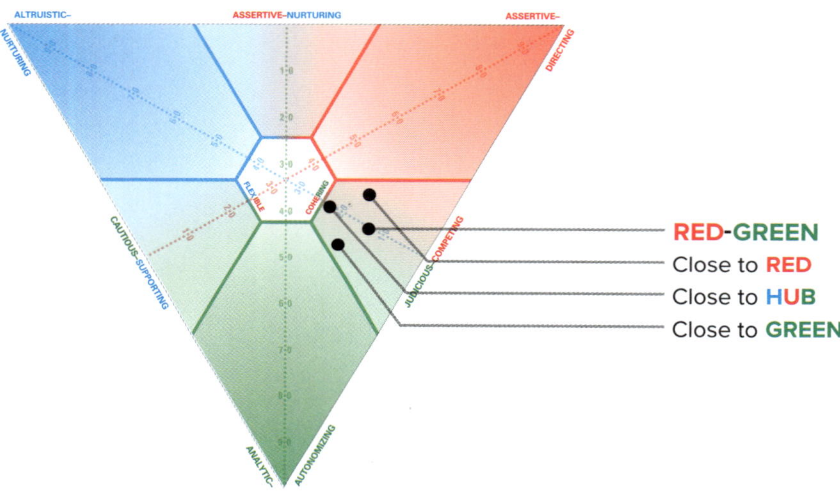

This descriptive text is written about an MVS dot in the center of the Red-Green MVS region. Individuals with MVS dots close to the borders (within 6 points) of other MVS regions may differ slightly from this description. Individuals with MVS dots in the Red-Green MVS region close to the borders (within six points) of other MVS regions may differ slightly from this description. They will likely find that the descriptions of the neighboring region(s) also influence their understanding of themselves and the way they are perceived by others.

RED-GREEN MOTIVES AND VALUES

The motivation of people with a Judicious-Competing Motivational Value System (hereafter referred to as Red-Greens) is to achieve feelings of self-worth by using carefully thought-out strategies to achieve ambitious and rational objectives.

Red-Greens tend to find satisfaction in life by providing rational leadership that assesses risk and opportunity, integrating those components into elegantly planned victories. Red-Greens' self-worth is affirmed by the efficient execution of logical plans and complex strategies. The accomplishment process must be logical, and the achievement of desired goals must come through an orderly action plan. Red-Greens value the power of systemic, strategic planning and implementation.

Red-Greens' sense of personal integrity comes from using strategies and efficient tactics to maximize the use of resources. They are supportive and loyal to those who will help them, without hesitation or qualification, to be successful. They integrate planning and implementation, viewing the concepts as virtually indistinguishable.

For Red-Greens, there is a clear understanding of the rational use of power and the desire to act promptly with good judgment in matters affecting their competitive edge. Red-Greens tend to be strong and principled. They want to earn recognition and respect. They feel responsible for developing and leading winning strategies, and they want to direct others in an impartial, efficient manner.

OBSERVING RED-GREEN BEHAVIORS

While motives cannot be directly observed, consistencies in behavior can offer insight into a person's underlying motives. Red-Greens are motivated by intelligent assertiveness and fairness in competition. They have a strong desire to develop strategy and assess risks and opportunities. They express their motives through behavior and tend to:

- Provide rational leadership that can assess risks and opportunities.
- Be decisive and proactive when all the facts are in.
- Challenge opposition through thoughtful process and strategy.
- Demonstrate understanding of the situation, and get to the point deliberately.
- Have facts available to support a winning strategy.
- Confidently communicate relevant facts that lead to justifiable action.
- Compete against others and against their own past performances.
- Be challenging, realistic, and open to a well-thought-out response.
- Think strategically and logically.
- Defend logical positions with energy and forcefulness.

Red-Green strengths confirm the self-worth of both people in a relationship. When Red-Green strengths are overdone, they may threaten the self-worth of

Red-Greens or other people who perceive these strengths as overdone. Table 2.5 illustrates two examples:

Table 2.5 *Examples of Red-Green Overdone Strengths*

Productive Strength	Effect of Overdone Strength
When Red-Greens compete toward shared goals or objectives, everyone benefits from the success.	When Red-Greens are overly competitive, they may disregard how others feel about the goals.
When Red-Greens are strategic, they can identify the most efficient method of accomplishing something.	When Red-Greens are overly strategic, their methods may be viewed as manipulative or self-serving.

REASONS THAT RED-GREENS ENTER CONFLICT

Red-Greens tend to go into conflict about things that block their ability to plan or implement logical plans. They have difficulty with people who give up too easily, who are overly emotional, intrusive, or who think illogically. Awareness of the potential causes of conflict can help Red-Greens manage their own reactions to conflict triggers and can help others adjust their behavior in an attempt to prevent conflict.

Red-Greens may experience conflict when they perceive any of the following conflict triggers:

- They are required to slow down for what they determine to be an invalid reason.
- An important decision is being made without adequate thought and analysis, possibly resulting in a rash or unexpected result.
- There is too much emphasis on the interpersonal aspects of a task.
- Others are behaving in an impulsive or emotional way.
- Logic is overlooked in the planning process.
- They are treated with passivity or ignorance.
- Others perceive their choices as mindless or aggressive.
- They are operating in an environment that does not recognize achievement or an environment where achievement is difficult to quantify.
- They must comply with a system that requires unnecessary steps.
- They are being forced to operate within the constraints of rules that are illogical or counterproductive.

When in conflict, Red-Greens want to defend their values, so they can get back to relating to others productively. The way they defend their MVS in an effort to return to feeling good about themselves will vary, depending on their Conflict Sequence.

PRODUCTIVE RESULTS OF CONFLICT FOR RED-GREENS

When in conflict, regardless of their individual different Conflict Sequences, Red-Greens share a desire to return to feelings of self-worth and activities that are rational and strategic. They are more likely to resolve conflict when they see the potential for some of these outcomes:

- Quick, clear action will be supported by a logical plan.
- Better alignment will be achieved, because the thinking behind the action will be understood and accepted.
- Appropriate but not excessive time will be allocated to develop an action plan.
- Problems will be solved efficiently and without emotion so resolution will be both fair and actionable.
- Goals will be clarified, so the conversation can shift to methods.

HOW RED-GREENS CAN IMPROVE INTERACTIONS

Red-Greens' preferred approach to situations and other people may not always result in outcomes that are valuable to Red-Greens or to others. Judicious strengths may not fit certain situations, or they may be perceived as overdone, possibly triggering conflict in others. Adjusting behavior is most effective when considering the MVS of others, and advice about how to approach people with different Motivational Value Systems can be found in the other MVS sections of this book.

Red-Greens may bear the burdens of pride from Red and certainty from Green. When they develop strategies to achieve desired results, they analyze situations and logically craft their approaches. The Green in the blend contributes certainty that these approaches are the correct ways to solve problems and get outcomes. The Red in the blend adds great pride in a history of developing excellent and pragmatic solutions. When Red-Greens encounter a failure of their strategies, they have to face the reality that not only were they incorrect, but that they also lost. Pride and certainty together make it difficult for Red-Greens to objectively assess their positions and remain open to others' ideas about improvement.

In general, Red-Greens may be able to improve the quality of their interactions, and the results they produce, by deploying some behaviors that are not typical of their MVS. Some examples include:

- Taking time to check in with people on a personal level.
- Making people's issues or the affect on people part of every strategy.
- Being tolerant of people who are not focused primarily on the big picture.
- Accepting the suggestions of others as tentative revisions to collaboratively explore.
- Including all people who could be affected in planning processes.
- Recognizing and rewarding people for meeting expectations, rather than only for exceeding expectations.

THE RED-GREEN STYLE OF PERSONAL LEADERSHIP

When leading others, Red-Greens tend to focus on the effective execution of plans, believing that a clear strategy is a mandate for action. Red-Greens view the purpose of leadership as rationally using power to increase the probability of success. The Red-Green leadership style is precise, principled, and decisive when the facts are in, optimizing resources and overpowering obstacles to assure victory. Their leadership style is often characterized by:

- Figuring all the angles and developing winning strategies.
- Organizing commitment and resources to get to the goal in the most streamlined manner.
- Building the capacity of an organization for low maintenance and high performance.
- Seeking tactical leverage points to multiply the effects of people's efforts and invested resources.

Working with RED-GREENS

LISTENING TO RED-GREENS

Working effectively with Red-Greens means you will need to understand what they are saying. Listening well to Red-Greens will ensure that they feel heard, and know that you understand what they see as the most logical course of action. When you are listening, and engaging in dialogue, keep these points in mind:

- When listening, interpret through the lens of how things fit with the bigger strategy.

- Don't mistake comments about problems as resistance; they are trying to identify and solve issues so things will be more efficient.
- Be direct, logical, assertive, and objective.
- Don't prioritize emotion over reason. Avoid small-talk until the main topics are covered.
- Take time to clarify goals. Move quickly when plans are clear.

REWARDING AND RECOGNIZING RED-GREENS

Red-Greens like to be valued for their pragmatic and strategic skills and their ability to condense large volumes of information into actionable plans. Red-Greens prefer that rewards be clearly structured and administered, so they can control the inputs to the system and justifiably claim the rewards.

The best compliments are about the design or implementation of strategy and the specific results that were produced. Some compliments might include:

- "That was elegantly planned and masterfully executed."
- "Your strategic insight into the challenge made it possible for us to close the deal."
- "Your analytical work and sheer force of will made the difference between success and failure."
- "You saw the opportunity in a complex situation and turned it to our advantage, while everyone else only saw the risks."

HOW TO APPROACH RED-GREENS

- Demonstrate understanding of the situation, and get to the point quickly.
- Have facts readily available to support a winning strategy.
- Confidently communicate relevant facts that lead to justifiable action.
- Be challenging, realistic, and open.
- Think strategically, logically, and impartially.

THINGS TO AVOID WHEN APPROACHING RED-GREENS

- Emotional decision-making or personalizing issues.
- Being passive, uninvolved, ambivalent, or vague.
- Giving in or giving up, unless there's a logical reason to do so.
- Accepting everything without challenging anything.
- Resisting logical solutions and related actions for emotional reasons.

PREVENTING CONFLICT WITH RED-GREENS

Much conflict with Red-Greens can be prevented by acting or communicating in ways that recognize and respect Red-Greens' MVS and do not introduce conflict triggers. Proactive conflict prevention strategies can be employed to reduce the chance the self-worth of Red-Greens will be threatened.

- Be unemotional and direct.
- Own your role in the interaction, and calmly explain the reasons behind the behaviors chosen.
- Discuss the thought processes that decisions are based upon before action is taken.
- If challenged, be prepared to stand and engage with the analysis.
- Know your position, and be prepared to defend it rationally.

INFLUENCING RED-GREENS

The key to influencing Red-Greens is to create or communicate conditions that are intrinsically rewarding to Red-Greens. The more what you want them to do is clearly linked to strategic accomplishment and fairness in competition, the more willing Red-Greens will generally be to engage their strengths in those activities.

Red-Greens will tend to feel more motivated in complex, challenging environments that offer opportunities to calculate, compete, and win. They are likely to follow people who are supportive and loyal and who will help them achieve success.

To influence Red-Greens, engage them in a conversation about how a desired action will:

- Allow them to craft and implement strategy.
- Improve their ability to compete.
- Enable them to fully survey the risks and potential rewards in a situation.
- Engage them in a rational challenge.

BLUE-GREEN MVS

CAUTIOUS-SUPPORTING

Cau•tious—careful to avoid potential problems or dangers
Sup•port•ing—providing encouragement, comfort, and emotional help

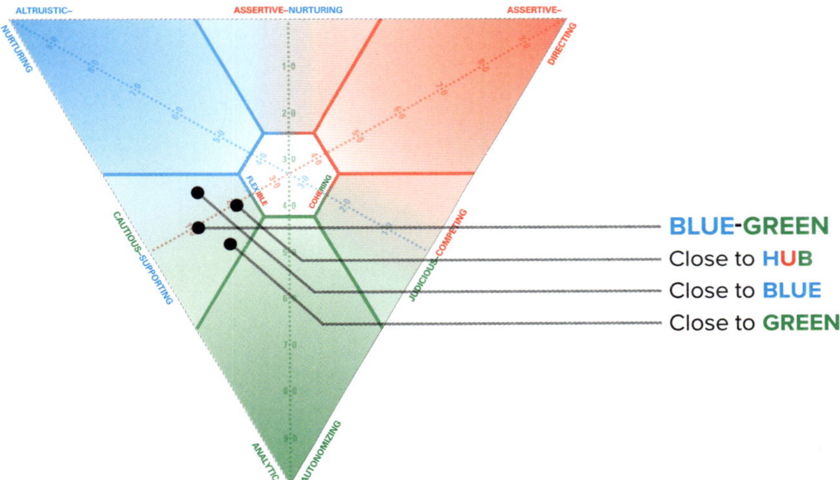

This descriptive text is written about an MVS dot in the center of the Blue-Green MVS region. Individuals with MVS dots in the Blue-Green MVS region close to the borders (within six points) of other MVS regions may differ slightly from this description. They will likely find that the descriptions of the neighboring region(s) also influence their understanding of themselves and the way they are perceived by others.

BLUE-GREEN MOTIVES AND VALUES

The motivation of people with a Cautious-Supporting Motivational Value System (hereafter referred to as Blue-Greens) is to achieve feelings of self-worth by being genuinely helpful to others while maintaining self-sufficiency for both themselves and the people they help.

Blue-Greens tend to find satisfaction in life through accurately assessing other people's needs and contributing to their self-reliance. Blue-Greens value giving assistance to people who are genuinely in need of help and are willing to utilize the help offered. Blue-Greens tend to understand and value the productivity behind moving quietly to the aid of others with an efficient plan. Blue-Greens tend to believe in prudent helpfulness, setting limits on assistance to others in order to develop their self-sufficiency. Blue-Greens value the power of building the capacity of self and others.

Blue-Greens' sense of personal integrity comes from creating fair processes that help people become self-reliant. For Blue-Greens, the real measure of success is how helpful they can be without threatening their own sense of independence or the independence of those they are helping. Blue-Greens believe in the balance of principles and feelings, of logic and emotion. Blue-Greens tend to feel rewarded when their well-planned help brings out the best in others.

For Blue-Greens, life is often about clearly understanding the use of feelings and reason to better the welfare and independence of others. Blue-Greens tend to alert others to risks they may not have considered. Blue-Greens prefer a conscientious, patient environment that respects the feelings of others and adheres to fair principles.

OBSERVING BLUE-GREEN BEHAVIORS

While motives cannot be directly observed, consistencies in behavior can offer insight into a person's underlying motives. Blue-Greens are motivated by developing self-sufficiency in self and others. They have a strong desire to analyze the needs of others and to help others help themselves. They express their motives through behavior and tend to:

- Be patient, soft-spoken, and conscientious when relating with others.
- Be fair, logical, and principled in the consideration of other people's needs.
- Help people who truly need or deserve help and who will be able to help themselves later.
- Quietly move to the aid of others using both feelings and reason.
- Defend the rights and values of others.
- Nurture the growth of other people's self-reliance through an analysis of their needs.

- Be warm and principled, combining compassion and logic to guide others.
- Be reserved and cautious about expressing their own needs, refraining from self-assertion.
- Limit the amount of help provided to others to maintain their own independence.
- Want to be included in decisions about matters affecting the welfare of others.

Blue-Green strengths confirm the self-worth of both people in a relationship. When Blue-Green strengths are overdone, they may threaten the self-worth of Blue-Greens or other people who perceive these strengths as overdone. Table 2.6 illustrates two examples:

Table 2.6 *Examples of Blue-Green Overdone Strengths*

Productive Strength	Effect of Overdone Strength
When Blue-Greens are self-sufficient, they can be productive without imposing on others.	When Blue-Greens are overly self-sufficient, they may refuse assistance and become isolated from others.
When Blue-Greens thoughtfully support others, they guide them toward future independence.	When Blue-Greens are overly supportive, they may sacrifice their own needs in the continued service of others.

REASONS THAT BLUE-GREENS ENTER CONFLICT

Blue-Greens tend to go into conflict about things that block their ability to thoughtfully encourage growth and independence or systematically bring forth the best in others. They have difficulty with people who impose their will, help, or principles on others. Awareness of the potential causes of conflict can help Blue-Greens to manage their own reactions to conflict triggers and can help others adjust their behavior in an attempt to prevent conflict.

Blue-Greens may experience conflict when they perceive any of the following conflict triggers:

- Others are being intrusive, confrontational, or invading their personal space.
- They are being pushed to move ahead before they are ready.

- People appear to be braggarts and meddlers, who presume upon and compete with others in any situation.
- They are being treated with anger or disdain and are accused of fostering child-like dependence.
- They are being pushed for an answer without being allowed time to think.
- Solutions are being dictated, and power is being used to force outcomes.
- Interactions with others are not carefully thought out, lacking the analysis to appropriately aid those who might be in need.
- Change is required before the rational justification of the need for that change is satisfactorily proven, and before the impact the change will make on others is duly considered.
- They are being pressured to get involved in something that may result in a high, personal cost to them.
- Clarification of issues and emotions is blocked, forcing action without reflective discussion.

When in conflict, Blue-Greens want to defend their values, so they can get back to relating to others productively. The way they defend their MVS in an effort to return to feeling good about themselves will vary, depending on their Conflict Sequence.

PRODUCTIVE RESULTS OF CONFLICT FOR BLUE-GREENS

When in conflict, regardless of their individual different Conflict Sequences, Blue-Greens share a desire to return to feelings of self-worth and activities that are rational and compassionate. They are more likely to resolve conflict when they see the potential for some of these outcomes:

- Balance between the problem's solution and the emotions related to the problem will be maintained.
- People who truly need and deserve help will get it.
- Expectations and boundaries will be clarified.
- Principles that were disregarded by others during the conflict will be reaffirmed and protected.
- Self-sufficiency of others and themselves will be re-established.

HOW BLUE-GREENS CAN IMPROVE INTERACTIONS

Blue-Greens' preferred approach to situations and other people may not always result in outcomes that are valuable to Blue-Greens or to others. Cautious strengths may not fit certain situations, or they may be perceived as overdone, possibly triggering conflict in others. Adjusting behavior is most effective when considering the MVS of others, and advice about how to approach people with different Motivational Value Systems can be found in the other MVS sections of this book.

Blue-Greens may bear the burden of guilt from Blue and certainty from Green. Blue-Greens feel gratified when they can accurately assess others' needs and create solutions that help them become more self-sufficient. When Blue-Greens create plans to help, they analyze situations and try to deliver just the right amount of help to make a sustainable difference for the other person. The Green in the blend is certain that the plan is logically appropriate for the need. When such a plan does not work as expected, and therefore does not help as planned, Blue-Greens may feel discouraged that they wasted their efforts and were incorrect. They may also feel guilty because help was not provided.

In general, Blue-Greens may be able to improve the quality of their interactions, and the results they produce, by deploying some behaviors that are not typical of their MVS. Some examples include:

- Clearly and assertively stating personal preferences and desires.
- Taking small risks as a way of testing plans.
- Offering opinions about things without being asked.
- Clarifying the urgency and importance of tasks with others.
- Being bold and decisive when the course of action is clear.
- Being forceful and persuasive in the defense of the rights of self and others.

THE BLUE-GREEN STYLE OF PERSONAL LEADERSHIP

When leading others, Blue-Greens tend to focus on creating structures and environments that facilitate self-reliance, believing that the people they lead are capable of making excellent decisions. Blue-Greens view the purpose of leadership as enabling others to act independently and responsibly. The Blue-Green leadership style is calm and contemplative, using analysis to minimize risk and maximize personal and professional development. Their leadership is often characterized by:

- Establishing systems that help others become self-reliant.
- Creating an environment in which people can be authentic and productive.
- Serving the needs of people who are implementing the vision.
- Quietly moving to the aid of others, using feelings and reason to guide their approach.

Working with BLUE-GREENS

LISTENING TO BLUE-GREENS

Working effectively with Blue-Greens means you will need to understand what they are saying. Listening well to Blue-Greens will ensure that they feel heard, and know that you understand the principles that guide them. When you are listening, and engaging in dialogue, keep these points in mind:

- When listening, interpret through the lens of security and predictability.
- Don't mistake caution for unwillingness; they want to identify risks so they can give you appropriate warning.
- Be calm, caring, complete, and compassionate.
- Don't push too hard. Don't surprise them with last-minute changes.
- Take time to consider the implications of decisions and how they will affect others.

REWARDING AND RECOGNIZING BLUE-GREENS

Blue-Greens like to be recognized for their self-reliance and for maintaining environments where others are able to grow and act independently. Blue-Greens appreciate reasonable and justifiable rewards that are shared fairly with all of those who contributed to success.

The best compliments tend to be specific about providing structured guidance, protecting the rights of others, or avoiding problems by anticipating and addressing potential risks. Some compliments might include:

- "Your careful, well thought-out plan made a positive difference for the people involved."
- "You gave me just enough help and just enough space so that I was able to finish it myself."
- "Your patience and willingness to work with others resulted in a sustainable solution."
- "Thank you. Your calm, careful approach allowed us to stop that from becoming a problem and to maintain harmony on the team."

HOW TO APPROACH BLUE-GREENS

- Be calm, patient, open, and genuine.
- Be considerate and respectful of others' space and of their processing time.
- Ask their opinion before sharing your own.

- Offer logical proposals without pushing too assertively.
- Emphasize principles and fairness, and recognize how the process will affect others.

THINGS TO AVOID WHEN APPROACHING BLUE-GREENS

- Bragging or being overly enthusiastic or confident.
- Being intrusive and confrontational, or speaking loudly.
- Violating their personal space.
- Pushing them to engage before they are ready, without appropriate time to think about the outcomes.
- Forcing them to compete with others or appearing to take advantage of others.

PREVENTING CONFLICT WITH BLUE-GREENS

Much conflict with Blue-Greens can be prevented by acting or communicating in ways that recognize and respect Blue-Greens' MVS and do not introduce conflict triggers. Proactive conflict prevention strategies can be employed to reduce the chance that the self-worth of Blue-Greens will be threatened.

- Avoid raised voices and appearing aggressive or confrontational.
- Be calm and logical in support of your opinions, while keeping an eye on the relationship cost of any potential disagreement.
- Allow time for thoughtful consideration without rushing ahead or forcing compliance.
- Resist isolating them from others or being indecisive in matters that affect their welfare.
- De-personalize the problem, and reassure them that the relationship matters.
- Consider the logic of your request and how that request will impact others involved in the situation.
- Make a genuine inquiry about their welfare and how the situation is affecting them.

INFLUENCING BLUE-GREENS

The key to influencing Blue-Greens is to create or communicate conditions that are intrinsically rewarding to Blue-Greens. The more what you want them to do is clearly linked to social justice or the establishment and maintenance of self-sufficiency, the more willing Blue-Greens will generally be to engage their strengths in those activities.

Blue-Greens will tend to feel more motivated in fair, conscientious, and respectful environments that thoughtfully bring out the best in others. They are likely to follow people who are cautious, rational, respectful, and thorough in whatever they do.

To influence Blue-Greens, engage them in a conversation about how a desired action will:

- Provide learning and guidance for others.
- Create processes that will protect others or enhance their well-being.
- Bring out the best in others.
- Enable them to systematically support people who need support.

HUB MVS

FLEXIBLE-COHERING

Flex•i•ble—able to respond to changing circumstances and conditions
Co•her•ing—bringing together to form a united whole

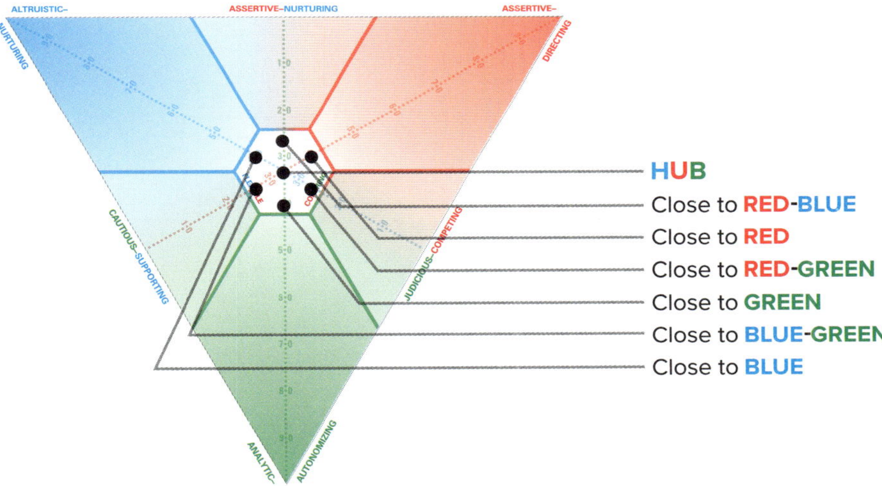

This descriptive text is written about an MVS dot in the center of the Hub MVS region. Individuals with MVS dots close to the borders (within 6 points) of other MVS regions may differ slightly from this description. They will likely find that the descriptions of the neighboring region(s) also influence their understanding of themselves and the way they are perceived by others.

HUB MOTIVES AND VALUES

The motivation of people with a Flexible-Cohering Motivational Value System (hereafter referred to as Hubs) is to achieve feelings of self-worth by finding and meeting the needs of groups, remaining open to seeing all sides of situations, and working with others in ways that are appropriate to various situations.

Hubs tend to find satisfaction in life by being flexible in approach and responsive and adaptable in relating to others. They collect information about the needs of the group in order to find common ground and meet the group's needs. Hubs want to see all sides of a situation, demonstrating empathy with a variety of different types of people, situations, and challenges. Hubs can be described as tolerant, social, creative, and versatile. They value the power of sharing perspective and building consensus.

Hubs' sense of personal integrity comes from exercising their ability to read situations and respond to them in situationally appropriate means. Hubs strive to meet the needs of the moment while maintaining future flexibility. Hubs tend to promote cohesiveness by getting others together to share ideas and consider alternatives. They want to unite people in a common cause, and they are willing to play whatever role is necessary to do so.

For Hubs, there is a desire to coordinate their efforts with others in some common undertaking that involves closeness, clear lines of authority, and opportunities for self-reliance. Hubs want to be good team members and loyal followers who know how to exercise authority, when to follow the rules, and when to use good judgment. They tend to be friendly, democratic, and playful. Hubs value building consensus through encouraging interactions and exploring points of view.

OBSERVING HUB BEHAVIORS

While motives cannot be directly observed, consistencies in behavior can offer insight into a person's underlying motives. Hubs are motivated by flexibility and adapting to others or situations. They have a strong desire to collaborate with others and to remain open to different options and viewpoints. They express their motives through behavior and tend to:

- Be curious about what others think and feel.
- Be open-minded and willing to adapt.
- Experiment with different ways of behaving.
- Be flexible, social, playful, and collaborative.
- Maintain an appropriate balance between process, people, and performance.
- Include other people, and recognize their contributions.

- Remain open to new ideas, options, and possibilities.
- Examine the situation from multiple perspectives.
- Have multiple goals and more than one area of focus.
- Use social skills and personal charm to cope with realities in the world.

Hub strengths confirm the self-worth of both people in a relationship. When Hub strengths are overdone, they may threaten the self-worth of Hubs or other people who perceive these strengths as overdone. Table 2.7 illustrates two examples:

Table 2.7 *Examples of Hub Overdone Strengths*

Productive Strength	Effect of Overdone Strength
When Hubs are flexible, they can assess a situation from multiple perspectives and aid in collective understanding.	When Hubs are overly flexible, they can agree with different things at different times, which appears inconsistent and unpredictable.
When Hubs are curious, they bring novel and useful ideas to relationships and situations that others may have missed.	When Hubs are overly curious, they may be easily distracted by options and lose focus on the current situation.

REASONS THAT HUBS ENTER CONFLICT

Hubs tend to go into conflict about things that block their flexibility or restrict their options until the best solution or plan is developed. They have difficulty with people who don't participate in group activities or who do not see the merit of reconsidering plans when new information is known. Awareness of the potential causes of conflict can help Hubs to manage their own reactions to conflict triggers and can help others adjust their behavior in an attempt to prevent conflict.

Hubs may experience conflict when they perceive any of the following conflict triggers:

- They must operate in an environment that doesn't allow enough time to explore the opinions of others.
- Others restrict their ability to change, insisting on only one approach or solution.
- They are required to interact with others who are strict, unyielding, or domineering.
- Others are excluded from the group or treated indifferently.
- Consensus-building is not valued or allowed.

- They are not being heard, or they fear that their input is unwelcome or undesirable.
- They are managed in a style that rewards compliance and does not value their innovative efforts and contributions.
- They are being locked into a rigid and inflexible future without any opportunity to reconsider or reevaluate their options.
- They can see that several mutually exclusive opportunities have equal value, and it is not clear that any one of them is better than the others.

When in conflict, Hubs want to defend their values, so they can get back to relating to others productively. The way they defend their MVS in an effort to return to feeling good about themselves will vary, depending on their Conflict Sequence.

PRODUCTIVE RESULTS OF CONFLICT FOR HUBS

When in conflict, regardless of their individual different Conflict Sequences, Hubs share a desire to return to feelings of self-worth and activities that are inclusive and flexible. They are more likely to resolve conflict when they see the potential for some of these outcomes:

- Consensus will lead to implementation of the best possible solution for the situation.
- There will be restored flexibility in approach and an agreement to revisit plans when new information is available.
- There will be effective and fun-filled collaboration among those involved in the situation.
- People will be open-minded about alternative solutions, as well as feelings about those solutions.
- People will be included, and a sense of camaraderie and shared purpose will be created.

HOW HUBS CAN IMPROVE INTERACTIONS

Hubs' preferred approach to situations and other people may not always result in outcomes that are valuable to Hubs or to others. Adaptable strengths may not fit certain situations, or they may be perceived as overdone, possibly triggering conflict in others. Adjusting behavior is most effective when considering the MVS of others, and advice about how to approach people with different Motivational Value Systems can be found in the other MVS sections of this book.

Hubs have all three primary motives blended about equally; they may carry the burdens of guilt from Blue, pride from Red, and certainty from Green. These integrated colors may also cause additional challenges. Hubs may bear the burden of appropriateness, the desire to be whatever someone (or a situation) needs them to be. They may lose their true sense of self by constantly checking the appropriateness of their behavior with others. Hubs also may find maintaining focus and making a decision that eliminates other options to be frustrating.

In general, Hubs may be able to improve the quality of their interactions, and the results they produce, by deploying some behaviors that are not typical of their MVS. Some examples include:

- Discussing contingencies with others, as well as the types of new information that would require reconsideration of an agreement.
- Setting and disclosing deadlines for decisions.
- Selecting any option and acting on it in situations where all options seem equally attractive.
- Describing the process that led to a decision, so others can be aware of the internal logic and how it fits the situation.
- Clearly articulating the principles and critical issues that will remain constant in their decision-making process.
- Clearly and assertively stating personal preferences.

THE HUB STYLE OF PERSONAL LEADERSHIP

When leading others, Hubs tend to focus on creating an inclusive environment that fosters collaboration and consensus, believing that the best ideas will come from the synergy of diverse perspectives. Hubs view the purpose of leadership as adapting to and responding appropriately to each situation. The Hub leadership style is flexible and team-based, finding and filling in the gaps, then moving back to the periphery to assess the next move. Their leadership is often characterized by:

- Keeping options open until the most appropriate or most widely acceptable one can be identified and implemented.
- Focusing on the group, making sure that everyone is included and that work is playful and social.
- Valuing creativity, problem-solving, and novelty.
- Being open to contrasting opinions and the relative merits embodied in different points of view.

Working with HUBS

LISTENING TO HUBS

Working effectively with Hubs means you will need to understand what they are saying. Listening well to Hubs will ensure that they feel heard, and know that you want them to be included. When you are listening, and engaging in dialogue, keep these points in mind:

- When listening, interpret through the lens of how they are trying to maintain future flexibility.
- Don't mistake their consideration of options as being indecisive; they don't want to get locked into a set course of action.
- Allow or encourage moments of fun and spontaneity.
- Don't restrict options or cast options in mutually exclusive terms.
- Compare diverse perspectives, and don't force a decision unless time is of the essence.

REWARDING AND RECOGNIZING HUBS

Hubs like to be appreciated for responding appropriately to people's needs in the moment, being flexible with regard to tasks, and being tolerant with regards to people. Hubs prefer to be rewarded as part of a group, and if rewarded individually, for their contributions to the group. Some compliments might include:

- "You are a natural translator, helping us all to understand one another's perspectives."
- "Thanks for filling in. We know we can always count on you to step in and do whatever is needed for the team."
- "You always seem to be able to sense what's going on around you and then do whatever is appropriate in the situation."
- "The recent decisions you made will give us a lot more flexibility in the future."

HOW TO APPROACH HUBS

- Be flexible, sociable, playful, and collaborative.
- Maintain an appropriate balance between process, people, and goals.
- Include other people, and recognize their contributions.
- Remain open to new ideas, options, and possibilities.
- Examine the situation from multiple perspectives.

THINGS TO AVOID WHEN APPROACHING HUBS

- Disregarding group camaraderie or the opinions of others.
- Accepting the first option without hearing others.
- Restricting the ability to change, insisting on only one approach or solution.
- Being strict, unyielding, or domineering.
- Excluding people or being inconsiderate of others.

PREVENTING CONFLICT WITH HUBS

Much conflict with Hubs can be prevented by acting or communicating in ways that recognize and respect Hubs' MVS and that do not introduce conflict triggers. Proactive conflict prevention strategies can be employed to reduce the chance that the self-worth of Hubs will be threatened.

- Remain open to various ideas, allowing flexibility in the approach to solutions.
- Focus on the attributes of a situation and the different perspectives that people have about it.
- Keep your sense of humor.
- Use a collaborative style to get valuable input into the process.
- Set aside preconceived notions, and explore the possibilities.

INFLUENCING HUBS

The key to influencing Hubs is to create or communicate conditions that are intrinsically rewarding to Hubs. The more what you want them to do is linked to current and future flexibility and the welfare of the group and its members, the more willing Hubs will generally be to engage their strengths in those activities.

Hubs will tend to feel more motivated in democratic, playful, and social environments that encourage consensus. They are likely to follow people who are appropriately balanced, who are generous, strong, and patient.

To influence Hubs, engage them in a conversation about how a desired action will:

- Enable them to use their judgment based on the situation.
- Let them alternate between leading and following, depending on the circumstances.
- Encourage the solicitation of points of view and perspectives.
- Involve others in a collaborative endeavor.

3 CONFLICT SEQUENCES

What is a Conflict Sequence?

A Conflict Sequence (CS), as its name suggests, is an order or pattern of conflict. In SDI terms, a Conflict Sequence is the order in which a person experiences Blue (Accommodate), Red (Assert), and Green (Analyze) motives during the course of conflict.

A Conflict Sequence is a consistent, predictable pattern of changes in motives during conflict. Motives give purpose and meaning to activities and relationships.

Figure 3.1 *The 13 Conflict Sequences*

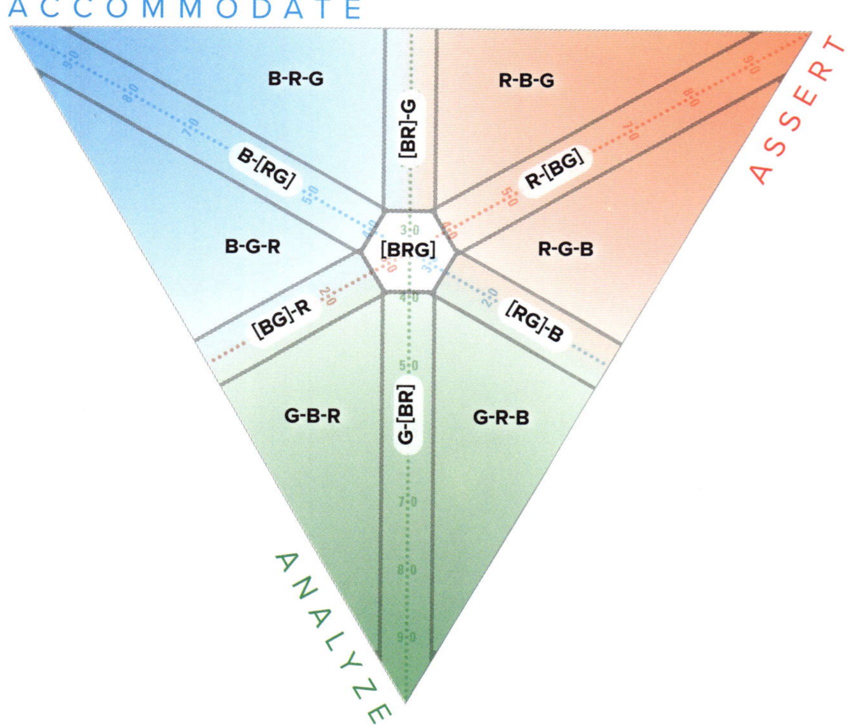

Differences in motives during conflict are a significant part of personality. A Conflict Sequence is a simple and practical way of thinking about the complex reasons why people do the things they do when they are faced with conflict.[1]

While all people share a desire to feel good about themselves and to experience feelings of self-worth, all people also experience threats to their sense of self-worth. A threat to self-worth is a definitive characteristic of conflict, and these threats can be real or perceived. Different people experience these threats in different ways.

The SDI shows how everyone has all three motives (Blue, Red, and Green) and that the motives may be experienced in different orders as conflict progresses. The different combinations produce 13 distinct Conflict Sequences (described in detail in the following pages). Nine of them have a single color in the first stage, three more have two colors blended in stages one and two, and one has all three colors blended in all three stages.

The scores from the conflict portion of the SDI are charted as an arrowhead on the SDI triangle to represent a person's Conflict Sequence. The location of the arrowhead suggests one of the 13 Conflict Sequences. When an arrowhead is close to another region (within six points[2] as illustrated in Figure 3.2), however, the person may identify with portions of the descriptions of more than one Conflict Sequence. Unlike a typecasting exercise, the goal is not to force people to choose only one of the descriptions. Instead, the goal is to allow the flexibility to identify the most characteristic portions of each description.

Figure 3.2 *Example of Test/Retest Reliability*

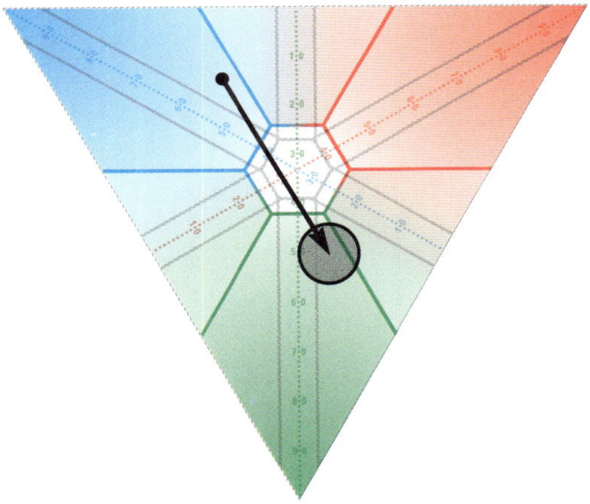

WHAT DOES THE CONFLICT SEQUENCE DO?

As people's motives undergo changes during conflict, so do their behaviors.[3] A person who moves from wanting to accommodate in Stage 1 to wanting to assert themselves in Stage 2 will usually behave differently in Stage 1 and Stage 2.

One thing that everyone shares during conflict is the desire to return to feeling good again. Feeling good again involves the removal of threats to self-worth.

The Conflict Sequence also describes the way people's focus and energy is concentrated as conflict progresses through stages.[4]

1. In the **first stage,** the intent is to respond to conflict in a way that is acceptable to everyone involved; the focus is on the self, the problem, and other people.
2. The transition to the **second stage** is characterized by a narrowed focus and a concentration of energy on the self and the problem. Other people can be out of focus in the second stage, where the intent is to resolve the conflict in a way that is acceptable to the individual in conflict.
3. The transition to the **third stage** is characterized by a further concentration of energy and focus on the self. The problem can be dropped from focus in the third stage, where the motive is to protect, defend, or preserve the individual's sense of self.

Table 3.1 *Stages of Conflict by Color*

AREAS OF FOCUS	BLUE *Accommodate*	RED *Assert*	GREEN *Analyze*
STAGE 1: Responding			
Self, Problem, Other	Wanting to accommodate the other person's needs	Wanting to rise to the challenge being offered	Wanting to be prudently cautious
STAGE 2: Narrowing			
Self, Problem, ~~Other~~	Wanting to conditionally give in or defer to the other person	Wanting to prevail against the issue or other person	Wanting to escape from the other person or delay the issue
STAGE 3: Defending			
Self, ~~Problem,~~ ~~Other~~	Feeling driven to give up completely	Feeling driven to fight for one's life	Feeling driven to retreat completely

Each Conflict Sequence can be understood as though it were assembled from different blocks, as shown in Table 3.1. For example, the Conflict Sequence of R-G-B is:

- Stage 1 Red—wanting to rise to the challenge being offered.
- Stage 2 Green—wanting to escape from the other person or delay the issue.
- Stage 3 Blue—feeling driven to give up completely.

A Conflict Sequence with letters in brackets means the two colors of motive are, for practical purposes, equal. For example, the Conflict Sequence of [RG]-B is:

- Stage 1 Red or Green—wanting to rise to the challenge being offered or wanting to be prudently cautious (or a combination of the two).
- Stage 2 Red or Green—wanting to prevail against the issue or person or wanting to escape from the other person or delay the issue (or a combination of the two).
- Stage 3 Blue—feeling driven to give up completely.

WHAT ARE CONFLICT FILTERS?

The Conflict Sequence can act as a filter through which life is perceived, interpreted, and understood. Filters stop some things and allow other things through. The Conflict Sequence filters and influences perception. Information deemed important is readily received, but information deemed irrelevant is actively or even subconsciously screened out of awareness.

Differences in conflict filters can help explain why two people can have entirely different memories of a shared experience or why one person believes there is a conflict when another person does not. For example, a team leader could express frustration with the progress on a project, and one team member could believe the leader was angry, accusatory, and hostile, while another team member could believe the leader simply and appropriately stated the facts and asked people to take ownership for their actions.

Since behavior is a choice (even during conflict) and choices are limited to options that people perceive, the Conflict Sequence acts to constrain or expand the range of choices that people believe they have. The less choice people believe they have, the less accountable they will feel for their actions and results. The more choice people believe they have, the more accountable they will feel for their actions and results. Therefore, expanding people's views and perceived freedom of choice during conflict can also increase personal accountability.

WHAT DOESN'T THE CONFLICT SEQUENCE DO?

The Conflict Sequence does not indicate skills. However, people may want to develop skills in their first stage of conflict, so they can resolve conflict in the first stage and less frequently experience stages two and three. The Conflict Sequence is not an indicator of effectiveness; it describes what people want to do, not how well they do it. For example, people may want to be prudently cautious, but their caution during conflict may be exercised to such a degree that they do not actively engage in solving problems.

The Conflict Sequence is not a forecast or guarantee of behavior. While it helps to understand, anticipate, and perhaps even predict the way people's motives change in conflict, people still have the ability to choose to act differently. Just because someone feels like fighting does not mean they will fight.

The Conflict Sequence and the numerical results that indicate it do not predict the speed with which people will enter conflict or go through the stages. Nor does it foretell the amount of time people will spend in the stages. It shows the order of the motivational changes that people experience as conflict intensifies. Other factors, such as the history of conflict in the relationship or the importance or severity of the conflict trigger, may affect the speed or duration of conflict. A conflict can be resolved or left unresolved at any stage. If a conflict is resolved in Stage 1, there is no need to enter Stage 2 or Stage 3. A conflict does not need to go through all three stages to be resolved. Resolution can happen quickly, or it can take a long time.

WHAT VARIABLES AFFECT CONFLICT?

There are 13 Conflict Sequences. People with the same Conflict Sequence generally agree about why they do things during conflict, but they may not necessarily agree about what to do in each situation. Over time, however, patterns of common behavior can be observed. Each Conflict Sequence covers a region of the SDI triangle that includes many possible SDI scores. Within each region, many differences are possible for scores and also for people. The Conflict Sequence scores show the order of changes in motives.

Conflict can be a complex topic, with many variables affecting the way people approach it. If a conflict involves a core personal value or has some other strong tie to a person's sense of self-worth, it's possible that they will be willing to engage in deeper stages of conflict. Conflicts involving less significant values may be more readily released in earlier stages.

The way people express their motives in conflict may also be subject to situational or cultural expectations. For example, a person could feel similarly in two conflicts, one with a boss and one with a peer. It's possible that role expectations will influence the selection of different behaviors in these two situations, even though the feelings and motives are the same.

The history of conflict in a relationship may affect future conflicts. People who have repeatedly been unable to resolve conflict in Stage 1 may move quickly into Stage 2. This may cause it to appear that Stage 1 was skipped. However, when a current event is viewed as a continuation of a past conflict and not as a new conflict, a different conclusion is possible. People may re-enter or re-engage a conflict at the point at which they previously left it; they go "in through the out door."

WHAT'S NOT CONFLICT?

Conflict is different from opposition. It is possible to experience disagreements, differences of opinion, and uncertainty without also experiencing a threat to self-worth. These non-threatening differences are opposition and can be managed from the going-well state (the MVS), rather than the conflict state. Two people may have legitimate differences of opinion regarding the budget or deadline for a project; this is opposition. But oppositions can turn into conflict if the disagreement gets personalized, such as with accusations that one person always wastes money or that the other always takes too long to get things done.

The word conflict is often used to describe opposition or even negotiation. While it is tempting to connect the idea of a win-win solution to Stage 1 conflict, a win-lose solution to Stage 2 conflict, and a lose-lose solution to Stage 3 conflict, the Conflict Sequence describes changes in motives, not the quality of outcomes. Winners and losers can be found in all stages of conflict. However, practical experience suggests that a win-win solution becomes less likely and more difficult to achieve as people get deeper into the stages of their Conflict Sequences.

THE CRAFT OF CONFLICT QUESTIONS

The Conflict Sequences also provides a framework to guide conflict resolution conversations. The goal of conflict resolution is to defend what matters and get back to the MVS. Therefore, the conversation guide essentially works backward through the sequence: Stage 3, Stage 2, Stage 1, and then back to the MVS. The example questions are paired with the focus of the person who is experiencing

Table 3.2 *Conflict Questions*

Potential Emotional State and Focus of Person in Conflict	Intent of Conversation	Example Questions
STAGE 3 CONFLICT Focus: Self	Discover values of the person who is in conflict. If the person is in Stage 3, answering these questions can help them move to Stage 2.	What's really most important to you? How are you feeling now? What are your priorities? Fundamentally, what is wrong here? What do you most need right now?
STAGE 2 CONFLICT Focus: Self and Problem	Define the problem as viewed by the person who is in conflict. If the person is in Stage 2, answering these questions can help them move to Stage 1.	Ideally, what would solve this problem for you? What are some other acceptable solutions for you? If you had total control of this situation, what would you do? What could make this go away? What's the bare minimum solution, in your opinion?
STAGE 1 CONFLICT Focus: Self, Problem, and Others	Expand the focus of the person who is in conflict. If they are in Stage 1, they will be more open to others' views and desires than they were in Stages 2 or 3.	Would you be interested to hear what's important to me in this? May I share how I feel about it? May I express my priorities? Would you like to hear my ideal outcome? What else would you like to know from my perspective?
MOTIVATIONAL VALUE SYSTEM Focus: Relationship and Elements of Opposition	Reach agreement, resolution, or reconciliation. Connect the experience in Stage 1 to the MVS of the person in conflict. See the "path-back" section of each Conflict Sequence chapter for examples.	What common ground or shared interests do we have? What do we still objectively disagree about? How should we make our decision? What would help us both feel good about the outcome? How can we prevent similar issues in the future?

conflict. For example, in Stage 2, where the focus is on the self and the problem, the questions are about the person's view of the problem, but they do not include anything about the other people involved.

WHAT NEXT?

As you read the following sections, start with your own Conflict Sequence. When you find something useful, make it easy to find again. Remember that each section is written with a standard Conflict Sequence type in mind and that you will probably not agree with everything as presented, especially if your Conflict Sequence arrowhead is close to the border of another Conflict Sequence region on the triangle. It's also useful to keep some past conflicts in mind as you read. Ask yourself the conflict questions (Table 3.2) about the past conflicts and see what you can learn from them.

Don't stop with the Conflict Sequence. Understand more about yourself by considering how your Conflict Sequence connects to your MVS. Then do the same for other people; build your Relationship Intelligence. While the SDI is about you, it has the most value when you consider yourself in the context of your relationships. Understanding MVS and Conflict Sequence for yourself and others will help you understand the real-time dynamics of relationships when things are going well, how conflict gets triggered, and how to manage and resolve conflict.

B-R-G

CONFLICT SEQUENCE

This Conflict Sequence describes people who want to keep peace and harmony. If that does not work, they want to take a stand for their rights. If that does not work, they may feel compelled to withdraw as a last resort.

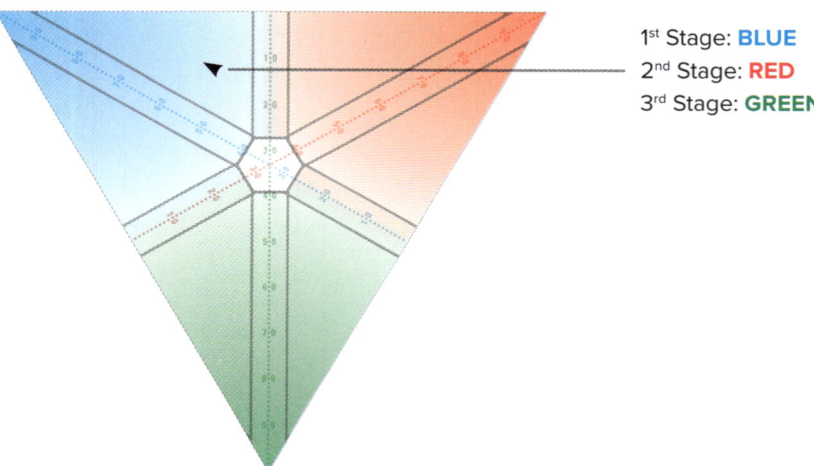

This descriptive text is written with a Conflict Sequence arrowhead located about centrally in the Conflict Sequence region in mind. People whose arrowheads are close to the borders (within six points) of other Conflict Sequence regions may find that some text from the neighboring regions' descriptions is more accurate or useful.

While the following text describes the B-R-G Conflict Sequence, it should also be considered in light of the MVS of the person who has this Conflict Sequence. Since there are seven Motivational Value Systems, there are at least seven different ways to enter conflict and many different issues that can trigger conflict. These differences will affect the way people experience conflict and how they will resolve conflict. The first stage of this Conflict Sequence is Blue. People with a short arrow whose MVS is also Blue may experience a less noticeable transition from their MVS to the first stage of conflict than people whose MVS is a different color will.

STAGE 1 BLUE CONFLICT

People in first stage Blue conflict are motivated by a desire to accommodate the needs of others. They want most to keep harmony and goodwill and may continue to appease the opposition in order to do so.

People in first stage Blue tend to feel anxious or worried that things will get worse or that people could be hurt. They want to talk openly in order to prevent things from getting worse. They are curious about how other people feel, and why they feel that way.

In first stage Blue, people want to keep peace, harmony, and goodwill in the relationship. In order to avoid conversations that could be hurtful to others, they may deflect or minimize issues. They hope the conflict will pass without the need for direct intervention, but are usually open to talking about the conflict if they are invited to an honest conversation.

Productive first stage Blue conflict behaviors are typically used in an effort to minimize confrontation and to ensure that everyone is heard and that harmony is first pursued above individual resolution. They want to create an environment where those in conflict feel accommodated, so that resolution can occur in a non-threatening way.

When unproductive, people in first stage Blue may sacrifice their own rights or refuse to acknowledge that there is a problem. This may cause them to appear subservient or in denial. They may simply hope that the problem goes away on its own and avoid any potential confrontation.

How People in Stage 1 Blue Can Improve Interactions

People who are experiencing the first stage of conflict may act as described previously. However, people may also adjust behavior or examine their perceptions during conflict in an effort to be more effective.

In Stage 1 Blue, people may be more effective if they:

- Consider the issue from as objective a vantage point as possible.
- Clearly state their personal priorities and boundaries.

- Determine whether they are able to accommodate and let go, or whether the accommodation will create an implied obligation on another person's part.
- Consider subtle signs of discomfort and what deeper issue they may represent.

STAGE 2 RED CONFLICT

When initial efforts to maintain harmony and accommodate the needs of others are not effective at resolving conflict, people who then move into the second stage of Red (following Blue) carry a desire for peace and an awareness of others' needs with them.

In second stage Red (following Blue), people are frustrated and perhaps even hurt that they have not been heard. Their accommodation in Stage 1 may be missed by others or misperceived as compliance, or even agreement. Now, they feel totally justified in asserting their positions, often with energized words that may seem abrupt and hurtful to others involved in the conflict. At this point, the assertion is viewed as a justifiable use of force to win the battle. By standing up for their rights, they get others to understand the problem and return to a more harmonious state.

In second stage Red (following Blue), people may act more energetically, closing space and increasing volume in order to be heard. Feeling hurt by a lack of understanding, they actively assert their position. Their sense of being overlooked or unacknowledged results in a burst of emotion, which is intended to get others' attention and ensure that they are heard. By demanding a platform for expressing their concerns, they hope to restore the initial harmony.

People with a B-R-G Conflict Sequence generally work very hard in Stage 2 Red to prevent going to Stage 3 Green. They may continue to elevate the importance and urgency of the situation and the intensity of their reaction. They may believe that they are acting on their last chance to stay involved with a person or situation and that the fight, no matter how difficult, is better than walking away in Stage 3 Green.

STAGE 3 GREEN CONFLICT

In third stage Green (following Blue and Red), people tend to abandon or insulate themselves from all feeling for the issue and the people involved. They tend to believe that their assertive and accommodating approaches to conflict have been met with a lack of cooperation or fair play and that no option remains except to disengage.

In the third stage of Green (following Blue and Red), people will typically withdraw and cut off contact in order to preserve whatever they can salvage from the situation. They may refuse to even talk about the past issue because they think there is no remaining possibility of resolving it. If the conflict is severe, they may end the relationship and avoid all further interaction with the people involved.

The Green Stage 3 Filter

Green is the third stage of conflict in the B-R-G sequence. While in first stage Blue and observing Green behavior in another person, some projection of the third stage experience onto the other is possible. Analytical behavior in others may be perceived as cold detachment without first considering the needs of others or engaging in problem-solving efforts.

Working with B-R-G

CONFLICT RESOLUTION

Conflict is resolved when the elements of opposition are addressed, and the people involved are able to return to feeling good about themselves again.

The Path Back to the MVS from Stage 1 Blue

Each person has a path back from conflict to their MVS and feelings of self-worth. Even though many people may feel and act similarly in the first stage of conflict, there may be differences that are related to the MVS they are trying to return to. Conflict management efforts can be improved by keeping these differences in mind.

The path back to the MVS will be different for every person. Table 3.3 features some general illustrations of the path from Stage 1 Blue back to MVS.

Figure 3.3 *Paths back to MVS from B-R-G*

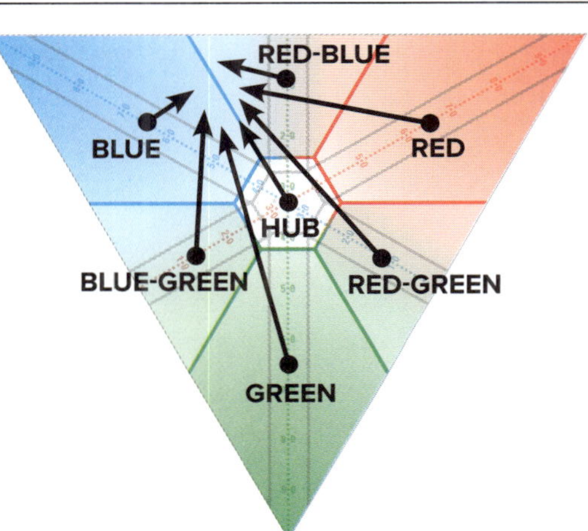

Table 3.3 *Illustrations of the path back to MVS from Stage 1 Blue*

Blue MVS	Restoring peace and reestablishing the value of the relationship
Red MVS	Smoothing things over and refocusing on results
Green MVS	Accepting the logic of others and clarifying underlying principles
Red-Blue MVS	Restoring, developing, and strengthening the relationship
Red-Green MVS	Letting go of small things to focus on the bigger strategy
Blue-Green MVS	Accommodating others and learning from mistakes
Hub MVS	Calming the situation so everyone can get reunited

For more detailed information and ideas about resolving conflict with people who have this Conflict Sequence, also consult the "Productive Results of Conflict" sections in the chapters that describe the MVS of those people. No matter the MVS of the people in the conflict, there are some things that can help them transition out of Stage 1 Blue.

LISTENING TO STAGE 1 BLUE

Working effectively with people in Stage 1 Blue conflict means you will need to understand what they are saying. Listening well will ensure that they feel heard, and know that you would also prefer a harmonious resolution. When you are listening, and engaging in dialogue, keep these points in mind:

- Hear them as attempting to be peacemakers and restore harmony.
- Don't mistake apologies as acceptance of blame.
- Be open, accepting, and affirming.
- Avoid public confrontation.
- Talk fully about issues; explore thoughts and feelings.

HOW TO APPROACH PEOPLE WHILE THEY ARE IN STAGE 1 BLUE CONFLICT

- Affirm the relationship, and depersonalize the conflict.
- Be pleasant and genuine and invite responses.
- Be calm and non-confrontational.
- Allow the person to lead the conversation toward the point they really want to make.
- Listen, and ask more than once if needed.
- Respect the person's request for time and space.

THINGS TO AVOID WHEN APPROACHING PEOPLE WHILE THEY ARE IN STAGE 1 BLUE CONFLICT

- Focusing on resolving the conflict quickly or exclusively on the facts.
- Being aggressive toward the person or confronting them in public.
- Being sarcastic or patronizing.

MANAGING CONFLICT IN STAGES 2 AND 3

Conflict resolution is most likely to be effective from Stage 1, where self, problem, and others are in focus. If you are working with someone who has moved to Stage 2 or 3, you may need to de-escalate the conflict back to Stage 1 before you can reconcile your differences.

If the person is in Stage 2 Red:

- Listen without making judgments, because they may say things they later regret.
- Try to identify at least one immediate action you can take that is in their self-interest.

If the person is in Stage 3 Green:

- Make sure they know you are available and willing to participate, but do not try to force an immediate conversation.
- Emphasize your desire to restore the relationship. Ask what additional information, or how much time they need.

B-G-R

CONFLICT SEQUENCE

This Conflict Sequence describes people who want to keep harmony and goodwill. If that does not work, they want to disengage and save what they can. If that does not work, they may feel compelled to fight, possibly in an explosive manner.

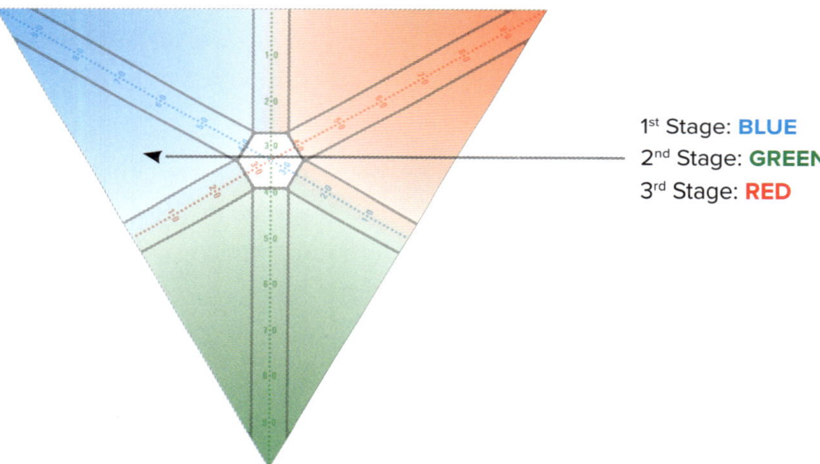

This descriptive text is written with a Conflict Sequence arrowhead located about centrally in the Conflict Sequence region in mind. People whose arrowheads are close to the borders (within six points) of other Conflict Sequence regions may find that some text from the neighboring regions' descriptions is more accurate or useful.

While the following text describes the B-G-R Conflict Sequence, it should also be considered in light of the MVS of the person who has this Conflict Sequence. Since there are seven Motivational Value Systems, there are at least seven different ways to enter conflict and many different issues that can trigger conflict. These differences will affect the way people experience conflict and how they will resolve conflict. The first stage of this Conflict Sequence is Blue. People with a short arrow whose MVS is also Blue, may experience a less noticeable transition from their MVS to the first stage of conflict than people whose MVS is a different color will.

STAGE 1 BLUE CONFLICT

People in first stage Blue conflict are motivated by a desire to accommodate the needs of others. They want most to keep harmony and goodwill and may continue to appease the opposition in order to do so.

People in first stage Blue tend to feel anxious or worried that things will get worse or that people could be hurt. They want to talk openly in order to prevent things from getting worse. They are curious about how other people feel, and why they feel that way.

In first stage Blue, people want to keep peace, harmony, and goodwill in the relationship. In order to avoid conversations that could be hurtful to others, they may deflect or minimize issues. They hope the conflict will pass without the need for direct intervention, but are usually open to talking about the conflict if they are invited to an honest conversation.

Productive first stage Blue conflict behaviors are typically used in an effort to minimize confrontation and to ensure that everyone is heard and that harmony is first pursued above individual resolution. They want to create an environment where those in conflict feel accommodated, so that resolution can occur in a non-threatening way.

When unproductive, people in first stage Blue may sacrifice their own rights or refuse to acknowledge that there is a problem. This may cause them to appear subservient or in denial. They may simply hope that the problem goes away on its own and avoid any potential confrontation.

How People in Stage 1 Blue Can Improve Interactions

People who are experiencing the first stage of conflict may act as described previously. However, people may also adjust behavior or examine their perceptions during conflict in an effort to be more effective.

In Stage 1 Blue, people may be more effective if they:

- Consider the issue from as objective a vantage point as possible.
- Clearly state their personal priorities and boundaries.

- Determine whether they are able to accommodate and let go or whether the accommodation will create an implied obligation on another person's part.
- Consider subtle signs of discomfort and what deeper issue they may represent.

STAGE 2 GREEN CONFLICT

When initial efforts to maintain harmony and accommodate the needs of others are not effective at resolving the conflict, people who then move into the second stage of Green (following Blue) carry a desire for peace and an awareness of others' needs with them.

In second stage Green (following Blue), people feel unable to restore harmony and goodwill. In fact, it is possible that the efforts to restore that goodwill in Stage 1 may be missed or misperceived as compliance or even agreement. Therefore, they try to disengage and save what can be saved. They may feel the need to become quiet and withdrawn as they try to think through a solution that regains the harmony that is lost. They want to come up with "just the right words" to resolve the confrontation.

In second stage Green (following Blue), people may become quiet and distance themselves from others. They consider and reconsider their position, gathering information to give their position strength. At this point, they try an objective approach to the situation, stepping back from their feelings and their anxiety about those feelings. They focus on solving whatever can be solved, attempting to understand and make adjustments in the conflict, while always thinking about how to restore harmony and goodwill.

People with a B-G-R Conflict Sequence generally work very hard in Stage 2 Green to prevent going to Stage 3 Red. They may continue to collect information about the situation and the people involved in an effort to find some sort of rational solution to the problem. They may hold their position and wait, even for extended periods of time, believing that waiting is better than allowing themselves to slip into the potentially explosive situation of Stage 3 Red.

STAGE 3 RED CONFLICT

In third stage Red (following Blue and Green), people tend to feel intensely angry, energized, and potentially out of control, demanding an "all or nothing" solution. They tend to feel that all of their efforts to resolve the issue logically and without confrontation have failed. They feel that the desired outcome must be forcibly taken or forcibly denied to the other person, regardless of cost.

In the third stage of Red (following Blue and Green), people will typically challenge others or fight others, potentially in an explosive manner. They may say that they no longer care what other people think or want, forcibly implementing whatever they originally thought was the best solution. If the conflict is severe, the relationship may be irreparably damaged by the harshness of personal attacks or by the negative reactions of people who view this third stage red behavior as overblown and uncalled for.

The Red Stage 3 Filter

Red is the third stage of conflict in the B-G-R sequence. While in first stage Blue and observing Red behavior in another person, some projection of the third stage experience on the other is possible. Assertive behavior of others may be perceived as angry overreaction without first taking the time to consider the needs of others or the facts of the situation.

Working with B-G-R

CONFLICT RESOLUTION

Conflict is resolved when the elements of opposition are addressed and the people involved are able to return to feeling good about themselves again.

The Path Back to the MVS from Stage 1 Blue

Each person has a path back from conflict to their MVS and feelings of self-worth. Even though many people may feel and act similarly in the first stage of conflict, there may be differences that are related to the MVS they are trying to return to. Conflict management efforts can be improved by keeping these differences in mind.

The path back to the MVS will be different for every person. Table 3.4 features some general illustrations of the path from Stage 1 Blue back to MVS.

Figure 3.4 *Paths back to MVS from B-G-R*

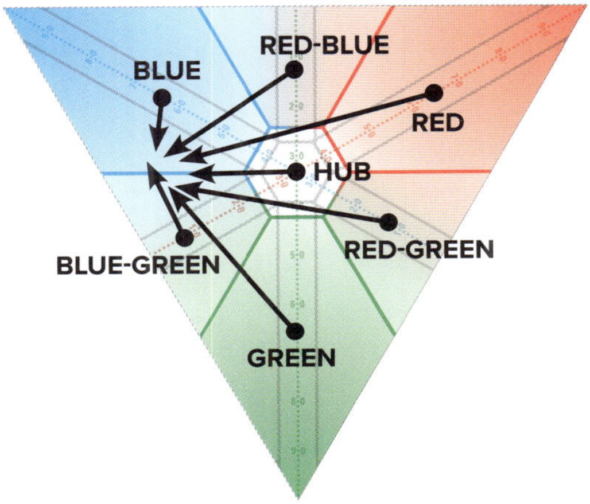

Table 3.4 *Illustrations of the path back to MVS from Stage 1 Blue*

Blue MVS	Restoring peace and reestablishing the value of the relationship
Red MVS	Smoothing things over and refocusing on results
Green MVS	Accepting the logic of others and clarifying underlying principles
Red-Blue MVS	Restoring, developing, and strengthening the relationship
Red-Green MVS	Letting go of small things to focus on the bigger strategy
Blue-Green MVS	Accommodating others and learning from mistakes
Hub MVS	Calming the situation so everyone can get reunited

For more detailed information and ideas about resolving conflict with people who have this Conflict Sequence, also consult the "Productive Results of Conflict" sections in the chapters that describe the MVS of those people. No matter the MVS of people in the conflict, there are some things that can help them transition out of Stage 1 Blue.

LISTENING TO STAGE 1 BLUE

Working effectively with people in Stage 1 Blue conflict means you will need to understand what they are saying. Listening well will ensure that they feel heard, and know that you would also prefer a harmonious resolution. When you are listening, and engaging in dialogue, keep these points in mind:

- Hear them as attempting to be peacemakers and restore harmony.
- Don't mistake apologies as acceptance of blame.
- Be open, accepting, and affirming.
- Avoid public confrontation.
- Talk fully about issues; explore thoughts and feelings.

HOW TO APPROACH PEOPLE WHILE THEY ARE IN STAGE 1 BLUE CONFLICT

- Affirm the relationship, and depersonalize the conflict.
- Be pleasant and genuine, and invite responses.
- Be calm and non-confrontational.
- Allow the person to lead the conversation toward the point they really want to make.
- Listen, and ask more than once if needed.
- Respect the person's request for time and space.

THINGS TO AVOID WHEN APPROACHING PEOPLE WHILE THEY ARE IN STAGE 1 BLUE CONFLICT

- Focusing on resolving the conflict quickly or exclusively on the facts.
- Being aggressive toward the person or confronting them in public.
- Being sarcastic or patronizing.

MANAGING CONFLICT IN STAGES 2 AND 3

Conflict resolution is most likely to be effective from Stage 1, where self, problem, and others are in focus. If you are working with someone who has moved to Stage 2 or 3, you may need to de-escalate the conflict back to Stage 1 before you can reconcile your differences.

If the person is in Stage 2 Green:

- Listen objectively and patiently, because they may need to replay the events.
- Try to find at least one principle that you can agree on, or at least agree on what is currently unknown.

If the person is in Stage 3 Red:

- Create a safe space for them to say everything that's on their mind. They have probably been trying not to say these things.
- Emphasize your desire to restore the relationship. Ask what is most important to them at this moment.

B-[RG]

CONFLICT SEQUENCE

This Conflict Sequence describes people who want to keep harmony and accommodate the opposition. If that does not work, they want to make a choice based on what's best for everyone: to rely on logic and principle or to employ assertive strategies to prevent defeat.

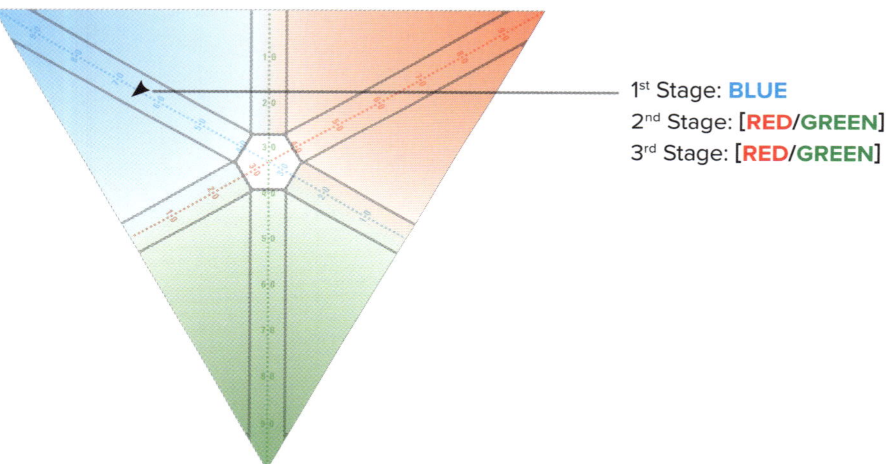

This descriptive text is written with a Conflict Sequence arrowhead located centrally in the Conflict Sequence region in mind. People whose arrowheads are close to the borders (within six points) of other Conflict Sequence regions may find that some text from the neighboring regions' descriptions is more accurate or useful.

While the following text describes the B-[RG] Conflict Sequence, it should also be considered in light of the MVS of the person who has this Conflict Sequence. Since there are seven Motivational Value Systems, there are at least seven different ways to enter conflict and many different issues that can trigger conflict.

These differences will affect the way people experience conflict and how they will resolve conflict. The first stage of this Conflict Sequence is Blue. People with a short arrow whose MVS is also Blue, may experience a less noticeable transition from their MVS to the first stage of conflict than people whose MVS is a different color will.

STAGE 1 BLUE CONFLICT

People in first stage Blue conflict are motivated by a desire to accommodate the needs of others. They want most to keep harmony and goodwill and may continue to appease the opposition in order to do so.

People in first stage Blue tend to feel anxious or worried that things will get worse or that people could be hurt. They want to talk openly in order to prevent things from getting worse. They are curious about how other people feel, and why they feel that way.

In first stage Blue, people want to keep peace, harmony, and goodwill in the relationship. In order to avoid conversations that could be hurtful to others, they may deflect or minimize issues. They hope the conflict will pass without the need for direct intervention, but are usually open to talking about the conflict if they are invited to an honest conversation.

Productive first stage Blue conflict behaviors are typically used in an effort to minimize confrontation and to ensure that everyone is heard and that harmony is first pursued above individual resolution. They want to create an environment where those in conflict feel accommodated, so that resolution can occur in a non-threatening way.

When unproductive, people in first stage Blue may sacrifice their own rights or refuse to acknowledge that there is a problem. This may cause them to appear subservient or in denial. They may simply hope that the problem goes away on its own and avoid any potential confrontation.

How People in Stage 1 Blue Can Improve Interactions

People who are experiencing the first stage of conflict may act as described previously. However, people may also adjust behavior or examine their perceptions during conflict in an effort to be more effective.

In Stage 1 Blue, people may be more effective if they:

- Consider the issue from as objective a vantage point as possible.
- Clearly state their personal priorities and boundaries.

- Determine whether they are able to accommodate and let go or whether the accommodation will create an implied obligation on another person's part.
- Consider subtle signs of discomfort and what deeper issue they may represent.

STAGE 2 [RG] CONFLICT

When initial efforts to maintain harmony and accommodate the needs of others are not effective at resolving the conflict, people who then move into the second stage of [RG] carry their desire for peace and awareness of others' needs with them.

People in this blended second and third stage may take different approaches based on their perception of the situation. They may go to Red followed by Green if the results are more important than the principles involved or to Green followed by Red if the principles are more important than the results. In these cases, conflict can be understood more fully by referring to the B-R-G and B-G-R pages. It is also possible that the Red and Green conflict stages will be combined for a blended conflict experience.

When Red and Green are blended in Stages 2 and 3, people are done with accommodating others to solve the problem. Pressed far enough, they now feel the need to fall back on logical and assertive strategies to preserve their integrity and to prevent unfair accommodation of others. These people have a strong desire to find an effective strategy, which they are willing to implement forcefully if necessary.

Once a strategy has been identified, they want to drive their agenda and decisively overcome objections. If a rational end to the conflict cannot be achieved quickly, they may begin to formulate worst-case scenarios or ultimatums, which may be acted on from the third stage.

STAGE 3 [RG] CONFLICT

While Red and Green are blended in Stages 2 and 3, people will experience an internal difference between these stages. Stage 2 is characterized by a focus on the self and the problem, and Stage 3 is focused on the self. Therefore, the Stage 3 experience of [RG] is a more intense and self-focused version of the Stage 2 experience. If a person concentrated on an assertive, Red approach in Stage 2, their third stage is likely to be the detached withdrawal typical of Stage 3 Green. If they concentrated on the analytical, Green approach to Stage 2, their third stage is likely to be the explosive fighting typical of Stage 3 Red.

[RG] Stage 3 Filter

[RG] is the blended second and third stage of conflict in the B-[RG] sequence. While in first stage Blue and observing Red-Green behavior in another person, some projection of the second or third stage experience on the other is possible. Strategic behavior of others may be perceived as manipulative and without regard for the needs of others.

Working with B-[RG]

CONFLICT RESOLUTION

Conflict is resolved when the elements of opposition are addressed, and the people involved are able to return to feeling good about themselves again.

The Path Back to the MVS from Stage 1 Blue

Each person has a path back from conflict to their MVS and feelings of self-worth. Even though many people may feel and act similarly in the first stage of conflict, there may be differences that are related to the MVS they are trying to return to. Conflict management efforts can be improved by keeping these differences in mind.

The path back to the MVS will be different for every person. Table 3.5 features some general illustrations of the path from Stage 1 Blue back to MVS.

Figure 3.5 *Paths back to MVS from B-[RG]*

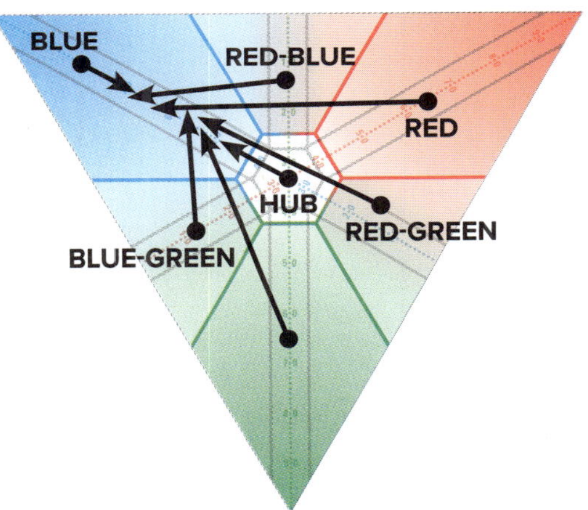

Table 3.5 *Illustrations of the path back to MVS from Stage 1 Blue*

Blue MVS	Restoring peace and reestablishing the value of the relationship
Red MVS	Smoothing things over and refocusing on results
Green MVS	Accepting the logic of others and clarifying underlying principles
Red-Blue MVS	Restoring, developing, and strengthening the relationship
Red-Green MVS	Letting go of small things to focus on the bigger strategy
Blue-Green MVS	Accommodating others and learning from mistakes
Hub MVS	Calming the situation so everyone can get reunited

For more detailed information and ideas about resolving conflict with people who have this Conflict Sequence, also consult the "Productive Results of Conflict"sections in the chapters that describe the MVS of those people. No matter the MVS of people in the conflict, there are some things that can help them transition out of Stage 1 Blue.

LISTENING TO STAGE 1 BLUE

Working effectively with people in Stage 1 Blue conflict means you will need to understand what they are saying. Listening well will ensure that they feel heard, and know that you would also prefer a harmonious resolution. When you are listening, and engaging in dialogue, keep these points in mind:

- Hear them as attempting to be peacemakers and restore harmony.
- Don't mistake apologies as acceptance of blame.
- Be open, accepting, and affirming.
- Avoid public confrontation.
- Talk fully about issues; explore thoughts and feelings.

HOW TO APPROACH PEOPLE WHILE THEY ARE IN STAGE 1 BLUE CONFLICT

- Affirm the relationship and depersonalize the conflict.
- Be pleasant and genuine, and invite responses.
- Be calm and non-confrontational.
- Listen, and ask more than once if needed.
- Allow the person lead to the conversation toward the point they really want to make.
- Respect the person's request for time and space.

THINGS TO AVOID WHEN APPROACHING PEOPLE WHILE THEY ARE IN STAGE 1 BLUE CONFLICT

- Focusing on resolving the conflict quickly or exclusively on the facts.
- Being aggressive toward the person or confronting them in public.
- Being sarcastic or patronizing.

MANAGING CONFLICT IN STAGES 2 AND 3

Conflict resolution is most likely to be effective from Stage 1, where self, problem, and others are in focus. If you are working with someone who has moved to Stage 2 or 3, you may need to de-escalate the conflict back to Stage 1 before you can reconcile your differences.

If the person is in Stage 2 [RG]

- Listen carefully to understand their view of the problem and the rationale for their expectations.
- Try to agree on at least one logical next step that you can take action on.

If the person is in Stage 3 [RG]

- Be responsive and engaged, yet allow time for reflection or data collection if needed.
- Emphasize your desire to restore the relationship. Ask what they see as the most logical next step.

R-B-G

CONFLICT SEQUENCE

This Conflict Sequence describes people who want to challenge conflict directly. If that does not work, they want to restore or preserve harmony. If that does not work, they may want to withdraw from the situation or end the relationship.

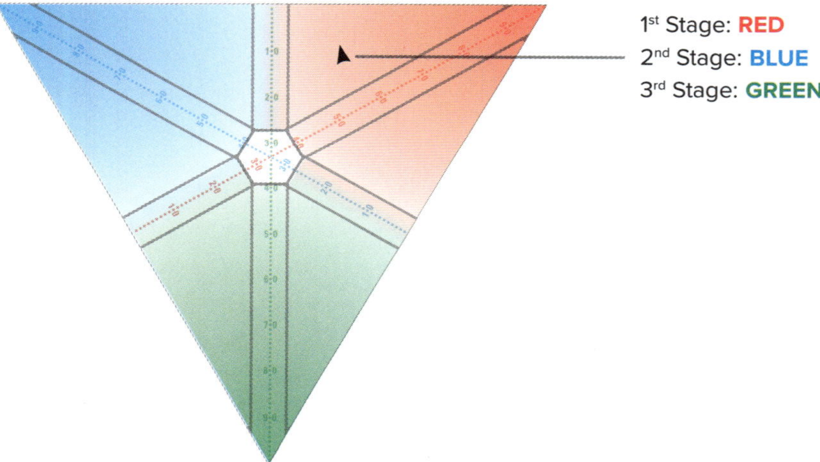

This descriptive text is written with a Conflict Sequence arrowhead located centrally in the Conflict Sequence region in mind. People whose arrowheads are close to the borders (within six points) of other Conflict Sequence regions may find that some text from the neighboring regions' descriptions is more accurate or useful.

While the following text describes the R-B-G Conflict Sequence, it should also be considered in light of the MVS of the person who has this Conflict Sequence. Since there are seven Motivational Value Systems, there are at least seven different ways to enter conflict and many different issues that can trigger conflict. These differences will affect the way people experience conflict and how they will resolve conflict. The first stage of this Conflict Sequence is Red. People with a short arrow whose MVS is also Red, may experience a less noticeable transition from their MVS to the first stage of conflict than people whose MVS is a different color will.

STAGE 1 RED CONFLICT

People in first stage Red conflict are motivated by the desire to rise to the challenge being offered. They tend to meet conflict head-on, with strong self-assertion and challenge to the opposition.

In first stage Red, people tend to feel energized and have a sense of certainty about what needs to be done. They feel a sense of urgency about solving the conflict and expect others to reflect that urgency back to them by taking action. If they do not sense that others feel a similar sense of urgency, they may press others for an immediate response.

In Stage 1 Red, people tend to come out competing to prevail over the opposition. They are quick to assert their rights and to argue persuasively for them in the moment. They press for an immediate resolution of the conflict. Their intensity may cause others to back away from the interaction, unintentionally delaying the engagement that people in first stage Red want.

Productive first stage Red conflict behaviors are typically targeted directly at the problem and the people involved. First stage Reds want to engage the issue as quickly as possible. The desire is to solve the problem rapidly and with the best possible result. Their assertive behaviors are intended to provide a quick answer to the opposition and an expedient response to the conflict issue.

When unproductive, people in first stage Red may push too hard or act too quickly. This may cause them to appear argumentative, angry, pushy, or rash. They may become so focused on the need for action and the urgency of the situation that they are not open to others' ideas.

How People in Stage 1 Red Can Improve Interactions

People who are experiencing the first stage of conflict may act as described previously. However, people may also adjust behavior or examine their perceptions during conflict in an effort to be more effective.

In Stage 1 Red, people may be more effective if they:

- Take time to consider the issue from as neutral a vantage point as possible.
- Listen carefully to the facts and feelings expressed by others.

- Determine whether there are alternative approaches to the one that seems most obvious in the moment.
- Consider the implications of doing nothing or waiting.

STAGE 2 BLUE CONFLICT

When initial actions to meet the challenge decisively are not effective at resolving the conflict, people who then move into the second stage of Blue (following Red) carry their passion for the issue and their desire for results with them.

In second stage Blue (following Red), people may feel they have pushed too hard or overreacted and now want to restore harmony or repair any unintentional damage they may have done. This second stage is about putting aside their ambitions in order to get other people back on board with the vision. They may also feel tired of the struggle and just want people to get along, even if the results are slightly less than optimal.

In second stage Blue (following Red), people want to let go of the struggle. They may still hold a strong position, but they no longer want to talk about it. If they are pushed further at this point, they may throw up their hands and respond with, "OK, fine. Whatever." Although this appears to be a sort of surrender, it is conditional, and they may still be upset. They may be back to re-engage after they have recovered their energy for the issue.

People with a R-B-G Conflict Sequence generally work very hard in Stage 2 Blue to prevent going to Stage 3 Green. They may continue to appease others through accommodation or apology if they believe they overreacted in Stage 1 Red. They may put aside their own wishes, believing that sacrifice allows them to stay engaged and is better than walking away in Stage 3 Green.

STAGE 3 GREEN CONFLICT

In third stage Green (following Red and Blue), people tend to abandon or insulate themselves from feelings for the issue and the people involved. They tend to believe that their assertive and accommodating approaches to conflict have been met with a lack of cooperation or fair play and that no option remains except to disengage.

In the third stage of Green (following Red and Blue) people will typically withdraw and cut off contact in order to preserve whatever they can salvage from the situation. They may refuse to even talk about the past issue because they think there is no remaining possibility of resolving it. If the conflict is severe, they may end the relationship and avoid all further interaction with the people involved.

The Green Stage 3 Filter

Green is the third stage of conflict in the R-B-G sequence. When in first stage Red and observing Green behavior in another person, some projection of the third stage experience on the other is possible. Analytical behavior of others may be perceived as uncommitted detachment without first taking a stand, sensing the urgency of the situation, or engaging in problem-solving efforts.

Working with R-B-G

CONFLICT RESOLUTION

Conflict is resolved when the elements of opposition are addressed and the people involved are able to return to feeling good about themselves again.

The Path Back to the MVS from Stage 1 Red

Each person has a path back from conflict to their MVS and feelings of self-worth. Even though many people may feel and act similarly in the first stage of conflict, there may be differences that are related to the MVS they are trying to return to. Conflict management efforts can be improved by keeping these differences in mind.

The path back to the MVS will be different for every person. Table 3.6 features some general illustrations of the path from Stage 1 Red back to MVS.

Figure 3.6 *Paths back to MVS from R-B-G*

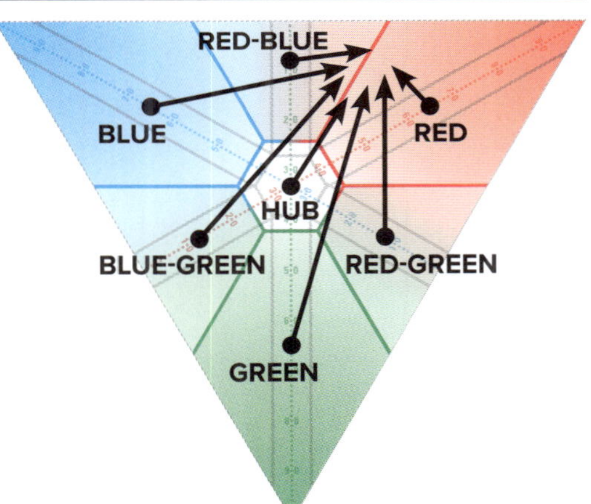

Table 3.6 *Illustrations of the path back to MVS from Stage 1 Red*

Blue MVS	Taking immediate action that benefits others
Red MVS	Meeting the challenge and refocusing on the results
Green MVS	Acting with urgency to restore order and logic
Red-Blue MVS	Challenging others to grow by overcoming obstacles
Red-Green MVS	Proving the validity of a strategy through decisive action
Blue-Green MVS	Fighting for principles to restore fairness and self-sufficiency
Hub MVS	Choosing the least constraining option and acting swiftly on it

For more detailed information and ideas about resolving conflict with people who have this Conflict Sequence, also consult the "Productive Results of Conflict" sections in the chapters that describe the MVS of those people. No matter the MVS of people in the conflict, there are some things that can help them transition out of Stage 1 Red.

LISTENING TO STAGE 1 RED

Working effectively with people in Stage 1 Red conflict means you will need to understand what they are saying. Listening well will ensure that they feel heard, and know that you understand the importance of the issue. When you are listening, and engaging in dialogue, keep these points in mind:

- Hear them as attempting to solve the problem as quickly as possible.
- Don't mistake passion and energy for anger.
- Be confident and direct; focus on outcomes.
- Don't be dismissive or passive.
- Show a sense of urgency and willingness to act.

HOW TO APPROACH PEOPLE WHILE THEY ARE IN STAGE 1 RED CONFLICT

- Listen and acknowledge their position, then respond directly, openly, and honestly.
- Take a confident stand, discussing your point of view and raising relevant issues.
- Be prepared for a robust exchange of views.
- Be purposeful and direct.
- Focus on resolving the issue and taking action.
- Be energetic and passionate, demonstrating an understanding of the issue's importance.

THINGS TO AVOID WHEN APPROACHING PEOPLE WHILE THEY ARE IN STAGE 1 RED CONFLICT

- Focusing on minor details or emotional issues.
- Trivializing, walking away, or giving in without reason.
- Telling them they are angry or telling them to "calm down."

MANAGING CONFLICT IN STAGES 2 AND 3

Conflict resolution is most likely to be effective from Stage 1, where self, problem, and others are in focus. If you are working with someone who has moved to Stage 2 or 3, you may need to de-escalate the conflict back to Stage 1 before you can reconcile your differences.

If the person is in Stage 2 Blue:

- Be open to apologies; they may feel that they were too abrupt or demanding in Stage 1.
- Focus on repairing any damage and quickly returning to action.

If the person is in Stage 3 Green:

- Make sure they know you are available and willing to participate, but do not try to force an immediate conversation.
- Emphasize your understanding of the importance of the issue to them. Ask what additional information, or how much time they need.

R-G-B

CONFLICT SEQUENCE

This Conflict Sequence describes people who want to prevail through competition. If that does not work, they want to use logic, reason, and rules. If that does not work, they may feel compelled to surrender as a last resort.

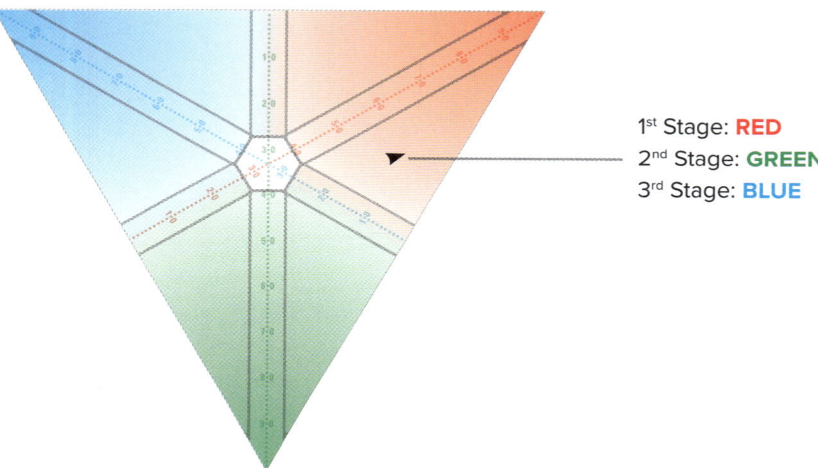

This descriptive text is written with a Conflict Sequence arrowhead located centrally in the Conflict Sequence region in mind. People whose arrowheads are close to the borders (within six points) of other Conflict Sequence regions may find that some text from the neighboring regions' descriptions is more accurate or useful.

While the following text describes the R-G-B Conflict Sequence, it should also be considered in light of the MVS of the person who has this Conflict Sequence. Since there are seven Motivational Value Systems, there are at least seven different ways to enter conflict and many different issues that can trigger conflict. These differences will affect the way people experience conflict and how they will resolve conflict. The first stage of this Conflict Sequence is Red.

People with a short arrow whose MVS is also Red may experience a less noticeable transition from their MVS to the first stage of conflict than people whose MVS is a different color will.

STAGE 1 RED CONFLICT

People in first stage Red conflict are motivated by the desire to rise to the challenge being offered. They tend to meet conflict head-on, with strong self-assertion and challenge to the opposition.

In first stage Red, people tend to feel energized and have a sense of certainty about what needs to be done. They feel a sense of urgency about solving the conflict and expect others to reflect that urgency back to them by taking action. If they do not sense that others feel a similar sense of urgency, they may press others for an immediate response.

In Stage 1 Red, people tend to come out competing to prevail over the opposition. They are quick to assert their rights and to argue persuasively for them in the moment. They press for an immediate resolution of the conflict. Their intensity may cause others to back away from the interaction, unintentionally delaying the engagement that people in first stage Red want.

Productive first stage Red conflict behaviors are typically targeted directly at the problem and the people involved. First stage Reds want to engage the issue as quickly as possible. The desire is to solve the problem rapidly and with the best possible result. Their assertive behaviors are intended to provide a quick answer to the opposition and an expedient response to the conflict issue.

When unproductive, people in first stage Red may push too hard or act too quickly. This may cause them to appear argumentative, angry, pushy, or rash. They may become so focused on the need for action and the urgency of the situation that they are not open to others' ideas.

How People in Stage 1 Red Can Improve Interactions

People who are experiencing the first stage of conflict may act as described previously. However, people may also adjust behavior or examine their perceptions during conflict in an effort to be more effective.

In Stage 1 Red, people may be more effective if they:

- Take time to consider the issue from as neutral a vantage point as possible.
- Listen carefully to the facts and feelings expressed by others.

- Determine whether there are alternative approaches to the one that seems most obvious in the moment.
- Consider the implications of doing nothing or waiting.

STAGE 2 GREEN CONFLICT

When initial actions to meet the challenge decisively are not effective at resolving the conflict, people who then move into the second stage of Green (following Red) carry their passion for the issue and their desire for results with them.

In second stage Green (following Red), people feel that since competition and challenge did not produce a quick and desirable solution, they now need to fall back on analysis and logic. They may still feel a strong sense of rightness about their prior position, but they are willing to look at facts that will either support or challenge their initial position. They want some time and space away from others in order to think about how they can strengthen or improve their plan.

In second stage Green (following Red), people step back, taking the time to logically and thoughtfully assess the situation. Setting aside the desire to win in the moment, they analyze the situation and people's roles in it in order to identify a strategy to resolve the conflict more efficiently.

People with an R-G-B Conflict Sequence generally work very hard in Stage 2 Green to prevent going to Stage 3 Blue. They may continue to collect information to support or challenge positions held by themselves and others. They may become rigid and inflexible, believing that they are building a case that, if lost, cannot be salvaged if they are forced into a Stage 3 Blue experience.

STAGE 3 BLUE CONFLICT

In third stage Blue (following Red and Green), people tend to feel completely defeated, not by others, but by the inability to find and implement a solution. They tend to feel that all of their efforts to resolve the issue logically and forcefully have failed, and all that remains is to give up on the issue and figure out how to live with the pain of defeat.

In the third stage of Blue (following Red and Green), people will typically end association with the issue and the people. They may say that they no longer care about the conflict or the impact on the people involved. If the conflict is severe, the relationship may be irreparably damaged by the inability to become emotionally involved again.

The Blue Stage 3 Filter

Blue is the third stage of conflict in the R-G-B sequence. When in first stage Red and observing Blue behavior in another person, some projection of the third stage experience onto the other is possible. Accommodating behavior of others may be perceived as weakness, giving up, or lack of commitment, without any attempt to stand up for themselves or assert their rights.

Working with R-G-B

CONFLICT RESOLUTION

Conflict is resolved when the elements of opposition are addressed and the people involved are able to return to feeling good about themselves again.

The Path Back to the MVS from Stage 1 Red

Each person has a path back from conflict to their MVS and feelings of self-worth. Even though many people may feel and act similarly in the first stage of conflict, there may be differences that are related to the MVS they are trying to return to. Conflict management efforts can be improved by keeping these differences in mind.

The path back to the MVS will be different for every person. Table 3.7 features some general illustrations of the path from Stage 1 Red back to MVS.

Figure 3.7 *Paths back to MVS from R-G-B*

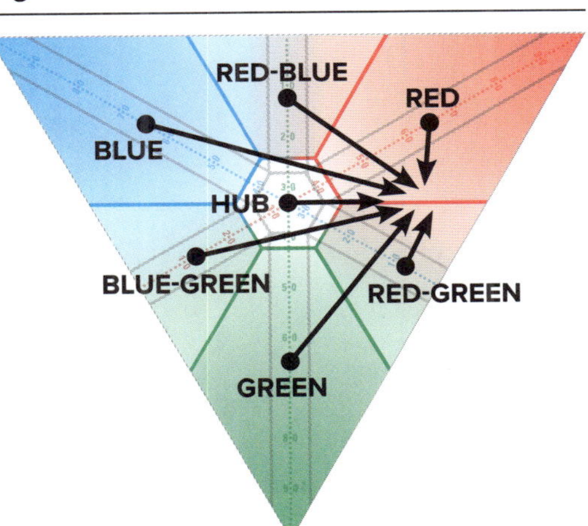

Table 3.7 *Illustrations of the path back to MVS from Stage 1 Red*

Blue MVS	Taking immediate action that benefits others
Red MVS	Meeting the challenge and refocusing on the results
Green MVS	Acting with urgency to restore order and logic
Red-Blue MVS	Challenging others to grow by overcoming obstacles
Red-Green MVS	Proving the validity of a strategy through decisive action
Blue-Green MVS	Fighting for principles to restore fairness and self-sufficiency
Hub MVS	Choosing the least constraining option and acting swiftly on it

For more detailed information and ideas about resolving conflict with people who have this Conflict Sequence, also consult the "Productive Results of Conflict"sections in the chapters that describe the MVS of those people. No matter the MVS of people in the conflict, there are some things that can help them transition out of Stage 1 Red.

LISTENING TO STAGE 1 RED

Working effectively with people in Stage 1 Red conflict means you will need to understand what they are saying. Listening well will ensure that they feel heard, and know that you understand the importance of the issue. When you are listening, and engaging in dialogue, keep these points in mind:

- Hear them as attempting to solve the problem as quickly as possible.
- Don't mistake passion and energy for anger.
- Be confident and direct; focus on outcomes.
- Don't be dismissive or passive.
- Show a sense of urgency and willingness to act.

HOW TO APPROACH PEOPLE WHILE THEY ARE IN STAGE 1 RED CONFLICT

- Listen and acknowledge their position, then respond directly, openly, and honestly.
- Take a confident stand, discussing your point of view and raising relevant issues.
- Be prepared for a robust exchange of views.
- Be purposeful and direct.
- Focus on resolving the issue and taking action.
- Be energetic and passionate, demonstrating an understanding of the issue's importance.

THINGS TO AVOID WHEN APPROACHING PEOPLE WHILE THEY ARE IN STAGE 1 RED CONFLICT

- Focusing on minor details or emotional issues.
- Trivializing, walking away, or giving in without reason.
- Telling them they are angry or telling them to "calm down."

MANAGING CONFLICT IN STAGES 2 AND 3

Conflict resolution is most likely to be effective from Stage 1, where self, problem, and others are in focus. If you are working with someone who has moved to Stage 2 or 3, you may need to de-escalate the conflict back to Stage 1 before you can reconcile your differences.

If the person is in Stage 2 Green:

- Allow time for analysis; they may not know why their initial assertive approach didn't work.
- Focus on clarifying their objectives or desired outcomes.

If the person is in Stage 3 Blue:

- Apologize, if appropriate, and express your willingness to try again.
- Emphasize your understanding of the importance of the issue to them. Ask what you can do to set things right.

R-[BG]

CONFLICT SEQUENCE

This Conflict Sequence describes people who want to assert their rights and win. If that does not work, they want to make a choice, depending on what's better in the situation: to give in with conditions or to disengage and save what they can.

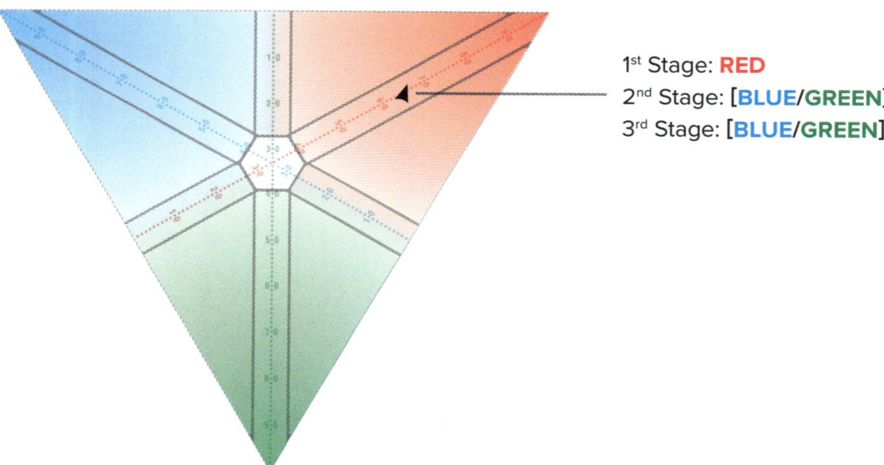

This descriptive text is written with a Conflict Sequence arrowhead located centrally in the Conflict Sequence region in mind. People whose arrowheads are close to the borders (within six points) of other Conflict Sequence regions may find that some text from the neighboring regions' descriptions is more accurate or useful.

While the following text describes the R-[BG] Conflict Sequence, it should also be considered in light of the MVS of the person who has this Conflict Sequence. Since there are seven Motivational Value Systems, there are at least seven different ways to enter conflict, and many different issues that can trigger conflict. These differences will affect the way people experience conflict and how they will resolve conflict. The first stage of this Conflict Sequence is Red. People with a short arrow whose MVS is also Red may experience a less noticeable transition from their MVS to the first stage of conflict than people whose MVS is a different color will.

STAGE 1 RED CONFLICT

People in first stage Red conflict are motivated by the desire to rise to the challenge being offered. They tend to meet conflict head-on, with strong self-assertion and challenge to the opposition.

In first stage Red, people tend to feel energized and have a sense of certainty about what needs to be done. They feel a sense of urgency about solving the conflict and expect others to reflect that urgency back to them by taking action. If they do not sense that others feel a similar sense of urgency, they may press others for an immediate response.

In Stage 1 Red, people tend to come out competing to prevail over the opposition. They are quick to assert their rights and to argue persuasively for them in the moment. They press for an immediate resolution of the conflict. Their intensity may cause others to back away from the interaction, unintentionally delaying the engagement that people in first stage Red want.

Productive first stage Red conflict behaviors are typically targeted directly at the problem and the people involved. First stage Reds want to engage the issue as quickly as possible. The desire is to solve the problem rapidly and with the best possible result. Their assertive behaviors are intended to provide a quick answer to the opposition and an expedient response to the conflict issue.

When unproductive, people in first stage Red may push too hard or act too quickly. This may cause them to appear argumentative, angry, pushy, or rash. They may become so focused on the need for action and the urgency of the situation that they are not open to others' ideas.

How People in Stage 1 Red Can Improve Interactions

People who are experiencing the first stage of conflict may act as described previously. However, people may also adjust behavior or examine their perceptions during conflict in an effort to be more effective.

In Stage 1 Red, people may be more effective if they:

- Take time to consider the issue from as neutral a vantage point as possible.
- Listen carefully to the facts and feelings expressed by others.

- Determine whether there are alternative approaches to the one that seems most obvious in the moment.
- Consider the implications of doing nothing or waiting.

STAGE 2 [BG] CONFLICT

When initial actions to meet the challenge decisively are not effective at resolving the conflict, people who then move into the second stage of [BG] carry their passion for the issue and their desire for results with them.

People in this blended second and third stage may take different approaches based on their perception of the situation. They may go to Blue followed by Green if the relationship is more important than the principles involved or to Green followed by Blue if the principles are more important than the relationship. In these cases, conflict can be understood more fully by referring to the R-B-G and R-G-B pages. It is also possible that the Blue and Green conflict stages will be combined for a blended conflict experience.

When Blue and Green are blended in Stages 2 and 3 (following Red), people feel that they have pushed the issue hard enough and want to back off a bit. They want to take some time to reconsider the issue and their role in it. Because their direct engagement did not result in resolution, they may give in temporarily, apologizing for their assertiveness, conceding to their opposition, or doing some additional research about the conflict.

Ideally, they will be able to reconcile their differences and solve the problem. If they cannot and they do not openly concede or apologize, they may instead choose to wait the issue out, hoping that circumstances will change.

STAGE 3 [BG] CONFLICT

While Blue and Green are blended in Stages 2 and 3, people will experience an internal difference between these stages. Stage 2 is characterized by a focus on the self and the problem, and Stage 3 is focused on the self. Therefore, the Stage 3 experience of [BG] is a more intense and self-focused version of the Stage 2 experience. If a person concentrated on a conditionally accommodating, Blue approach in Stage 2, their third stage is likely to be the detached withdrawal typical of Stage 3 Green. If they concentrated on the analytical, Green approach to Stage 2, their third stage is likely to be the painful defeat or surrender typical of Stage 3 Blue.

[BG] STAGE 3 FILTER

(Blue-Green) is the blended second and third stage of conflict in the R-[BG] sequence. When in first stage Red and observing Blue-Green behavior in another person, some projection of the second or third stage experience on the other is possible. The cautious behavior of others may be perceived as passive-aggressive and without concern for the issue at hand.

Working with R-[BG]

CONFLICT RESOLUTION

Conflict is resolved when the elements of opposition are addressed and the people involved are able to return to feeling good about themselves again.

The Path Back to the MVS from Stage 1 Red

Each person has a path back from conflict to their MVS and feelings of self-worth. Even though many people may feel and act similarly in the first stage of conflict, there may be differences that are related to the MVS they are trying to return to. Conflict management efforts can be improved by keeping these differences in mind.

The path back to the MVS will be different for every person. Table 3.8 features some general illustrations of the path from Stage 1 Red back to MVS.

Figure 3.8 *Paths back to MVS from R-[BG]*

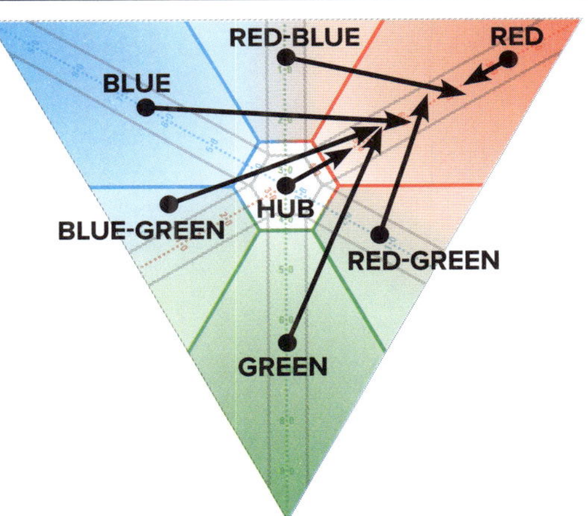

Table 3.8 *Illustrations of the path back to MVS from Stage 1 Red*

Blue MVS	Taking immediate action that benefits others
Red MVS	Meeting the challenge and refocusing on the results
Green MVS	Acting with urgency to restore order and logic
Red-Blue MVS	Challenging others to grow by overcoming obstacles
Red-Green MVS	Proving the validity of a strategy through decisive action
Blue-Green MVS	Fighting for principles to restore fairness and self-sufficiency
Hub MVS	Choosing the least constraining option and acting swiftly on it

For more detailed information and ideas about resolving conflict with people who have this Conflict Sequence, also consult the "Productive Results of Conflict"sections in the chapters that describe the MVS of those people. No matter the MVS of people in the conflict, there are some things that can help them transition out of Stage 1 Red.

LISTENING TO STAGE 1 RED

Working effectively with people in Stage 1 Red conflict means you will need to understand what they are saying. Listening well will ensure that they feel heard, and know that you understand the importance of the issue. When you are listening, and engaging in dialogue, keep these points in mind:

- Hear them as attempting to solve the problem as quickly as possible.
- Don't mistake passion and energy for anger.
- Be confident and direct; focus on outcomes.
- Don't be dismissive or passive.
- Show a sense of urgency and willingness to act.

HOW TO APPROACH PEOPLE WHILE THEY ARE IN STAGE 1 RED CONFLICT

- Listen and acknowledge their position, then respond directly, openly, and honestly.
- Take a confident stand, discussing your point of view and raising relevant issues.
- Be prepared for a robust exchange of views.
- Be purposeful and direct.
- Focus on resolving the issue and taking action.
- Be energetic and passionate, demonstrating an understanding of the issue's importance.

THINGS TO AVOID WHEN APPROACHING PEOPLE WHILE THEY ARE IN STAGE 1 RED CONFLICT

- Focusing on minor details or emotional issues.
- Trivializing, walking away, or giving in without reason.
- Telling them they are angry or telling them to "calm down."

MANAGING CONFLICT IN STAGES 2 AND 3

Conflict resolution is most likely to be effective from Stage 1, where self, problem, and others are in focus. If you are working with someone who has moved to Stage 2 or 3, you may need to de-escalate the conflict back to Stage 1 before you can reconcile your differences.

If the person is in Stage 2 [BG]

- Allow time for reconsideration of the issue; they may feel that they acted too quickly.
- Focus on what is fair to everyone and what can be done next.

If the person is in Stage 3 [BG]

- Hear them out fully; they may feel uncertain about what to do.
- Emphasize your understanding of the importance of the issue to them. Ask when you could talk about setting things right.

G-B-R

CONFLICT SEQUENCE

This Conflict Sequence describes people who want to carefully examine the situation. If that does not work, they want to defer to other people in the interest of harmony. If that does not work, they may feel compelled to fight, possibly in an explosive manner.

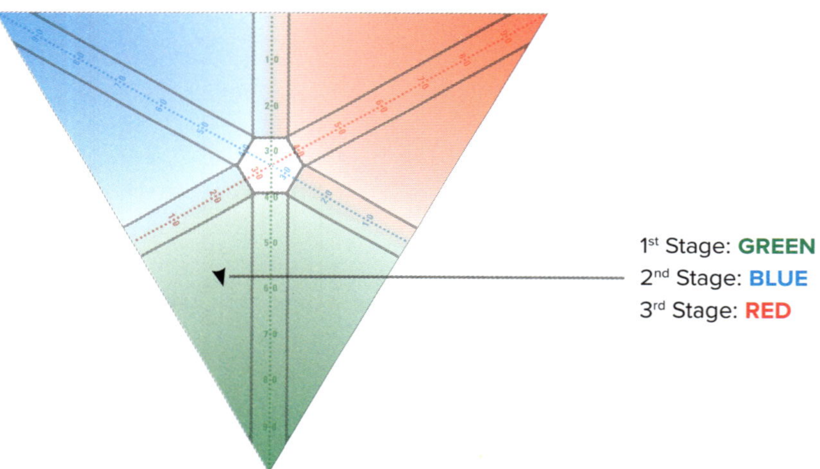

This descriptive text is written with a Conflict Sequence arrowhead located about centrally in the Conflict Sequence region in mind. People whose arrowheads are close to the borders (within six points) of other Conflict Sequence regions may find that some text from the neighboring regions' descriptions is more accurate or useful.

While the following text describes the G-B-R Conflict Sequence, it should also be considered in light of the MVS of the person who has this Conflict Sequence. Since there are seven Motivational Value Systems, there are at least seven different ways to enter conflict and many different issues that can trigger conflict. These differences will affect the way people experience conflict and how they will resolve conflict. The first stage of this Conflict Sequence is Green. People with a short arrow whose MVS is also Green may experience a less noticeable transition from their MVS to the first stage of conflict than people whose MVS is a different color will.

STAGE 1 GREEN CONFLICT

People in first stage Green conflict are motivated by a desire to carefully examine the situation. They want to be prudently cautious, checking and/or conserving resources and collecting information to make logical decisions.

They tend to minimize their feelings, instead focusing on non-emotional issues to clarify the conflict. If they do talk about feelings, they tend to say they feel uncertain or hesitant, or they say they are in need of more information. If coming from an MVS other than Green, they may feel a lower level of energy.

In first stage Green, people tend to take time and space to analyze the problem objectively. This may be perceived as pulling away from others or the issue; however, people in first stage Green are quietly and analytically engaged in the issue. They may prefer to be alone for a period of time to reflect on the issue and design a fair solution.

Productive first stage Green conflict behaviors are typically used in an effort to create rational, well-thought-out solutions that are fair and unbiased. Their analysis is targeted at discovering facts or connections that were previously overlooked. The intent is to create better understanding and processes.

When unproductive, people in first stage Green may take too long to complete their analysis or overly focus on details. This may cause them to appear withdrawn or unconcerned about the problem. They may become rigidly adherent to certain principles and take a purely objective, almost clinical approach to things.

How People in Stage 1 Green Can Improve Interactions

People who are experiencing the first stage of conflict may act as described previously. However, people may also adjust behavior or examine their perceptions during conflict in an effort to be more effective.

In Stage 1 Green, people may be more effective if they:

- Ask people for their deadlines or reasons for urgency and negotiate a time for a decision.
- Analyze the emotions of others as additional data regarding the problem.

- Suggest a tentative, non-binding solution or involve other people in generating alternative scenarios.
- Consider delegating the issue or partnering with someone else.

STAGE 2 BLUE CONFLICT

When an initial stand on logic, principles, and fairness is not effective at resolving the conflict, people who then move into the second stage of Blue (following Green) carry their analysis, data, information, and thought processes with them.

In second stage Blue (following Green), the needs of others are viewed as less important, and the primary motivation is to escape from the opposition without giving up anything of significant value. The desire for objectivity, fairness, and logic is replaced by a desire to give in for the moment and to let go of less important things. There is a feeling of justification in letting go of the preferred solution and allowing other people to have their way, because it is hoped that a small sacrifice will appease the other person and resolve the issue.

In second stage Blue (following Green), people tend to conditionally surrender, letting go of things that were deemed less important during their prior analysis.

Prepared with an abundance of logic and strategies, people in second stage Blue may choose to let their argument go, even encouraging others to try solutions that may be ineffective. They may use phrases such as, "Whatever!" "I don't care; do what you want," or, "If that's what you think... fine," to distance themselves from the decision and place accountability for negative outcomes on the other person. "Letting go" at this stage may be done deliberately to prevent the experience of moving into Stage 3 Red and potentially doing more damage.

People with a G-B-R Conflict Sequence generally work very hard in Stage 2 Blue to prevent going to Stage 3 Red. They may make larger and larger concessions in an effort to make the conflict go away, believing that the concessions are worth avoiding the discomfort and explosive potential of Stage 3 Red.

STAGE 3 RED CONFLICT

In third stage Red (following Green and Blue), people tend to feel intensely angry, energized, and potentially out of control, demanding an "all or nothing" solution. They tend to feel that all of their efforts to resolve the issue logically and without confrontation have failed. They feel that the desired outcome must be forcibly taken from or forcibly denied to the other person, regardless of cost.

In the third stage of Red (following Green and Blue), people will typically challenge others or fight, potentially in an explosive manner. They may say that they no longer care what other people think or want, forcibly implementing whatever they originally thought was the best solution. If the conflict is severe, the relationship may be irreparably damaged by the harshness of personal attacks or by the negative reactions of people who view this third stage Red behavior as overblown and uncalled for.

The Red Stage 3 Filter

Red is the third stage of conflict in the G-B-R sequence. While in first stage Green and observing Red behavior in another person, some projection of the third stage experience on others is possible. Assertive behavior in others may be perceived as irrational overreaction without first taking the time to consider the facts of the situation or the needs of others.

Working with G-B-R

CONFLICT RESOLUTION

Conflict is resolved when the elements of opposition are addressed and the people involved are able to return to feeling good about themselves again.

The Path Back to the MVS from Stage 1 Green

Each person has a path back from conflict to their MVS and feelings of self-worth. Even though many people may feel and act similarly in the first stage of conflict, there may be differences that are related to the MVS they are trying to return to. Conflict management efforts can be improved by keeping these differences in mind.

The path back to the MVS will be different for every person. Table 3.9 features some general illustrations of the path from Stage 1 Green back to MVS.

Figure 3.9 *Paths back to MVS from G-B-R*

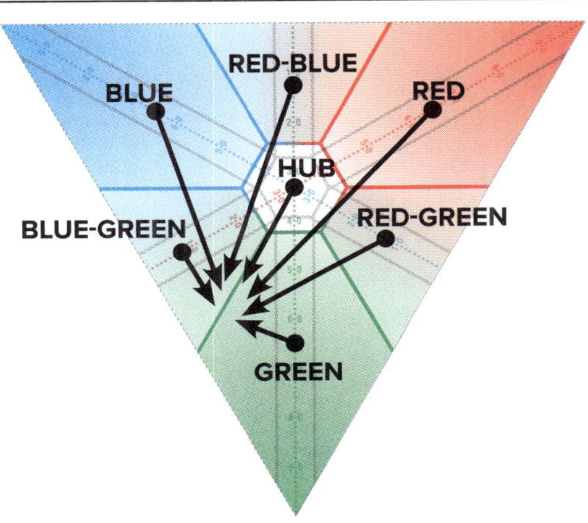

Table 3.9 *Illustrations of the path back to MVS from Stage 1 Green*

Blue MVS	Logically and fairly restoring harmony in the relationship
Red MVS	Collecting facts that can be used to accomplish tasks and goals
Green MVS	Clarifying principles and procedures that will restore order and assure a systematic solution
Red-Blue MVS	Creating a systematic way to assertively bring help to others
Red-Green MVS	Strengthening the strategy with additional facts and resources
Blue-Green MVS	Creating processes that help others help themselves
Hub MVS	Analytically generating options and making decisions that maintain future flexibility

For more detailed information and ideas about resolving conflict with people who have this Conflict Sequence, also consult the "Productive Results of Conflict" sections in the chapters that describe the MVS of those people. No matter the MVS of people in the conflict, there are some things that can help them transition out of Stage 1 Green.

LISTENING TO STAGE 1 GREEN

Working effectively with people in Stage 1 Green conflict means you will need to understand what they are saying. Listening well will ensure that they feel heard, and know that you understand their need for time and information. When you are listening, and engaging in dialogue, keep these points in mind:

- Hear them as attempting to find the most reasonable, logical solution.
- Don't mistake quiet for disinterest.
- Take time to get it right the first time.
- Don't push for quick decisions or guesses.
- Give them time to think or collect information before they respond.

HOW TO APPROACH PEOPLE WHILE THEY ARE IN STAGE 1 GREEN CONFLICT

- Respect the person's need for time to think things through.
- Listen attentively, then repeat or paraphrase key points to prove you are listening.
- After listening, explain your point of view.
- Keep calm and unemotional, presenting ideas in logical order.
- Listen to understand, not to respond.
- Focus on getting things right.

THINGS TO AVOID WHEN APPROACHING PEOPLE WHILE THEY ARE IN STAGE 1 GREEN CONFLICT

- Focusing on the urgency of the issue or on how others feel about the problem.
- Challenging aggressively or using feelings to justify decisions.
- Forcing them to decide quickly or making the decision without their input.

MANAGING CONFLICT IN STAGES 2 AND 3

Conflict resolution is most likely to be effective from Stage 1, where self, problem, and others are in focus. If you are working with someone who has moved to Stage 2 or 3, you may need to de-escalate the conflict back to Stage 1 before you can reconcile your differences.

If the person is in Stage 2 Blue:

- Tentatively accept if compromise is offered; check to ensure it is what they truly want to do.
- Focus on the potential costs of any concessions.

If the person is in Stage 3 Red:

- Create a safe space for them to say everything that's on their mind. They have probably been trying not to say these things.
- Emphasize your understanding of the facts of the matter. Ask what is most important to them at this moment.

G-R-B

CONFLICT SEQUENCE

This Conflict Sequence describes people who want to bring order and logic to the situation. If that does not work, they want to forcefully press for a logical resolution. If that does not work and others have more power in the situation, they may surrender.

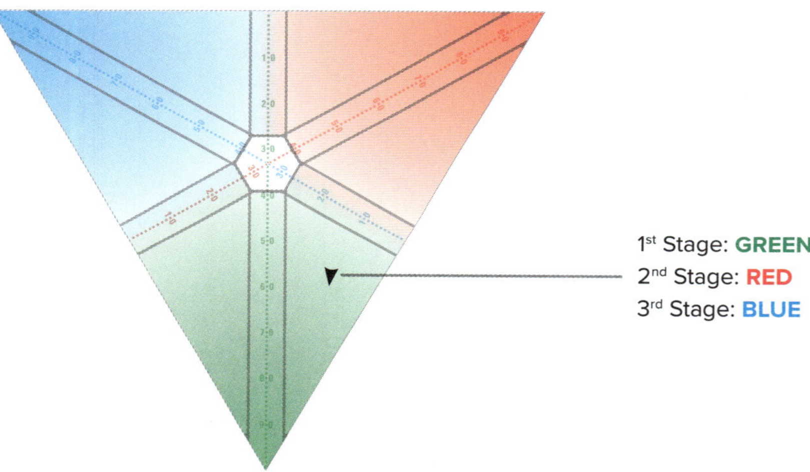

This descriptive text is written with a Conflict Sequence arrowhead located about centrally in the Conflict Sequence region in mind. People whose arrowheads are close to the borders (within six points) of other Conflict Sequence regions may find that some text from the neighboring regions' descriptions is more accurate or useful.

While the following text describes the G-R-B Conflict Sequence, it should also be considered in light of the MVS of the person who has this Conflict Sequence. Since there are seven Motivational Value Systems, there are at least seven different ways to enter conflict and many different issues that can trigger conflict. These differences will affect the way people experience conflict and how they will resolve conflict. The first stage of this Conflict Sequence is Green. People with a short arrow whose MVS is also Green may experience a less noticeable transition from their MVS to the first stage of conflict than people whose MVS is a different color will.

STAGE 1 GREEN CONFLICT

People in first stage Green conflict are motivated by a desire to carefully examine the situation. They want to be prudently cautious, checking and/or conserving resources and collecting information to make logical decisions.

They tend to minimize their feelings, instead focusing on non-emotional issues to clarify the conflict. If they do talk about feelings, they tend to say they feel uncertain or hesitant, or they say they are in need of more information. If coming from an MVS other than Green, they may feel a lower level of energy.

In first stage Green, people tend to take time and space to analyze the problem objectively. This may be perceived as pulling away from others or the issue; however, people in first stage Green are quietly and analytically engaged in the issue. They may prefer to be alone for a period of time to reflect on the issue and design a fair solution.

Productive first stage Green conflict behaviors are typically used in an effort to create rational, well-thought-out solutions that are fair and unbiased. Greens' analysis is targeted at discovering facts or connections that were previously overlooked. The intent is to create better understanding and processes.

When unproductive, people in first stage Green may take too long to complete their analysis or overly focus on details. This may cause them to appear withdrawn or unconcerned about the problem. They may become rigidly adherent to certain principles and take a purely objective, almost clinical approach to things.

How People in Stage 1 Green Can Improve Interactions

People who are experiencing the first stage of conflict may act as described previously. However, people may also adjust behavior or examine their perceptions during conflict in an effort to be more effective.

In Stage 1 Green, people may be more effective if they:

- Ask people for their deadlines or reasons for urgency and negotiate a time for a decision.
- Analyze the emotions of others as additional data regarding the problem.

- Suggest a tentative, non-binding solution or involve other people in generating alternative scenarios.
- Consider delegating the issue or partnering with someone else.

STAGE 2 RED CONFLICT

When an initial stand on logic, principles, and fairness is not effective at resolving the conflict, people who then move into the second stage of Red (following Green) carry their analysis, data, information, and thought processes with them.

In second stage Red (following Green), the needs of others are viewed as less important, and the primary motivation is to forcefully implement the logical solution that was previously not accepted. The desire for objectivity, fairness, and logic is replaced by a strong desire to win. There is an increased confidence in their solution and a diminished regard for the impact of that solution on others. If the other party has to be defeated to achieve the win, it is seen as an acceptable outcome.

In second stage Red (following Green), people tend to become more energized and animated, forcefully arguing their position and using whatever powers or resources are available to implement their desired solution. Armed with an abundance of logic and strategies, people in second stage Red may issue ultimatums and attack issues and others in an effort to prove that they are right and force compliance. They may use strong and intentionally hurtful language in an attempt to force the other party to surrender, ensuring that they themselves do not have to surrender and move into their third stage of Blue.

People with a G-R-B Conflict Sequence generally work very hard in Stage 2 Red to prevent going to Stage 3 Blue. They may continue to elevate the importance and urgency of the situation and the intensity of their reaction. They may become increasingly forceful and directive, based on their earlier analysis, believing that the fight, regardless of the potential damage, is better than being forced to surrender in Stage 3 Blue.

STAGE 3 BLUE CONFLICT

In third stage Blue (following Green and Red), people tend to feel completely defeated—not by others, but by the inability to find and implement a solution. They tend to feel that all of their efforts to resolve the issue logically and forcefully have failed. All that remains is to give up on the issue and figure out how to live with the pain of defeat.

In third stage Blue (following Green and Red), people will typically end their association with the issue and people. They may say that they no longer care about the conflict or the impact on the other people involved. If the conflict is severe, the relationship may be irreparably damaged, and they may refuse to become emotionally involved again with those other people.

The Blue Stage 3 Filter

Blue is the third stage of conflict in the G-R-B sequence. When in first stage Green and observing Blue behavior in another person, some projection of the third stage experience onto others is possible. Accommodating behavior in others may be perceived as irrationally surrendering without first taking the time to collect the facts or to stand up for themselves.

Working with G-R-B

CONFLICT RESOLUTION

Conflict is resolved when the elements of opposition are addressed and the people involved are able to return to feeling good about themselves again.

The Path Back to the MVS from Stage 1 Green

Each person has a path back from conflict to their MVS and feelings of self-worth. Even though many people may feel and act similarly in the first stage of conflict, there may be differences that are related to the MVS they are trying to return to. Conflict management efforts can be improved by keeping these differences in mind.

The path back to the MVS will be different for every person. Table 3.10 features some general illustrations of the path from Stage 1 Green back to MVS.

Figure 3.10 *Paths back to MVS from G-R-B*

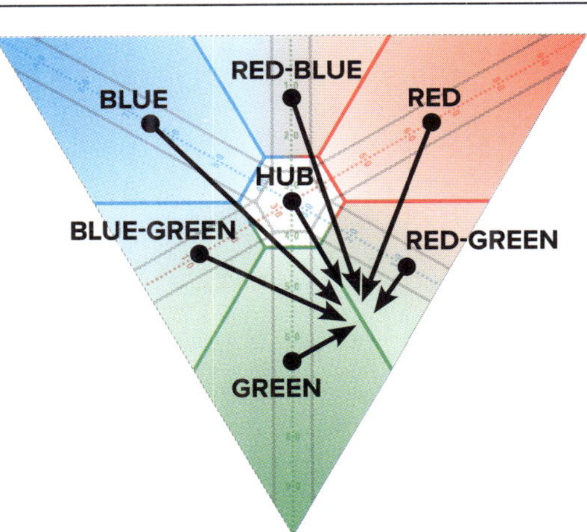

Table 3.10 *Illustrations of the path back to MVS from Stage 1 Green*

Blue MVS	Logically and fairly restoring harmony in the relationship
Red MVS	Collecting facts that can be used to accomplish tasks and goals
Green MVS	Clarifying principles and procedures that will restore order and assure a systematic solution
Red-Blue MVS	Creating a systematic way to assertively bring help to others
Red-Green MVS	Strengthening the strategy with additional facts and resources
Blue-Green MVS	Creating processes that help others help them-selves
Hub MVS	Analytically generating options and making decisions that maintain future flexibility

For more detailed information and ideas about resolving conflict with people who have this Conflict Sequence, also consult the "Productive Results of Conflict"sections in the chapters that describe the MVS of those people. No matter the MVS of people in the conflict, there are some things that can help them transition out of Stage 1 Green.

LISTENING TO STAGE 1 GREEN

Working effectively with people in Stage 1 Green conflict means you will need to understand what they are saying. Listening well will ensure that they feel heard, and know that you understand their need for time and information. When you are listening, and engaging in dialogue, keep these points in mind:

- Hear them as attempting to find the most reasonable, logical solution.
- Don't mistake quiet for disinterest.
- Take time to get it right the first time.
- Don't push for quick decisions or guesses.
- Give them time to think or collect information before they respond.

HOW TO APPROACH PEOPLE WHILE THEY ARE IN STAGE 1 GREEN CONFLICT

- Respect the person's need for time to think things through.
- Listen attentively, repeat or paraphrase key points to prove you are listening.
- After listening, explain your point of view.
- Keep calm and unemotional, stating ideas in a logical order.
- Listen to understand, not to respond.
- Focus on getting things right.

THINGS TO AVOID WHEN APPROACHING PEOPLE WHILE THEY ARE IN STAGE 1 GREEN CONFLICT

- Focusing on the urgency of the issue or on how others feel about the problem.
- Challenging aggressively or using feelings to justify decisions.
- Forcing them to decide quickly or making the decision without their input.

MANAGING CONFLICT IN STAGES 2 AND 3

Conflict resolution is most likely to be effective from Stage 1, where self, problem, and others are in focus. If you are working with someone who has moved to Stage 2 or 3, you may need to de-escalate the conflict back to Stage 1 before you can reconcile your differences.

If the person is in Stage 2 Red:

- Be prepared for an assertive statement of facts or rights; find points of agreement.
- Focus on the most likely outcomes of any proposed action.

If the person is in Stage 3 Blue:

- Apologize, if appropriate, and express your willingness to try again.
- Emphasize your understanding of the facts of the matter. Ask what you can do to set things right.

G-[BR]

CONFLICT SEQUENCE

This Conflict Sequence describes people who want to maintain order and principles. If that does not work, they want to make a choice, depending on what's more reasonable in the situation: to give in with conditions or to forcefully engage.

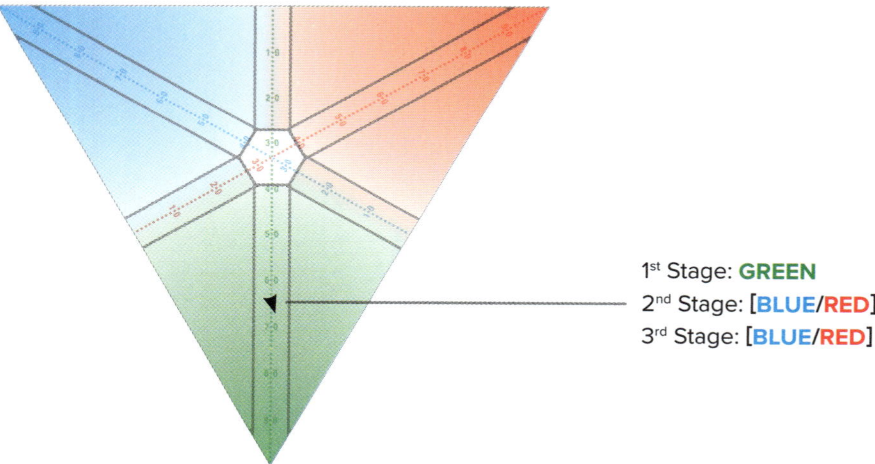

This descriptive text is written with a Conflict Sequence arrowhead located centrally in the Conflict Sequence region in mind. People whose arrowheads are close to the borders (within six points) of other Conflict Sequence regions may find that some text from the neighboring regions' descriptions is more accurate or useful.

While the following text describes the G-[BR] Conflict Sequence, it should also be considered in light of the MVS of the person who has this Conflict Sequence. Since there are seven Motivational Value Systems, there are at least seven different ways to enter conflict and many different issues that can trigger conflict. These differences will affect the way people experience conflict and how they will resolve conflict. The first stage of this Conflict Sequence is Green. People with a short arrow whose

MVS is also Green may experience a less noticeable transition from their MVS to the first stage of conflict than people whose MVS is a different color will.

STAGE 1 GREEN CONFLICT

People in first stage Green conflict are motivated by a desire to carefully examine the situation. They want to be prudently cautious, checking and/or conserving resources and collecting information to make logical decisions.

They tend to minimize their feelings, instead focusing on non-emotional issues to clarify the conflict. If they do talk about feelings, they tend to say they feel uncertain or hesitant, or they say they are in need of more information. If coming from an MVS other than Green, they may feel a lower level of energy.

In first stage Green, people tend to take time and space to analyze the problem objectively. This may be perceived as pulling away from others or the issue; however, people in first stage Green are quietly and analytically engaged in the issue. They may prefer to be alone for a period of time to reflect on the issue and design a fair solution.

Productive first stage Green conflict behaviors are typically used in an effort to create rational, well-thought-out solutions that are fair and unbiased. Their analysis is targeted at discovering facts or connections that were previously overlooked. The intent is to create better understanding and processes.

When unproductive, people in first stage Green may take too long to complete their analysis or overly focus on details. This may cause them to appear withdrawn or unconcerned about the problem. They may become rigidly adherent to certain principles and take a purely objective, almost clinical approach to things.

How People in Stage 1 Green Can Improve Interactions

People who are experiencing the first stage of conflict may act as described previously. However, people may also adjust behavior or examine their perceptions during conflict in an effort to be more effective.

In Stage 1 Green, people may be more effective if they:

- Ask people for their deadlines or reasons for urgency and negotiate a time for a decision.
- Analyze the emotions of others as additional data regarding the problem.
- Suggest a tentative, non-binding solution or involve other people in generating alternative scenarios.
- Consider delegating the issue or partnering with someone else.

STAGE 2 [BR] CONFLICT

When an initial stand on logic, principles and fairness is not effective at resolving the conflict, people who then move into the second stage of [BR] (following Green) carry their analysis, data, information, and thought processes with them.

People in this blended second and third stage may take different approaches based on their perception of the situation. They may go to Blue followed by Red if the relationship is more important than the result or to Red followed by Blue if the result is more important than the relationship. In these cases, conflict can be understood more fully by referring to the G-B-R and G-R-B pages. It is also possible that the Red and Blue conflict stages will be combined for a blended conflict experience.

In blended second and third stage [BR] (following Green), the needs of others are viewed as less important, and the motivation is to persuade people to accept the most important parts of the logical solution that has already been identified. The desire for objectivity, fairness, and logic is replaced by a desire to strongly communicate and delegate tasks, seeking immediate action, so people can move on to other, more rational issues. There is a feeling of rightness in disregarding the input of others because the solution will provide the final proof.

If they are unsuccessful in persuading others to act, they may forcefully restate their logic in an effort to overwhelm resistance, using phrases such as, "This is obviously the smartest thing to do," and, "Here's what you need to do."

STAGE 3 [BR] CONFLICT

While Blue and Red are blended in Stages 2 and 3, people will experience an internal difference between these stages. Stage 2 is characterized by a focus on the self and the problem, and Stage 3 is focused on the self. Therefore, the Stage 3 experience of [BR] is a more intense and self-focused version of the Stage 2 experience. If people concentrated on a conditionally accommodating, Blue approach in stage 2, their third stage is likely to be the explosive fighting typical of Stage 3 Red. If they concentrated on the assertive and argumentative Red approach to Stage 2, their third stage is likely to be the painful defeat or surrender typical of Stage 3 Blue.

[BR] Stage 3 Filter

[BR] is the blended second and third stage of conflict in the G-[BR]sequence. While in first stage Green and observing [BR] behavior in another person, some projection of the second or third stage experience on the other is possible.

Accommodating or confrontational behavior in others may be perceived as rash or irrational and not grounded in reality.

Working with G-[BR]

CONFLICT RESOLUTION

Conflict is resolved when the elements of opposition are addressed and the people involved are able to return to feeling good about themselves again.

The Path Back to the MVS from Stage 1 Green

Each person has a path back from conflict to their MVS and feelings of self-worth. Even though many people may feel and act similarly in the first stage of conflict, there may be differences that are related to the MVS they are trying to return to. Conflict management efforts can be improved by keeping these differences in mind.

The path back to the MVS will be different for every person. Table 3.11 features some general illustrations of the path from Stage 1 Green back to MVS.

Figure 3.11 *Paths back to MVS from G-[RB]*

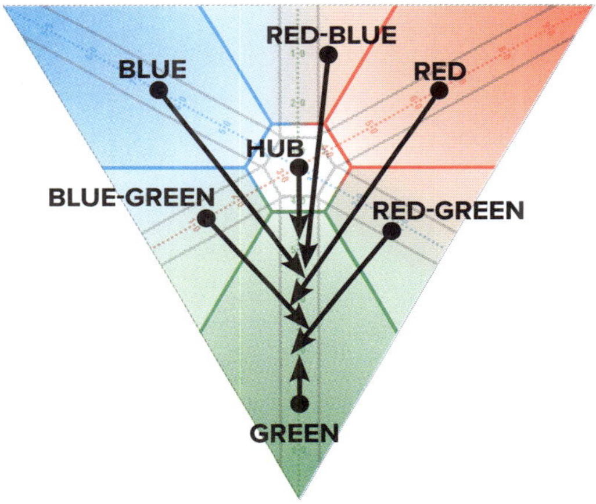

Table 3.11 *Illustrations of the path back to MVS from Stage 1 Green*

Blue MVS	Logically and fairly restoring harmony in the relationship
Red MVS	Collecting facts that can be used to accomplish tasks and goals
Green MVS	Clarifying principles and procedures that will restore order and assure a systematic solution
Red-Blue MVS	Creating a systematic way to assertively bring help to others
Red-Green MVS	Strengthening the strategy with additional facts and resources
Blue-Green MVS	Creating processes that help others help themselves
Hub MVS	Analytically generating options and making decisions that maintain future flexibility

For more detailed information and ideas about resolving conflict with people who have this Conflict Sequence, also consult the "Productive Results of Conflict" sections in the chapters that describe the MVS of those people. No matter the MVS of people in the conflict, there are some things that can help them transition out of Stage 1 Green.

LISTENING TO STAGE 1 GREEN

Working effectively with people in Stage 1 Green conflict means you will need to understand what they are saying. Listening well will ensure that they feel heard, and know that you understand their need for time and information. When you are listening, and engaging in dialogue, keep these points in mind:

- Hear them as attempting to find the most reasonable, logical solution.
- Don't mistake quiet for disinterest.
- Take time to get it right the first time.
- Don't push for quick decisions or guesses.
- Give them time to think or collect information before they respond.

HOW TO APPROACH PEOPLE WHILE THEY ARE IN STAGE 1 GREEN CONFLICT

- Respect the person's need for time to think things through.
- Listen attentively, then repeat or paraphrase key points to prove you are listening.
- After listening, explain your point of view.
- Keep calm and unemotional, presenting ideas in logical order.
- Listen to understand, not to respond.
- Focus on getting things right.

THINGS TO AVOID WHEN APPROACHING PEOPLE WHILE THEY ARE IN STAGE 1 GREEN CONFLICT

- Focusing on the urgency of the issue or on how others feel about the problem.
- Challenging aggressively or using feelings to justify decisions.
- Forcing them to decide quickly or making the decision without their input.

MANAGING CONFLICT IN STAGES 2 AND 3

Conflict resolution is most likely to be effective from Stage 1, where self, problem, and others are in focus. If you are working with someone who has moved to Stage 2 or 3, you may need to de-escalate the conflict back to Stage 1 before you can reconcile your differences.

If the person is in Stage 2 [BR]:

- Listen to all possible solutions; ask what is most logical.
- Focus on principles that are fair and practical.

If the person is in Stage 3 [BR]:

- Hear them out fully; they may feel that they are missing something.
- Emphasize your understanding of the facts of the matter. Ask what should be done next.

[BR]-G
CONFLICT SEQUENCE

This Conflict Sequence describes people who want to press assertively to maintain harmony and goodwill but do not want to sacrifice results for harmony. If that does not work, they may decide to withdraw from the situation.

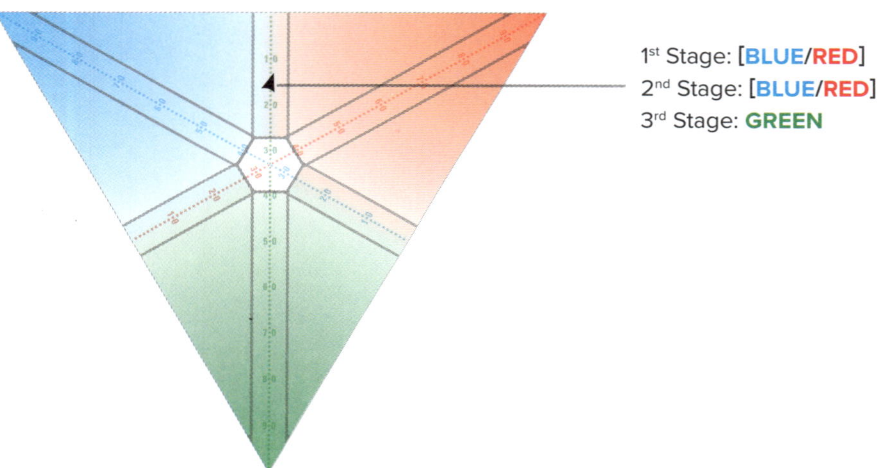

This descriptive text is written with a Conflict Sequence arrowhead located centrally in the Conflict Sequence region in mind. People whose arrowheads are close to the borders (within six points) of other Conflict Sequence regions may find that some text from the neighboring regions' descriptions is more accurate or useful.

While the following text describes the [BR]-G Conflict Sequence, it should also be considered in light of the MVS of the person who has this Conflict Sequence. Since there are seven Motivational Value Systems, there are at least seven different ways to enter conflict and many different issues that can trigger conflict.

These differences will affect the way people experience conflict and how they will resolve conflict. The first stage of this Conflict Sequence is a blend of Blue and Red. People with a short arrow whose MVS is also Red-Blue, may experience a less noticeable transition from their MVS to the first stage of conflict than people whose MVS is a different color will.

STAGE 1 [BR] CONFLICT

People in this blended first and second stage may take different approaches based on their perception of the situation. They may go to Red followed by Blue if the results are at least temporarily more important than the relationships involved, or to Blue followed by Red if the relationships are more important than the results. In these cases, conflict can be understood more fully by referring to the B-R-G and R-G-B pages. It is also possible that the Red and Blue conflict stages will be combined for a blended conflict experience.

When Red and Blue are blended in the first stage of conflict, people are motivated to quickly and kindly find an acceptable solution. They want others to get along and end the conflict. They want to get a good result as soon as possible but do not want any solution to be implemented in an authoritarian or domineering manner that would be hurtful to others.

They tend to feel alarmed when they are in conflict. To them, restoring the harmony in the relationship or team is a matter of greatest urgency. In addition to the conflict about the issue, people in the [BR] blend experience an internal tension between the two motives of asserting and accommodating. The internal dilemma is about how to integrate their competing priorities in the conflict: performance versus people, results versus relationships.

They may attempt to mediate a conversation, so everyone's concerns can be aired. They sense what other people need and will accommodate their needs if possible or take up their cause and seek accommodation of their needs from others. They may act quickly, believing that others will benefit by following their advice.

When unproductive, they may attempt to force people to talk to one another or make decisions on others' behalf. This may cause them to appear intrusive or controlling. They may believe it is better to ask for forgiveness than for permission and they may appear unconcerned about the rules.

How People in Stage 1 [BR] Can Improve Interactions

People who are experiencing the first stage of conflict may act as described previously. However, people may also adjust behavior or examine their perceptions during conflict in an effort to be more effective.

In Stage 1 [BR], people may be more effective if they:

- Take time to analyze as much detail about the issue as possible.
- Calmly state their personal priorities and boundaries.
- Consider whether others will view their actions as creating a precedent or a future obligation.
- Consider a Blue response when they feel Red, and a Red response when they feel Blue.

STAGE 2 [BR] CONFLICT

While Blue and Red are blended in Stages 1 and 2, people still experience a difference between Stage 1 and Stage 2. At first, they concentrate on themselves, the problem, and the other person. As the issue progresses to the second stage, they may drop the other person from focus, minimizing the importance of the other person's concerns and concentrating their energy on the problem and how it affects them. The second stage of conflict may appear similar to the first, but it is a more intensely experienced and self-focused version of problem-solving than the first stage.

People with a [BR]-G Conflict Sequence generally work very hard to prevent going to Stage 3 Green. They may continue to elevate the importance and urgency of the situation and the degree of sacrifice they are willing to make to resolve it. They may believe that they are acting on their last chance to stay involved with a person or situation and that the struggle, no matter how difficult, is better than walking away in Stage 3 Green.

STAGE 3 GREEN CONFLICT

In third Stage Green (following a blend of Blue and Red), people tend to abandon or insulate themselves from feelings about the issue and the people involved. They tend to believe that their assertive and accommodating approaches to conflict have been met with a lack of cooperation or fair play and that no option remains, except to disengage.

In third stage Green (following a blend of Blue and Red), people will typically withdraw and cut off contact in order to preserve whatever they can from the situation. They may refuse to even talk about the past issue, because they think there is no remaining possibility of resolving it. If the conflict is severe, they may end the relationship and avoid all further interaction with the people involved.

The Green Stage 3 Filter

Green is the third stage of conflict in the [BR]-G sequence. When in first stage [BR] and observing Green behavior in another person, some projection of the third stage experience on the other is possible. Analytical behavior in others may be perceived as abandonment or detachment without first taking a stand, sensing the needs of others, or engaging in problem-solving efforts.

Working with [BR]-G

CONFLICT RESOLUTION

Conflict is resolved when the elements of opposition are addressed and the people involved are able to return to feeling good about themselves again.

The Path Back to the MVS from Stage 1 [BR]

Each person has a path back from conflict to their MVS and feelings of self-worth. Even though many people may feel and act similarly in the first stage of conflict, there may be differences that are related to the MVS they are trying to return to. Conflict management efforts can be improved by keeping these differences in mind.

The path back to the MVS will be different for every person. Table 3.12 features some general illustrations of the path from Stage 1 [BR] back to MVS.

Figure 3.12 *Paths back to MVS from [BR]-G*

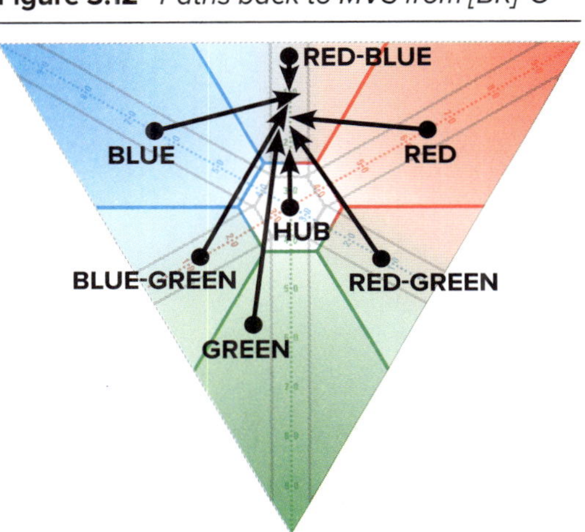

Table 3.12 *Illustrations of the path back to MVS from Stage 1 [BR]*

Blue MVS	Assertively restoring the peace and emphasizing the value of the relationship
Red MVS	Maintaining harmony and encouraging people to get behind a goal
Green MVS	Bringing people together to clarify objectives or processes
Red-Blue MVS	Pressing for harmony and refocusing on the need to develop others
Red-Green MVS	Collecting support and aligning people on strategy or tactics
Blue-Green MVS	Insisting on self-sufficiency for self and others
Hub MVS	Arguing kindly and persuasively to build consensus

For more detailed information and ideas about resolving conflict with people who have this Conflict Sequence, also consult the "Productive Results of Conflict" sections in the chapters that describe the MVS of those people. No matter the MVS of people in the conflict, there are some things that can help them transition out of Stage 1 [BR].

LISTENING TO STAGE 1 [BR]

Working effectively with people in Stage 1 [BR] conflict means you will need to understand what they are saying. Listening well will ensure that they feel heard, and know that you understand the tension they feel between asserting themselves and accommodating others. When you are listening, and engaging in dialogue, keep these points in mind:

- Hear them as attempting to meet other's needs as quickly as possible.
- Don't mistake speed for lack of consideration.
- Be energetic and show compassion for others.
- Don't get stuck in excessive detail.
- Focus on actions that restore or preserve relationships.

HOW TO APPROACH PEOPLE WHILE THEY ARE IN STAGE 1 [BR] CONFLICT

- Acknowledge the need for action that maintains the relationship.
- Show willingness to consider or work with possible solutions.
- Be energetic and genuinely concerned.
- Focus conversation on the big picture and move forward for quick resolution.
- Respect or mirror the behavior you are witnessing. For example, if the person is dealing with the conflict situation in a Blue way, use the recommendations for Blue.

THINGS TO AVOID WHEN APPROACHING PEOPLE WHILE THEY ARE IN STAGE 1 [BR] CONFLICT

- Dismissing the issue as trivial or unimportant.
- Putting off resolving the conflict.
- Presenting a long, detailed analysis of the issue.

MANAGING CONFLICT IN STAGES 2 AND 3

Conflict resolution is most likely to be effective from Stage 1, where self, problem, and others are in focus. If you are working with someone who has moved to Stage 2 or 3, you may need to de-escalate the conflict back to Stage 1 before you can reconcile your differences.

If the person is in Stage 2 [BR]:

- Acknowledge the tension between their desires to accommodate others and assert themselves.
- Focus on restoring a productive and harmonious relationship.

If the person is in Stage 3 Green:

- Make sure they know you are available and willing to participate, but do not try to force an immediate conversation.
- Emphasize your desire to get along well with them. Ask what additional information, or how much time they need.

[RG]-B
CONFLICT SEQUENCE

This Conflict Sequence describes people who want to engage conflict quickly but indirectly, with thoughtful strategies. If that does not work and others have more power in the situation, they may surrender.

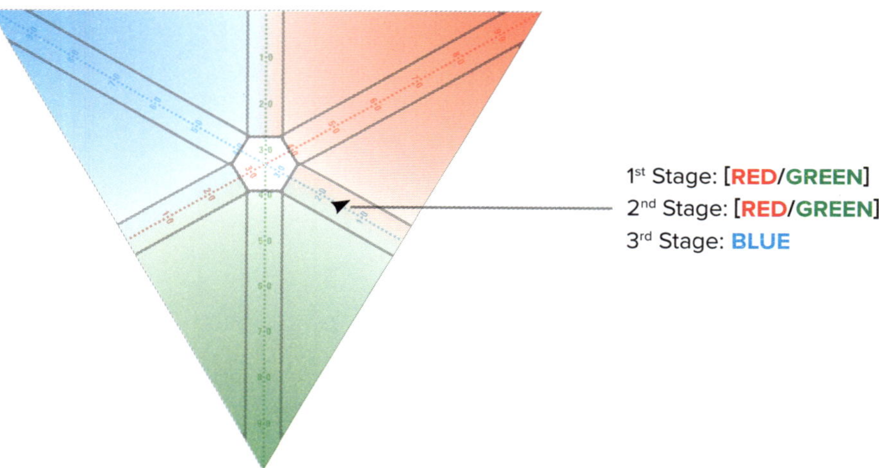

This descriptive text is written with a Conflict Sequence arrowhead located centrally in the Conflict Sequence region in mind. People whose arrowheads are close to the borders (within six points) of other Conflict Sequence regions may find that some text from the neighboring regions' descriptions is more accurate or useful.

While the following text describes the [RG]-B Conflict Sequence, it should also be considered in light of the MVS of the person who has this Conflict Sequence. Since there are seven Motivational Value Systems, there are at least seven different ways to enter conflict, and many different issues that can trigger conflict. These differences will affect the way people experience conflict and how they will resolve conflict. The first stage of this Conflict Sequence is a blend of

Red and Green. People with a short arrow whose MVS is also Red-Green may experience a less noticeable transition from their MVS to the first stage of conflict than people whose MVS is a different color will.

STAGE 1 [RG] CONFLICT

People in this blended first and second stage may take different approaches based on their perception of the situation. They may go to Red followed by Green if the results are at least temporarily more important than the principles involved, or to Green followed by Red if the principles are more important than the results. In these cases, conflict can be understood more fully by referring to the R-G-B and G-R-B pages. It is also possible that the Red and Green conflict stages will be combined for a blended conflict experience.

When Red and Green are blended in the first stage of conflict, people are motivated to quickly or fairly find a winning solution. They want to use their heads to win. They want to find a fair and rational solution to the problem, but they do not want rules enforced in ways that obstruct justifiable actions or results.

They tend to feel indignant when they are in conflict. To them, the facts of the matter are obvious and the right course of action is clear and urgent; they are frustrated when other people don't "get it." In addition to the conflict about the issue, people in the [RG] blend experience an internal tension between the two motives of asserting and analyzing. The internal dilemma is about how to integrate competing priorities in the conflict: performance versus principles, results versus rationality.

They prefer to take adequate time to think about the situation but also to act as quickly as reasonably possible. They engage others with well-crafted arguments that are intended to solidify their position and poke holes in the underlying assumptions of others' positions. They can be direct, believing that once the game is defined and the rules are clear, everyone can make their own decisions about how to compete.

When unproductive, they may engage in self-serving interpretations of rules or policy. This may cause them to appear manipulative or callous. They may become indignant or self-righteous and appear unconcerned about their effect on others.

How People in Stage 1 [RG] Can Improve Interactions

People who are experiencing the first stage of conflict may act as described previously. However, people may also adjust behavior or examine their perceptions during conflict in an effort to be more effective.

In Stage 1 [RG], people may be more effective if they:

- Take time to consider the emotional impact their desired actions could have on other people.
- Inquire about the personal priorities and boundaries of others.
- Calculate the personal cost of a firm and unyielding stance toward others.
- Consider a Green response when they feel Red, and a Red response when they feel Green.

STAGE 2 [RG] CONFLICT

While Red and Green are blended in Stages 1 and 2, people still experience a difference between Stage 1 and Stage 2. At first, they concentrate on themselves, the problem, and the other person. As the issue progresses to the second stage, they may drop the other person from focus, minimizing the importance of the other person's concerns and concentrating their energy on the problem and how it affects them. The second stage of conflict may appear similar to the first, but it is a more intensely experienced and self-focused version of problem-solving than the first stage.

People with a [RG]-B Conflict Sequence generally work very hard to prevent going to Stage 3 Blue. They may continue to argue and investigate the situation to find information to support or challenge positions held by themselves and others. They may become rigid and antagonistic, believing that they are defending a case that, if lost, cannot be salvaged if they are forced to surrender in Stage 3 Blue.

STAGE 3 BLUE CONFLICT

In the third stage of Blue (following a blend of Red and Green), people tend to feel completely defeated, not necessarily by others, but by the inability to find and implement a solution. They tend to feel that all of their efforts to resolve the issue logically and forcefully have failed, and all that remains is give up on the issue and figure out how to live with the pain of defeat.

In third stage Blue (following a blend of Red and Green), people will typically end association with the issue and others. They may say they no longer care about the conflict or the impact on the people involved. If the conflict is severe, the relationship may be irreparably damaged by the inability to *ever* become emotionally committed again.

The Blue Stage 3 Filter

Blue is the third stage of conflict in the [RG]-B sequence. When in first stage [RG] and observing Blue behavior in another person, some projection of the third stage experience onto the other is possible. Accommodating behavior of others may be perceived as spineless or lacking commitment or intelligence, without any attempt to defend or assert their rights.

Working with [RG]-B

CONFLICT RESOLUTION

Conflict is resolved when the elements of opposition are addressed and the people involved are able to return to feeling good about themselves again.

The Path Back to the MVS from Stage 1 [RG]

Each person has a path back from conflict to their MVS and feelings of self-worth. Even though many people may feel and act similarly in the first stage of conflict, there may be differences that are related to the MVS they are trying to return to. Conflict management efforts can be improved by keeping these differences in mind.

The path back to the MVS will be different for every person. Table 3.13 features some general illustrations of the path from Stage 1 [RG] back to MVS.

Figure 3.13 *Paths back to MVS from [RG]-B*

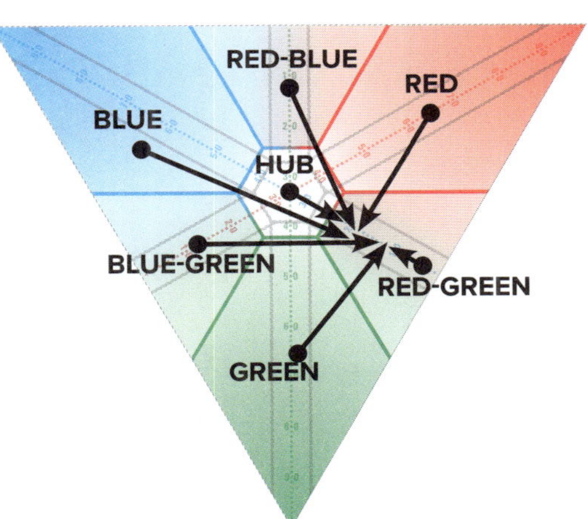

Table 3.13 *Illustrations of the path back to MVS from Stage 1 [RG]*

Blue MVS	Taking quick, logical action that brings help to others
Red MVS	Using the rules judiciously to produce results
Green MVS	Finding a flaw in a system and acting to improve that system
Red-Blue MVS	Clearly defining and dismantling the barriers to the growth of others
Red-Green MVS	Solidifying a position with additional evidence and action
Blue-Green MVS	Taking a strong and logical stand that enhances justice and equality
Hub MVS	Appropriately bending the rules to fit the situation

For more detailed information and ideas about resolving conflict with people who have this Conflict Sequence, also consult the "Productive Results of Conflict" sections in the chapters that describe the MVS of those people. No matter the MVS of people in the conflict, there are some things that can help them transition out of Stage 1 [RG].

LISTENING TO STAGE 1 [RG]

Working effectively with people in Stage 1 [RG] conflict means you will need to understand what they are saying. Listening well will ensure that they feel heard, and know that you understand the tension they feel between asserting themselves and analyzing the situation. When you are listening, and engaging in dialogue, keep these points in mind:

- Hear them as attempting to resolve issues as efficiently as possible.
- Don't mistake suggestions for orders.
- Make the best decision with available information.
- Don't be wishful or suggest improbable solutions.
- Maintain a balance between reflection and action.

HOW TO APPROACH PEOPLE WHILE THEY ARE IN STAGE 1 [RG] CONFLICT

- Listen and restate to prove your understanding.
- Acknowledge the need for a quick and logical response.
- Allow time for reflection, but maintain focus on resolution.
- Keep conversation rational and unemotional.
- Respect or mirror the behavior you are witnessing. For example, if the person is dealing with the conflict situation in a Red way, use the recommendations for Red.

THINGS TO AVOID WHEN APPROACHING PEOPLE WHILE THEY ARE IN STAGE 1 [RG] CONFLICT

- Minimizing the issue or dismissing it as trivial or unimportant.
- Responding without confidence or in an overly emotional manner.
- Avoiding the issue or thinking that the problem will go away on its own.

MANAGING CONFLICT IN STAGES 2 AND 3

Conflict resolution is most likely to be effective from Stage 1, where self, problem, and others are in focus. If you are working with someone who has moved to Stage 2 or 3, you may need to de-escalate the conflict back to Stage 1 before you can reconcile your differences.

If the person is in Stage 2 [RG]:

- Acknowledge the tension between their desires to assert themselves and analyze the situation.
- Focus on what is most efficient and logical.

If the person is in Stage 3 Blue:

- Apologize, if appropriate, and express your willingness to try again.
- Emphasize your objective understanding of the situation. Ask what you can do to set things right.

[BG]-R

CONFLICT SEQUENCE

This Conflict Sequence describes people who want to maintain peace and harmony but with caution regarding the personal costs of doing so. If that does not work, they may feel compelled to fight, possibly in an explosive manner.

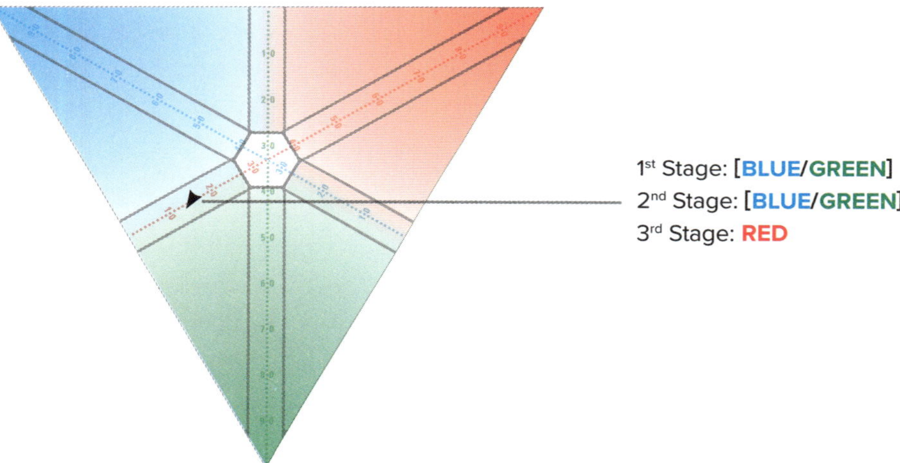

This descriptive text is written with a Conflict Sequence arrowhead located centrally in the Conflict Sequence region in mind. People whose arrowheads are close to the borders (within six points) of other Conflict Sequence regions may find that some text from the neighboring regions' descriptions is more accurate or useful.

While the following text describes the [BG]-R Conflict Sequence, it should also be considered in light of the MVS of the person who has this Conflict Sequence. Since there are seven Motivational Value Systems, there are at least seven different ways to enter conflict and many different issues that can trigger conflict. These differences will affect the way people experience conflict and how they will resolve conflict. The first stage of this Conflict Sequence is a blend of Blue and Green. People with a short arrow whose MVS is also Blue-Green may experience a less noticeable transition from their MVS to the first stage of conflict than people whose MVS is a different color will.

STAGE 1 [BG] CONFLICT

People in this blended first and second stage may take different approaches based on their perception of the situation. They may go to Blue followed by Green if the relationships are more important than the principles involved or to Green followed by Blue if the principles are more important than the relationships. In these cases, conflict can be understood more fully by referring to the B-G-R and G-B-R pages. It is also possible that the Blue and Green conflict stages will be combined for a blended conflict experience.

When Blue and Green are blended in the first stage of conflict, people are motivated to maintain peace and harmony and to minimize the personal cost of doing so. They want to find a fair and rational solution to the problem, but they do not want rules enforced in ways that would be harmful or unjust to anyone involved in the conflict.

They tend to feel surprised that they are in conflict. The moment they realize it may sometimes be described as a "deer in the headlights" experience, accompanied by similar body language. In addition to the conflict about the issue, people in the [BG] blend experience an internal tension between the two motives of accommodating and analyzing. The internal dilemma is about how to integrate their competing priorities in the conflict: people versus principles, reason versus relationships.

They prefer to take time to think about the situation, and their thoughts include the feelings and concerns of others. They ask questions about how the conflict started, whether it was warranted, what other people truly want, and what can be learned from the situation. They attempt to uncover the source of the misunderstanding, believing that if assumptions or intentions are clarified, understanding will result, and harmony will be restored.

When unproductive, they may become overly passive. This may cause them to appear unconcerned or incapable of addressing the problem. They may apologize excessively or isolate themselves from the problem, so they can wait it out.

How People in Stage 1 [BG] Can Improve Interactions

People who are experiencing the first stage of conflict may act as described previously. However, people may also adjust behavior or examine their perceptions during conflict in an effort to be more effective.

In Stage 1 [BG], people may be more effective if they:

- Focus on what to do next, instead of analyzing the sequence of events that led to the conflict.
- Clearly state their personal priorities, boundaries, and limits.
- Ask other people to suggest a potential solution as a starting point.
- Consider a Green response when they feel Blue, and a Blue response when they feel Green.

STAGE 2 [BG] CONFLICT

While Blue and Green are blended in Stages 1 and 2, people still experience a difference between Stage 1 and Stage 2. At first, they concentrate on themselves, the problem, and the other person. As the issue progresses to the second stage, they may drop the other person from focus, minimizing the importance of the other person's concerns and concentrating their energy on the problem and how it affects them. The second stage of conflict may appear similar to the first, but it is a more intensely experienced and self-focused version of problem-solving than the first stage.

People with a [BG]-R Conflict Sequence generally work very hard to prevent going to Stage 3 Red. They may make larger and larger concessions or engage in complex rationalizations in an effort to make the conflict go away, believing that no situation or person should be capable of provoking them to respond in the explosive and potentially hurtful manner of their third stage Red.

STAGE 3 RED CONFLICT

In third stage Red (following a blend of Blue and Green), people tend to feel intensely angry, energized, and potentially out of control, demanding an "all or nothing" solution. They tend to feel that all of their efforts to resolve the issue logically and without confrontation have failed. They feel that the desired outcome must be forcibly taken from or forcibly denied to the other person, regardless of cost.

In third stage Red (following a blend of Blue and Green), people will typically challenge others or fight, potentially in an explosive manner. They may say they no longer care what other people think or want, forcibly implementing whatever they originally thought was the best solution. If the conflict is severe, the relationship may be irreparably damaged by the harshness of personal attacks or by the negative reactions of people who view this third stage Red behavior as overblown and uncalled for.

The Red Stage 3 Filter

Red is the third stage of conflict in the [BG]-R sequence. When in first stage [BG] and observing Red behavior in another person, some projection of the third stage experience on the other is possible. Assertive behavior in others may be perceived as angry over-reaction without first taking the time to consider the facts of the situation or the needs of others.

Working with [BG]-R

CONFLICT RESOLUTION

Conflict is resolved when the elements of opposition are addressed and the people involved are able to return to feeling good about themselves again.

The Path Back to the MVS from Stage 1 [BG]

Each person has a path back from conflict to their MVS and feelings of self-worth. Even though many people may feel and act similarly in the first stage of conflict, there may be differences that are related to the MVS they are trying to return to. Conflict management efforts can be improved by keeping these differences in mind.

The path back to the MVS will be different for every person. Table 3.14 features some general illustrations of the path from Stage 1 [BG] back to MVS.

Figure 3.14 *Paths back to MVS from [BG]-R*

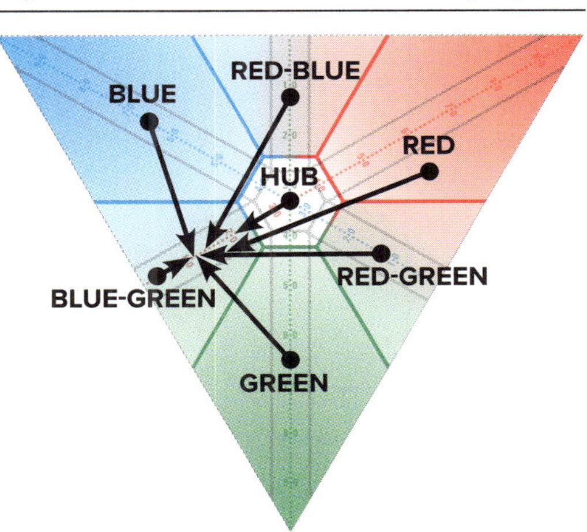

Table 3.14 *Illustrations of the path back to MVS from Stage 1 [BG]*

Blue MVS	Identifying the rights of others and seeing that they are supported
Red MVS	Clarifying issues and values and refocusing on action
Green MVS	Considering the logic of others and clarifying the process
Red-Blue MVS	Carefully considering the capabilities and potential of others
Red-Green MVS	Revising the strategy and improving the odds of its success
Blue-Green MVS	Reaffirming the value of people and principles
Hub MVS	Clarifying the rules of interaction and building consensus

For more detailed information and ideas about resolving conflict with people who have this Conflict Sequence, also consult the "Productive Results of Conflict"sections in the chapters that describe the MVS of those people. No matter the MVS of people in the conflict, there are some things that can help them transition out of Stage 1 [BG].

LISTENING TO STAGE 1 [BG]

Working effectively with people in Stage 1 [BG] conflict means you will need to understand what they are saying. Listening well will ensure that they feel heard, and that you understand the tension they feel between accommodating others and analyzing the situation. When you are listening, and engaging in dialogue, keep these points in mind:

- Hear them as attempting to calm the situation and avoid making things worse.
- Don't mistake silence for agreement.
- Be calm and show compassion for others.
- Don't be aggressive or confrontational.
- Maintain a balance between facts and feelings.

HOW TO APPROACH PEOPLE WHILE THEY ARE IN STAGE 1 [BG] CONFLICT

- Look for a reasonable solution that also maintains harmony.
- Make genuine inquiry about their welfare and how the conflict is affecting them.
- De-personalize the problem, reassuring them that the relationship is intact.
- Allow time for consideration, reframing mistakes or problems as learning opportunities.
- Respect or mirror the behavior you are witnessing. For example, if the person is dealing with the conflict situation in a Green way, use the recommendations for Green.

THINGS TO AVOID WHEN APPROACHING PEOPLE WHILE THEY ARE IN STAGE 1 [BG] CONFLICT

- Pushing for an answer without allowing time to think.
- Dictating solutions to conflict and using power to control the outcome.
- Raising your voice and appearing aggressive or overly competitive.

MANAGING CONFLICT IN STAGES 2 AND 3

Conflict resolution is most likely to be effective from Stage 1, where self, problem, and others are in focus. If you are working with someone who has moved to Stage 2 or 3, you may need to de-escalate the conflict back to Stage 1 before you can reconcile your differences.

If the person is in Stage 2 [BG]:

- Acknowledge the tension between their desires to accommodate others and analyze the situation.
- Focus on what is fair and does not require excessive sacrifice.

If the person is in Stage 3 Red:

- Create a safe space for them to say everything that's on their mind. They have probably been trying not to say these things.
- Emphasize your desire for a fair and harmonious relationship. Ask what is most important to them at this moment.

[BRG]

CONFLICT SEQUENCE

This Conflict Sequence describes people who want to determine the most appropriate response to each situation and to experiment with accommodating, assertive, and analytical approaches. If that does not work, they may feel compelled to use a non-preferred approach.

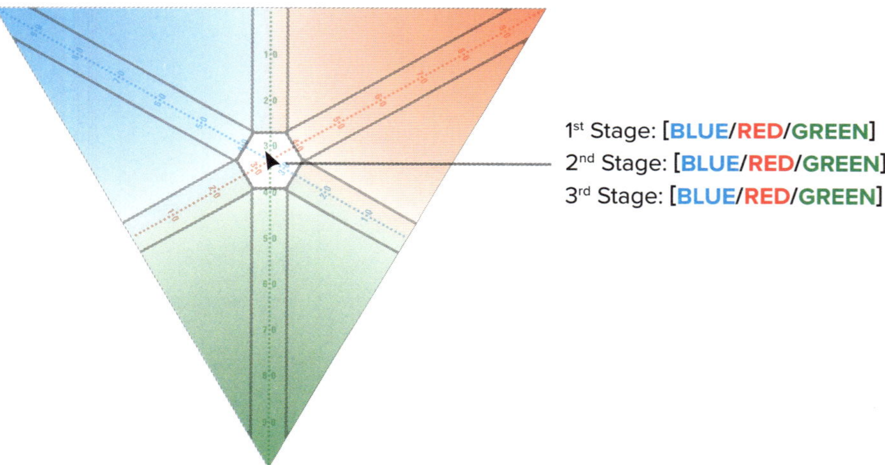

This descriptive text is written with a Conflict Sequence arrowhead located centrally in the Conflict Sequence region in mind. People whose arrowheads are close to the borders (within six points) of other Conflict Sequence regions may find that some text from the neighboring regions' descriptions is more accurate or useful.

While the following text describes the [BRG] Conflict Sequence, it should also be considered in light of the MVS of the person who has this Conflict Sequence. Since there are seven Motivational Value Systems, there are at least seven different ways to enter conflict and many different issues that can trigger conflict. These differences will affect the way people experience conflict and how they will resolve conflict. The first stage of this Conflict Sequence is a blend of Blue, Red, and Green. People with a short arrow whose MVS is Hub may experience a less noticeable transition from their MVS to the first stage of conflict than people whose MVS is a different color will.

STAGE 1 [BRG] CONFLICT

When all three stages and motives are blended in a [BRG] Conflict Sequence, people prefer to remain flexible in the way they approach each conflict situation. They want to come up with tailored solutions for those involved. They address each conflict differently, depending on the situation and circumstances.

In conflict, they may experience a range of emotions about conflict, depending on where it occurs and with whom it happens. Unlike others, whose motives are experienced in a predictable sequence during conflict, their motives in conflict all feel about equal. Instead of a predictable response, their behavior may reflect the way that others approach them. In each situation, they decide how to respond depending on the circumstances. They are natural problem solvers and tend to believe there isn't any challenge that doesn't have a solution. They are willing to keep trying different solutions until one works.

In conflict, they define the context in which to consider any problem. The context may include a combination of variables, such as the value of the relationship, the importance of the issue, or the environment in which the conflict occurs. Once the context is defined, the appropriate response can be selected.

When unproductive, they may show the sacrifice of Blue, the argumentativeness of Red, or the detachment of Green. They may also alternate between approaches and appear non-committal. This behavior may prove confusing to others and lead to the belief that the only thing truly predictable about them in conflict is that they are ***not*** predictable.

How People in Stage 1 [BRG] Can Improve Interactions

People who are experiencing the first stage of conflict may act as described previously. However, people may also adjust behavior or examine their perceptions during conflict in an effort to be more effective.

When all three colors blend in Stage 1, people may be more effective if they:

- Challenge their assumptions about why they are responding to conflict in a particular way.
- Clearly state their point of view as it relates to each specific situation.

- Let other people know where they are coming from with regards to each situation.

STAGE 2 [BRG] CONFLICT

When all three colors are blended, people will generally address conflict in flexible, situationally dependent ways throughout all three stages. However, there is a difference between this approach in Stage 2 because it is characterized by a focus on the problem and the self and less emphasis is given to the needs of others. Stage 2 may take the form of conditional accommodation, fighting, or arguing against others, or it might be independent analysis of the situation.

STAGE 3 [BRG] CONFLICT

While the situationally dependent response to conflict continues into Stage 3, there is a difference between this approach and Stage 2 because Stage 3 is characterized by a focus on the self and less emphasis is given to the needs of others and the problem at hand. Stage 3 may take the form of the least desired approach to the specific situation. It may look and feel like the unconditional surrender of Stage 3 Blue, the fighting for survival of Stage 3 Red, or the total withdrawal of Stage 3 Green.

[BRG] Stage 3 Filter

People with a [BRG] Conflict Sequence can experience any color as their third stage of conflict. While they are in conflict, they may perceive that other people with a clear first stage are inflexible and not able to adapt to the situation. They may think that people in Stage 1 Blue are blinded by emotion, believe that others in Stage 1 Red are impulsive, and think that others in Stage 1 Green are uncommunicative.

Working with [BRG]

CONFLICT RESOLUTION

Conflict is resolved when the elements of opposition are addressed and the people involved are able to return to feeling good about themselves again.

The Path Back to the MVS from Stage 1 [BRG]

Each person has a path back from conflict to their MVS and feelings of self-worth. Even though many people may feel and act similarly in the first stage of conflict, there may be differences that are related to the MVS they are trying to return to. Conflict management efforts can be improved by keeping these differences in mind.

The path back to the MVS will be different for every person. Table 3.15 features some general illustrations of the path from Stage 1 [BRG] back to MVS.

Figure 3.15 *Paths back to MVS from [BRG]*

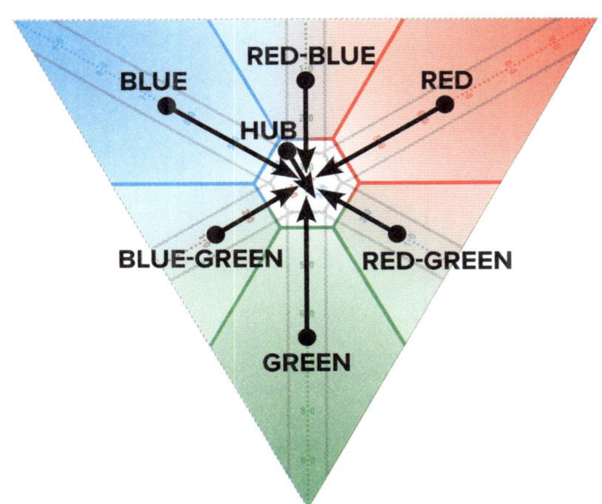

Table 3.15 *Illustrations of the path back to MVS from Stage 1 [BRG]*

Blue MVS	Going along with the option that is the least burdensome to others
Red MVS	Acting on the option most likely to succeed
Green MVS	Considering all the alternatives and selecting the most logical approach
Red-Blue MVS	Determining the best way forward for both parties
Red-Green MVS	Advancing the strategy in the best way possible for the situation
Blue-Green MVS	Searching for the best way to maintain self-sufficiency
Hub MVS	Experimenting with different approaches that do not restrict future options

For more detailed information and ideas about resolving conflict with people who have this Conflict Sequence, also consult the "Productive Results of Conflict" sections in the chapters that describe the MVS of those people. No matter the MVS of people in the conflict, there are some things that can help them transition out of Stage 1 [BRG].

LISTENING TO STAGE 1 [BRG]

Working effectively with people in Stage 1 [BRG] conflict means you will need to understand what they are saying. Listening well will ensure that they feel heard, and that you understand the tension they feel about choosing the best approach to the situation. When you are listening, and engaging in dialogue, keep these points in mind:

- Hear them as attempting to see all sides of an issue and adapt accordingly.
- Don't mistake changes in direction for lack of focus.
- Be receptive to options and different points of view.
- Don't be rigid or limit options or input.
- Explore the specific context before deciding on an approach.

HOW TO APPROACH PEOPLE WHILE THEY ARE IN STAGE 1 [BRG] CONFLICT

- Ask them to clarify the process and where they are "coming from" on the issue.
- Be open to their point of view and their potential solutions.
- Be willing to explore the situation as a unique situation.
- Respect or mirror the behavior you are witnessing. For example, if the person is dealing with the conflict situation in a Blue way, use the recommendations for Blue.
- Ask open-ended questions that will encourage them to clarify how they see this issue at this time.

THINGS TO AVOID WHEN APPROACHING PEOPLE WHILE THEY ARE IN STAGE 1 [BRG] CONFLICT

- Limiting ideas and showing lack of concern for the issue.
- Being rigid and dogmatic or not mirroring their approach.
- Expecting consistency in responses across multiple situations.

MANAGING CONFLICT IN STAGES 2 AND 3

Conflict resolution is most likely to be effective from Stage 1, where self, problem, and others are in focus. If you are working with someone who has moved to Stage 2 or 3, you may need to de-escalate the conflict back to Stage 1 before you can reconcile your differences.

If the person is in Stage 2 [BRG]:

- Acknowledge their efforts to clarify the context and address the situation appropriately.
- Focus on their perspective and how they are interpreting things.

If the person is in Stage 3 [BRG]:

- Acknowledge the frustration they feel; which may be due to perceived inflexibility in others.
- Emphasize your willingness to keep trying. Ask what matters most to them.

"In the art of living, we are both the artist and the object of our art; we are the sculptor and the marble; the physician and the patient."

— Erich Fromm

4 STRENGTH DEPLOYMENT

The SDI 2.0 provides two views of the way people deploy their strengths at work: the productive Strengths Portrait and the unproductive Overdone Strengths Portrait. Both of these views reflect the way people express their personality through behavior in the context of their work. The SDI 2.0 helps to explore questions such as "How do you find personal meaning and satisfaction in your work?" and "How can managers get people to want to do what they need to do in order to be effective in a given role or working environment?" This part of the book is about the intentional deployment of strengths (and perceptions of strengths) in working relationships.

Every person has some frequently used strengths, but strengths do not define people or their personalities. People also have free will, the ability to choose to bring any strength to a situation or relationship. Strengths that are intentionally connected to core motives, by way of authentic reasons, tend to be most effective and sustainable in working relationships. Becoming more effective implies that people need not be limited by their top strengths, but instead choose strengths that are most likely to produce the results they desire in their working relationships.

It is possible to become over-reliant on a particular strength, to the point that it can become limiting or even damaging. A good intention along with an expectation of effectiveness can cause a person to try harder with the same strength to the point that it becomes counterproductive. For example, a persuasive person with a lot of self-confidence can become arrogant and argumentative, which can cause problems in working relationships. But overdone strengths can be managed and returned to their productive form.

Understanding Strengths

The word strengths is used in many different ways to describe people. Sometimes it is meant to describe a person's talents, such as attention to detail or strategic thinking. It may also be used to describe virtues, such as courage or integrity.[1]

The SDI 2.0 views strengths in an interpersonal context and within a framework of personality types. Put simply, strengths, as described in the SDI 2.0, are behaviors. And behaviors are subject to interpretation.

People generally judge their own strengths based on their intentions, while observers generally judge others' strengths based on their interpretation of observed behaviors.[2] These judgements are subjective; they are influenced by people's personalities and preferences. Comparing two people's Strengths Portraits offers insight into the way these judgements are made.

For example, a person with a Blue MVS and Sociable at the top of their Strengths Portrait is likely to judge their Sociable behavior positively because it is a good way for them to stay connected with people who may need their help. However, a person with a Red-Green MVS who has Sociable at the bottom of their Strengths Portrait may judge the same sociability as intrusive (it's overdone form). Clearly, these judgments are not objective matters of fact; they are reactions based on each person's perception and priorities.

The Strengths Portrait shows the way a set of 28 strengths are prioritized in the context of work. The top boxes in the diamond-shaped pattern show the strengths a person is most likely to use at work, and the bottom boxes show those that are least likely to be used.

Figure 4.1 *Strengths Portrait Format*

All 28 strengths are ranked highest (1) to lowest (28), although strengths on the same row may feel about equal. Strengths near the top are best understood based on two influences, the person and the environment.[3]

The purpose of the diamond-shaped portrait is to display all the strengths in a way that represents their current deployment at work, but also facilitates choice of strengths in various situations and relationships. Think of strengths like tools, and the Strengths Portrait like a well-organized toolbox.

Strengths, like tools, are chosen with a specific task or outcome in mind. People do not reach for a hammer, then ask what needs to be pounded. Instead, they consider what needs to be done, then select the right tool for the job. Sometimes a relationship calls for trust; at other times, it may call for caution. If a person has Trusting near the top and Cautious near the bottom, it will generally be both easier and more preferable for them to deploy Trusting than Cautious in any given situation. This implies that when caution is required, it will take more effort.

The strengths are presented in four categories, Blue, Red, Green, and Hub. The colors correlate with the three primary motives and the key-words: people, performance, and process. The Hub strengths are grouped under the key-word "perspective."[4]

Table 4.1 *Four Categories of Strengths*

People	Performance	Process	Perspective
Caring	Ambitious	Analytical	Adaptable
Devoted	Competitive	Cautious	Flexible
Helpful	Forceful	Fair	Inclusive
Loyal	Persuasive	Methodical	Open-to-Change
Modest	Quick-to-Act	Persevering	Option-Oriented
Supportive	Risk-Taking	Principled	Sociable
Trusting	Self-Confident	Reserved	Tolerant

The 28 strengths were selected and refined over time on the basis that they correlate with underlying personality types. Traits such as honesty, sense of humor, and curiosity can be found in all types of people and are not part of the SDI 2.0 assessment.[5] One person may exhibit honesty, for example, through a combination of strengths such as Helpful and Risk-Taking, while another person's honesty is guided by being Principled and Tolerant.

Some combinations of strengths may feel, at first glance, that they do not fit together. For example, a person may have both Cautious and Quick-to-Act at the top of their Strengths Portrait. There could be several possible explanations for this (or any other pair of strengths that a person sees as opposites). Possible explanations include:

- **Self vs Role:** One strength is more like a value for the person, while the other is strongly influenced by the person's role. Cautious could be a core value, while Quick-to-Act is rewarded at work. An investment manager could be cautious in all aspects of life, including with other people's money, yet still be Quick-to-Act at work in response to threats or market opportunities.
- **Complementary Strengths:** The strengths may make sense when considered in context. For example, a firefighter can be Cautious and Quick-to-Act at the same time, driving rapidly to the scene without creating additional risk on the way or rushing into a burning building with adequate protective equipment.
- **Situational:** The two apparently opposite strengths are deployed at different times or in different situations. The person may not feel a need to use both strengths at the same time, but they use them both frequently. A scientist could be Cautious while conducting an experiment, and Quick-to-Act when the findings are ready to be shared.

STRENGTHS AND REASONS

The Strengths and Reasons tables that follow present all 28 strengths from the Strengths Portrait, along with two example reasons for choosing to use each of them. These examples are not the only possible connections between strengths and reasons. They are meant to help interpret past actions or to help describe intentions that could link people's motives to current or future actions. These example reasons are intended to help explore questions such as: What is the person trying to do? What is their intent? What is driving them to act that way? Your reasons may vary.

The simple, and most common interpretation of these tables is that Blues use Blue strengths for Blue reasons, Hubs use Hub strengths for Hub reasons, etc. But people have access to all the strengths on their Strengths Portrait. People are most likely to deploy strengths, of any color, for the reasons listed in the columns that correspond to their MVS. However, people do sometimes deploy strengths for reasons that relate to their lower MVS scores.

For example, consider Robin, a person whose MVS scores are 60 Blue, 25 Red, and 15 Green (a Blue MVS). From these scores, a general prediction can be made: Robin is most likely to deploy Blue strengths, such as Supportive, for Blue reasons — to protect or nurture others, and to enhance their general well-being (as in Figure 4.2).

Human motives and behavior are more complex than this simple example. The SDI shows how each person's three primary motives blend to create a

Motivational Value System. This systems-view of personality suggests that the motives interact; they are integrated. The scores from the SDI predict the relative frequency with which a person is likely to be motivated by concerns typical of that scale. It is likely that Robin will, on occasion, be Supportive for reasons that sound Red or Green, although Blue reasons will be the most frequent.

Figure 4.2 *Same Color Example*

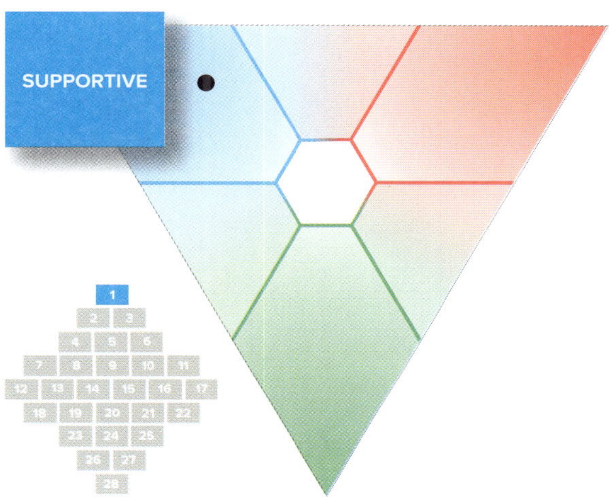

The color of the strength deployed does not always match the color of the reason for deploying it. Robin may prefer to use a Blue Strength, such as Supportive, in order to be helpful to someone. However, the best way to help may be to be Cautious (a Green strength) in order to help that person (a Blue reason) manage a risk in that person's situation (as in Figure 4.3). Robin may therefore feel very good about using the strength Cautious because there is a clear link to the Blue MVS and a way to fulfill the Blue motive. In this case, Robin chose to deploy a strength from the middle of the Strengths Portrait. This behavior was authentic because the strength was used with positive intent and driven by Robin's core motives. This behavior would not have been authentic if Robin felt forced to be Cautious in the situation due to someone else's expectations.

Figure 4.3 *Different Color Example*

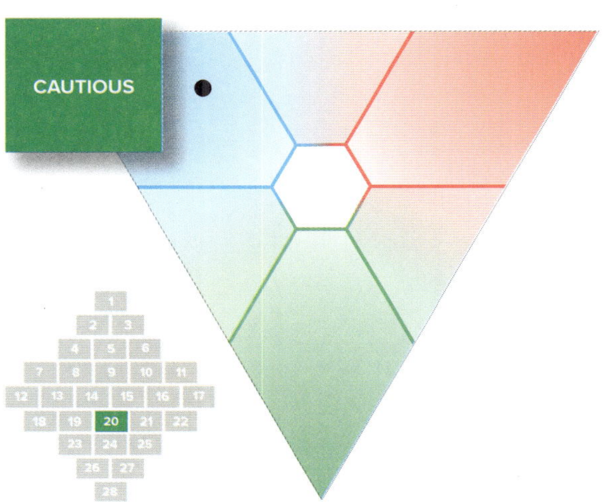

HOW TO USE THE STRENGTHS AND REASONS TABLES

These tables are example connections between strengths and underlying motives. You should consider the individuals you are working with, their specific needs, and the overall situation. Ideally, you will use these tables to get started, and you can find your own words to best describe the reasons for what you intend to do, what you have observed, or what you expect from others.

For Yourself

As you consider your choices of strengths for various situations, read the example reasons for deploying each of the strengths. Consider what motives are driving your choices. While it is most likely that the reasons in your MVS column drive many of your behavior choices, no one makes all their choices for only one type of reason. When you interact with others, remember that they cannot see your motives and reasons; they can only see your behavior. It is almost always helpful to communicate your motives, intentions, or purposes when you interact with others.

To Understand Others

If you've ever asked yourself, "Why are they doing that?" then these tables can help you ponder the possibilities. While the best possible source for the answers is dialogue with the people you're curious about, these tables can help you anticipate the types of answers you might get. If you are puzzled about a past interaction, these tables may offer insight to help you recast your view of the other person so that you more clearly perceive their intent.

To Coach Others

You may have a formal role, such as being a manager, that involves regular coaching. Or you may find yourself in conversations with peers where you provide informal coaching or mentoring. In either case, the Strengths and Reasons tables can help guide your conversations so that other people choose to deploy their strengths in the most authentic and effective way possible. When people make free choices, they also tend to be more accountable for the results of their actions.[6]

If you find yourself in a situation where different behavior from others is likely to be more effective, you need to help them see what's in it for them. First, ask them to identify the strengths they have been deploying, and to describe their underlying reasons for doing so. Then collaboratively identify the strength, or combination of strengths, that are most likely to produce the desired result. This is like choosing the right tool for the job. But choosing strengths that will work well with others requires more than an understanding of the task. You also need to consider other people's expectations and possible perceptions.

Once you have agreed on the strength(s) to deploy, talk about the reasons that can connect those strengths to that person's MVS. Coaching often involves behavior change, and intended changes are most sustainable when a person has a good reason to continue with the new behavior. Rather than pushing only on the metaphorical buoy of behavior, coaching for effective strength deployment involves helping them find a personally compelling reason to make the change.

Imagine a coaching conversation like helping a person move their behavioral buoy to a more effective location, as in figure 4.4. Say, for example, that you are coaching a person with a Green MVS who has been methodically executing a project plan. But this project is stagnating and could benefit from a shot of innovation. It's likely that your coachee would explain their methodical strength with Green reasons, such as giving the project plan and process enough time to work as intended.

Figure 4.4
Coaching for Strength Deployment

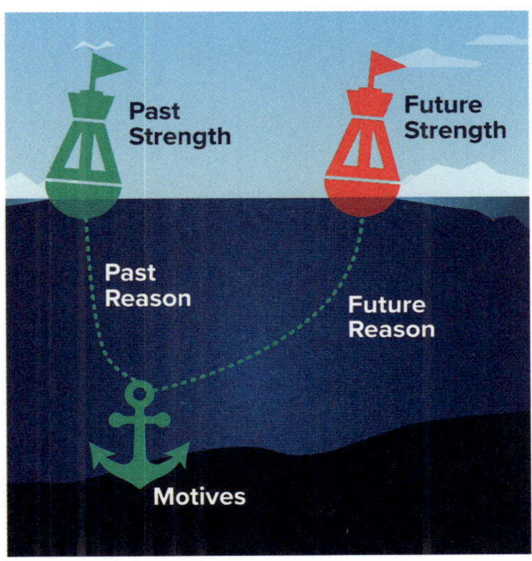

If you believe that some innovation would be beneficial, you don't have to change the person's underlying motives or personality; you don't need to move their anchor. Instead, you need to connect the new behavior to their existing motives with a compelling reason. Perhaps your coachee needs to take some more risk in the execution of the project, and perhaps they are generally not comfortable with risk. One of the Green reasons to deploy the risk-taking strength is "Because the risk-reward ratio justifies it." If your coachee does the mental calculus and agrees that the potential rewards outweigh the potential risks, then they will choose to use the Red Risk-Taking strength for a Green reason. This is how coaches use Relationship Intelligence to help coachees make sustainable behavior change, targeted at organizational results.

BLUE STRENGTHS AND EXAMPLE REASONS

BLUE STRENGTHS	BLUE REASONS	RED REASONS	GREEN REASONS
CARING I concern myself with the well-being of others.	So I will know what others need. So they will feel valued.	So others can perform at their best. To gain others' commitment to a task or purpose.	To be consistent with my principles. So I can accurately assess others' needs.
DEVOTED I am dedicated to some people, activities, or purposes.	To solidify my personal commitment to them. To further a cause that benefits people.	To create meaningful change. To show my commitment and passion.	To maintain focus on priorities. To keep striving for order and clarity.
HELPFUL I give assistance to others who are in need.	To show empathy for their situation. So they will feel better.	So others will help me when I need it. To help others overcome obstacles.	Because it is fair and reasonable. So others can carry their own weight.
LOYAL I remain faithful to the commitments I make to others.	So others know they can rely on me. To build trust in the relationship.	Because I expect loyalty in return. To deliver on my promises.	Because it is a matter of principle. To demonstrate that I am reliable.
MODEST I play down what I am capable of doing.	So others can get the credit they deserve. So others can show what they are capable of.	So others will rise to the challenge. So my results can speak for themselves.	To preserve my capacity in case it is needed later. So I don't promise something I can't do.
SUPPORTIVE I give encouragement and help to others.	To reassure people and help build their confidence. Because that will help them grow.	So others will help me achieve my goals. In order for others to achieve the best that they can.	So others will learn from information and experience. So others will be able to do things correctly.
TRUSTING I place my faith in others.	To show that I believe in others. To affirm our relationship.	So others will continue to perform. To give others the freedom to make decisions.	To honor my commitments. To show my support for others' plans.

RED-BLUE REASONS	RED-GREEN REASONS	BLUE-GREEN REASONS	HUB REASONS
To quickly identify how others can improve. So others will know they can rely on me when they need help.	So others see that they are important to success. To energize others and improve performance.	To help others be able to care for themselves. So I can understand others' needs and expectations.	So others will be able to participate. To keep lines of communication open.
To create enthusiasm for a cause. To lead people to what is best for them.	To concentrate on actions that produce results. To include people who have similar goals.	To maintain others' trust in me. To keep things fair and beneficial to everyone.	To keep outcomes in mind while testing options. To keep people united toward a common goal.
So others will be able to rise above a challenge. To know that I have given all I can.	So others' competence will increase. To speed up a process.	So others can focus on what is most important to them. So others' situation doesn't get worse.	To contribute whatever is needed in the moment. To join others in their struggle.
To develop a trusting connection. Because others will benefit when I fulfill my promise.	Because others are essential to my strategy. To affirm the understanding between us.	So others know that they can count on me. So I do not let others down.	To ensure that consensus is maintained. So I finish whatever I start.
To give other people a chance to do their best. So I can build up others' confidence.	Because I want to exceed expectations. So I do not over-commit myself.	To give me time before making a promise. To be considerate and not appear arrogant.	To get others' input and involvement. To make sure that everyone feels important and needed.
So others will feel good when they achieve their goals. So others will face and overcome obstacles.	To energize others to reach their potential. So others will understand their role in the strategy.	To show appreciation for others' efforts. To make sure that others have room to grow.	So others will do the same for me. So everyone will have access to the same opportunities.
To show my confidence in them. To inspire and encourage them.	So others will become stronger. To show how much I value others' abilities.	To affirm our mutual respect and understanding. So I do not need to worry about what they will do.	To bring people together. To create an open environment.

RED STRENGTHS AND EXAMPLE REASONS

RED STRENGTHS	BLUE REASONS	RED REASONS	GREEN REASONS
AMBITIOUS I am determined to succeed and to get ahead.	So I have the ability to help others. To show others that it can be done and to encourage them.	To drive others toward greater accomplishments. To be recognized for doing the best I can.	To be recognized for my expertise. To prove the validity of my plan.
COMPETITIVE I strive to win against others.	To support people or causes that I care about. To support my team against others.	To claim the rewards of victory. To improve on my own personal best.	To learn from it and improve myself. To show my expertise or knowledge.
FORCEFUL I act with conviction, power, and drive.	To nurture confidence in others. To protect someone's welfare.	To break through barriers. To minimize resistance and get people to follow.	To clarify a point when I know I'm right. To get the information I need.
PERSUASIVE I urge, influence, and convince others.	To defend others or to support a worthy cause. For their own benefit.	To direct action toward my goals. So others will move with me, not against me.	To have my ideas recognized. To set clear and reasonable expectations.
QUICK-TO-ACT I get things started without delay.	To show my commitment to others and focus my energy. To help others immediately.	To seize the opportunity before it is lost. So that I can finish the task as quickly as possible.	So there will be enough time to complete the process. To utilize available knowledge and resources.
RISK-TAKING I take chances on losses in pursuit of high gains.	To help someone who is in real trouble. To decrease the risk for someone else.	So I don't miss an opportunity. To test my limits and get stronger.	Because the risk-reward ratio justifies it. To improve overall efficiency.
SELF-CONFIDENT I believe in my own powers and strengths.	To encourage others and give them more confidence. To have the ability to help as much as needed.	To bolster my energy and focus. To be certain of my goals and abilities.	To identify the correct course of action. To get things done the right way.

RED-BLUE REASONS	RED-GREEN REASONS	BLUE-GREEN REASONS	HUB REASONS
To help my friends and colleagues benefit. To show others what it best for them.	To exceed performance standards and win. To prove the feasibility of my strategy.	To help others learn to succeed. To protect my independence.	So others will see me as a valuable contributor. So my ideas will be accepted as the best.
So I can share my success with others. To clear the way for others who also want to compete.	To test and refine my own skills. To get the optimal results from an opportunity.	To support someone else in their struggle. To re-establish or reinforce fair principles.	To have fun playing the game. So others will accept me as part of a team.
To challenge people to become their best. To get others what they need.	To compellingly communicate my strategy. To relentlessly pursue a goal.	To defend the rights of others. To protect boundaries or people.	To get cooperation. To adjust quickly to a changing situation.
To get people to do what they need to do to succeed. So they will let me help them.	To get buy-in and avoid using power over others. So others will accept my logic.	To get people to respect others. To stop people from making a mistake.	To get people to understand one another. To emphasize the importance of working together.
To match the urgency of the situation. So people don't have to wait for me.	To avoid last-minute mistakes. So there is time later to revise the plan, if needed.	To be responsive and considerate of others' time. So I do not hold up someone else's efforts.	So others will know what is important to me. To show my acceptance of others' ideas.
To show that I am fully invested in the situation. To address an urgent need.	To drive innovative and creative thinking. To remove the biggest obstacles first.	To protect important principles that are involved. To secure future independence.	To represent the interests of the group. To get unanimous support for an idea.
To set a good example that others can follow. To know what is best for others.	To drive action from analysis. To begin a difficult endeavor and expect to win.	To take credit for my own actions and achievements. To find a sustainable solution.	To remain flexible without losing focus. To build the confidence of the team.

GREEN STRENGTHS AND EXAMPLE REASONS

GREEN STRENGTHS	BLUE REASONS	RED REASONS	GREEN REASONS
ANALYTICAL I dissect and digest whatever is going on.	To learn how others are really feeling. To find the best way to be helpful.	To identify risks and opportunities. So I have the facts to support my direction.	To have a complete and accurate understanding. To identify and eliminate inefficiencies.
CAUTIOUS I am careful to make sure of what is going on.	To know what others really need. So I can manage any risk to relationships.	To make my next move at the right time. To make sure goals are realistic.	So there are no surprises. To make sure that nothing is missed or overlooked.
FAIR I act justly, equitably, and impartially.	So people get what they really need. So those most in need get the relevant support.	So there are no hidden agendas. To achieve a legitimate win.	To maintain my objectivity. So conclusions are supportable and defensible.
METHODICAL I am orderly in action, thought, and expression.	To make sure another person understands me. To create a structure that will benefit others.	To increase the chance of success. To make sure that I communicate clearly and effectively.	To ensure predictability or repeatability. To give the process a chance to work as intended.
PERSEVERING I maintain the same course of action in spite of obstacles.	To uphold a personal commitment. So obstacles do not prevent getting benefits to others.	To overcome the obstacles. To ensure that I keep the goal in sight.	To validate my method. To allow enough time for my actions to have an effect.
PRINCIPLED I follow certain rules of right conduct.	So people will not be harmed. So others will feel secure.	So competition will be fair. To correctly direct resources toward a desirable result.	To uphold the underlying logic of the rules. To ensure consistency and fairness.
RESERVED I practice self-restraint in expressing thoughts and feelings.	To encourage others to speak their minds. So I don't upset people if I disagree with them.	So I don't hurt people's feelings. To avoid getting distracted by insignificant differences.	To give me time to be sure I'm right. To defer a decision until the facts are available.

RED-BLUE REASONS	RED-GREEN REASONS	BLUE-GREEN REASONS	HUB REASONS
So I am clear about the task ahead. To help someone else make an important decision.	To solve a complex problem. To be correct the first time and prevent rework.	To find ways to build up others' capabilities. To identify and avoid potential risks.	To understand the social and political dynamics. To integrate others' views and facilitate agreement.
To give the best possible advice. So I don't lead others into danger.	To save time or effort in the long run. To make sure there is a viable way forward.	To prevent making mistakes. To get a good read on people and situations before acting.	So no viable option is overlooked. So I am not too easily swayed by opinions.
To give an advantage to a disadvantaged person. So others can make their own decisions.	To achieve justice in process and outcomes. To establish a level playing field.	So helping one person does not hurt another. To prevent any possible bias from affecting me.	To evaluate each option by its merits. To ensure that consensus is reached respectfully.
To make sure my decisions are valid. To help other people make effective choices.	To clarify my position regarding an issue. To lead people toward a logical course of action.	To prioritize what people need. So I don't need to worry about what is not done.	To consider all perspectives. To ensure that no person or issue is forgotten.
To convince someone of what is best for them. To encourage others to keep trying.	To achieve a predetermined outcome. To change the situation to better suit my objectives.	To guide people through complicated situations. So deviations do not cause problems.	To help the group get through a tough situation. To fully test a plan before changing it.
To correctly guide others' development. So people are protected from wrongdoing.	To make sure that my actions are guided by reason. To prevent compromises that weaken the strategy.	So that processes will be fair to people. To prevent errors or unintended consequences.	To adapt to the rules of a new situation. So that I can treat everyone equally.
So I don't say anything that might offend someone. To give others a chance to contribute.	To take enough time to clarify my own ideas. To avoid committing to something I might regret.	To learn others' thoughts and feelings. To give people a chance to succeed on their own.	To give everyone else a chance to have input. To respect others' thoughts and feelings.

HUB STRENGTHS AND EXAMPLE REASONS

HUB STRENGTHS	BLUE REASONS	RED REASONS	GREEN REASONS
ADAPTABLE I adjust readily to new or modified conditions.	To support and be responsive to someone. To make things easier on others.	To be agile and opportunistic. To recognize the urgent need for change.	To recognize the importance of new information. To remain open-minded.
FLEXIBLE I act in whatever manner is appropriate at the moment.	To help someone through a situation. To support others in their efforts.	To quickly achieve my goals. To take advantage of an opportunity.	To maintain fairness and boundaries. To recognize the facts as currently known.
INCLUSIVE I bring people together in order to reach consensus.	So each person feels valued. So that no one is left out of the process.	So everyone will be committed to the task. To ensure that we are all pulling in the same direction.	To make sure no vital information is overlooked. To establish clarity and shared meaning.
OPEN-TO-CHANGE I consider different perspectives, ideas, and opinions.	So people are being listened to. To be receptive to others' ideas.	To determine the best course of action. So significant differences can be addressed immediately.	To test options against my current belief. To be sure I am fully informed.
OPTION-ORIENTED I look for and suggest different ways of doing things.	To find a new way to help. To show alternatives when there is disagreement.	To keep trying until something works. To show that I care more about results than methods.	To challenge the underlying assumptions. To find the most efficient method.
SOCIABLE I engage easily in group conversations and activities.	To learn about people. To put everyone at ease and create harmony.	So I can add influential connections to my network. To find opportunities.	To exchange ideas with others. To learn what people think about things.
TOLERANT I respect differences, even when I don't agree.	To give each person a voice. To show people that I accept them for who they are.	To allow healthy debate and get better solutions. To keep people engaged in solving a problem.	To give new ideas time to be tested. To clarify people's positions and interests.

RED-BLUE REASONS	RED-GREEN REASONS	BLUE-GREEN REASONS	HUB REASONS
To be in the right position or relationship. To show others how to fit the situation	To preserve my ability to compete. To discard outdated or ineffective ideas.	To build a new process that fits the situation. To help others also adapt.	To go along with the group's wishes. To keep my options open.
To help someone achieve their goals. To find the most effective point of influence.	To make progress on my overall strategy. To secure a future advantage.	To help others navigate a process. To avoid unnecessary risk.	To fit into the situation. To let others participate in their own ways.
So we can move forward together. To create excitement about what we need to do.	To align people's actions toward an agreed goal. To make sure we do not have to revisit a decision later.	So each one of us will know our roles. So no one feels forced into a decision.	To create a sense of unity and belonging. So the group can fully consider the situation.
To encourage people to express themselves. To find the best way to help someone.	To adjust and improve my strategy. To be prepared for any potential opposition.	To see whether I have anything to contribute. To learn about other people or ideas.	To respect and honor diversity. To find something new everyone can agree on.
To encourage someone to try something new. To find the fastest way to get something done.	To find a way around a constraint or limit. To increase efficiency and effectiveness.	So people can make their own decisions about what to do. To hear what other people think about the options.	To find something that is appropriate to the situation. To involve other people in decisions.
So I can connect people to each other. To find out what others are capable of.	To break down barriers to interaction. To build stronger relations in case things gets tough.	To help create a safe and open environment. To bring out the best in others.	To meet and include new people. To understand where people are coming from.
To learn about people's priorities. To affirm the importance of a relationship.	To test ideas against each other. To remain open until a clear solution is found.	To recognize each person's individuality. To honor people's rights to be heard.	To allow new ideas to emerge. So group processes will be enriched by diversity.

Managing Overdone Strengths

FOCUS ON STRENGTHS AND WEAKNESSES

Many approaches to personal development advocate a focus on strengths to the exclusion of weaknesses. Developing and deploying strengths in relationships is different than applying skills or talents to tasks. People who have strong negotiation skills but are weak in computer programming should probably focus on their "strengths" and not bother to develop their "weaknesses." However, relationship strengths can become weaknesses when they are overused or misapplied. Too much ambition becomes ruthless, over-supporting others can lead to self-sacrifice, an abundance of caution becomes suspicious, being too flexible is unpredictable.

Habitually overdone strengths may even become part of the way people see themselves. An overly trusting person who is deceived yet again may say, "No surprise! I am gullible." An overly analytical person, when confronted with it, may reply, "Of course, I'm totally obsessive."

People who accentuate the strengths of their personality and ignore the effects of overdone strengths do so at their own peril. Overdone strengths can trigger conflict in relationships, but this type of conflict is preventable with some adjustments to behavior by the person who is at risk of overdoing—and adjustments to perception by the person who judges that a strength is overdone.

HOW STRENGTHS BECOME OVERDONE

If all behavior has purpose and all people want to feel worthwhile about themselves, how is it that strengths become weaknesses? How does a prudent risk-taker end up losing it all on an ill-advised gamble? How does an inclusive manager get mired in group-think?

Every behavior choice begins with a motive and an intended result. As people make the choice, they stand between experience and expectations. The choice is often guided by successful past experience with the strength and an expectation that the strength will continue to produce results. But in cases where the results are not produced, people try harder with the same strength if they feel certain that the strength should work. When a person believes they are doing the right thing, extra effort with the same strength can cause it to be overdone and unproductive. A person who over-supports others may find they have sacrificed so much that they have done harm to themselves. Negative effects, such as this, often come as a surprise to the person who has overdone the strength because their intentions were good, and they believed that providing support would be effective. Overdone strengths tend to result when people:

- are certain that they have chosen the correct behavior
- are not getting the results they want
- respond by trying harder with the same strength

Strengths can also become weaknesses when they pass through the perceptual filters of others. The confidence, speed, and persuasiveness of a Red leader may appear arrogant and rude when perceived through a Blue or Green MVS filter. The perception of overdone strengths tends to be a reaction to behavior in another person that would be considered inappropriate for oneself in the same circumstances. The more different two people's Motivational Value Systems are from each other, the more likely they are to choose different behavior in the same situation. Each person may feel certain that they have made the correct strength choice and that the other has made an unproductive choice.

OVERDONE STRENGTHS CAN TRIGGER CONFLICT

One of the principal causes of interpersonal conflict is the perceived overdoing of strengths. This type of conflict is largely preventable, as it involves interpersonal factors, not disagreements or opposition. Conflict can be triggered when one person judges that another person has overdone a strength in an unproductive or harmful manner. But these judgments tend to reveal as much about the observer as they do about the other person. They may be over-reactions to behaviors by others that are deemed inappropriate for oneself.

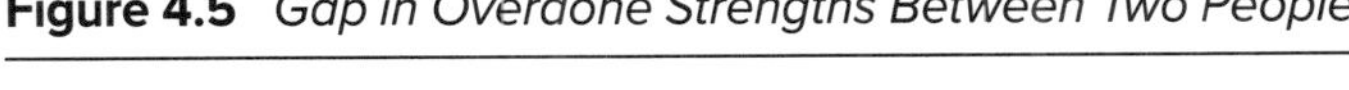

Figure 4.5 *Gap in Overdone Strengths Between Two People*

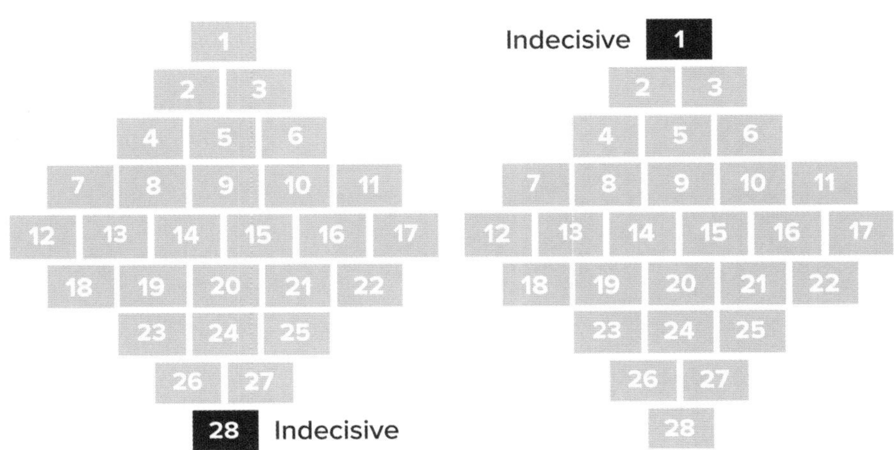

For example, a person who has Indecisive (overdone Option-Oriented) at the bottom of their Overdone Strength Portrait will probably be very sensitive to that behavior in others. Having Indecisive at the bottom suggests that the person would never want to be so Option-Oriented that they become Indecisive.

Therefore, when this person perceives indecisiveness in others, they tend to think "I would never do that." By implication, they tend to believe that other people should not be indecisive either. And this is the root of the interpersonal judgment, which if expressed or acted upon, can trigger conflict in the relationship. Statements like "You can never make up your mind." or sarcastic questions like "Can't you just pick something? Anything?" tend to generate defensiveness or conflict in others, especially when those others truly believe that they are effectively keeping their options open.

But overdone strengths do not have to trigger conflict. Both behavior and perception can be managed to prevent conflict.

MANAGING OVERDONE STRENGTHS: BEHAVIOR

Strengths can be reclaimed from overdone strengths by two principal strategies. 1) If we are aware that a strength may be perceived negatively, we can adjust our use of the strength or use a different strength. 2) When we are tempted to label another person with an overdone strength word (e.g. he is so rigid, or she is so distant) we can look for the positive intent behind the behavior that is bothering us.

Strengths can be overdone or misapplied in four ways: Frequency, Duration, Intensity, and Context. Knowing exactly how a strength is being overdone is the key to recapturing the productive strength. It's like when music is being played too loud, turning down the volume makes it enjoyable again. When your strength is too loud, you need to know which dial to turn down:

- **Frequency:** Any strength can be used too frequently. The regularity and predictability of a strength may begin to bother you or others, as in the saying "familiarity breeds contempt." You might get feedback or comments from others that give you clues about frequency, such as: You always...; That's a bad habit; Don't wear it out; Here we go again; or You do that every time. These are all indicators that you can be more effective if you reduce the frequency of deploying a specific strength.
- **Duration:** Once you get committed to a strength, it can go on too long. You may feel so certain about what you are doing that you don't notice when the strength has diminishing returns, and then when it starts working against you instead of for you. You might get feedback

or comments from others that give you clues about frequency, such as: Let go of it; Can we move on now?; Give it a rest; Do you ever stop?; or That's about all I can take. These are all indicators that you can be more effective if you shorten the duration of deploying a specific strength.

- **Intensity:** Any strength can be taken to an extreme, undiluted, too-intense level. A high level of passion or expertise can lead to over-intensity, as can a desire to compensate for not being noticed or appreciated. You might get feedback or comments from others that give you clues about intensity, such as: You need to tone that down; Wow, that was a bit over the top; Let's dial that back a bit; I can see that you're all-in; or That was harsh. These are all indicators that you can be more effective if you decrease the intensity of deploying a specific strength.
- **Context:** Strengths can be used at the wrong time or in the wrong place. Something that you're comfortable doing most of the time may be inappropriate in another context. You might get feedback or comments from others that give you clues about context, such as: Not here, not now; It's too late for that; Like a fish needs a bicycle; Your outgoing filter isn't working today; or Bad timing. These are all indicators that you can be more effective if you deploy a different strength in a specific context.

MANAGING OVERDONE STRENGTHS: PERCEPTION

One simple suggestion to have more productive relationships is to assume positive intent in others. But this is easier said than done, especially if another person's behavior looks like an overdone strength. Assuming positive intent increases the chance that you will perceive another person the way they see themselves, and it reduces the risk of misperceptions, which can turn into erroneous judgments and even into accusations and conflict. Any time you see another person's strengths as overdone, ask yourself: What positive intent could explain the behavior that is bothering me? The tables on the following pages present the 28 overdone strengths, along with their productive counterparts. Use them to help you assume positive intent in others and get better results in your relationships.

POSITIVE INTENT OF OVERDONE STRENGTHS

Overdone Strengths are almost always chosen with positive, productive intentions. The following tables link Overdone Strengths to their productive counterparts.

BLUE	
PRODUCTIVE STRENGTH	**OVERDONE STRENGTH**
SUPPORTIVE I give encouragement and help to others.	**SELF-SACRIFICING** Being so supportive that I give up my own interests and wishes for others.
CARING I concern myself with the well-being of others.	**SUBMISSIVE** Being so caring for others' well-being that I give or do anything they ask.
DEVOTED I am dedicated to some people, activities, or purposes.	**SUBSERVIENT** Being so devoted that I do what others want without question or resistance.
MODEST I play down what I am capable of doing.	**SELF-EFFACING** Being so modest that I don't take credit for my efforts or promote my ability.
HELPFUL I give assistance to others who are in need.	**SMOTHERING** Being so helpful to others that I do things for them that they do not want or need.
LOYAL I remain faithful to the commitments I make to others.	**BLIND** Being so loyal that I overlook or ignore problems with plans or people.
TRUSTING I place my faith in others.	**GULLIBLE** Being so trusting that I readily believe in people or things that I should not.

RED	
PRODUCTIVE STRENGTH	**OVERDONE STRENGTH**
RISK-TAKING I take chances on losses in pursuit of high gains.	**RECKLESS** Being risk-taking to the point of ignoring the potential consequences.
COMPETITIVE I strive to win against others.	**AGGRESSIVE** Being so competitive that I confront people in a combative or argumentative way.
QUICK-TO-ACT I get things started without delay.	**RASH** Being so quick-to-act that I overlook information that could be useful.
FORCEFUL I act with conviction, power, and drive.	**DOMINEERING** Being so forceful that I assert my will over others.
PERSUASIVE I urge, influence, and convince others.	**ABRASIVE** Being so persuasive that I disregard others' views and dispute their concerns.
AMBITIOUS I am determined to succeed and to get ahead.	**RUTHLESS** Being so ambitious with my goals that I don't have compassion for others.
SELF-CONFIDENT I believe in my own powers and strengths.	**ARROGANT** Being self-confident to the point of being convinced I know best.

GREEN	
PRODUCTIVE STRENGTH	**OVERDONE STRENGTH**
PERSEVERING I maintain the same course of action despite obstacles.	**STUBBORN** Being so persevering that I justify my course of action despite others' views or preferences.
FAIR I act justly, equitably, and impartially.	**COLD** Being so fair and impartial that I don't consider the affect on others.
PRINCIPLED I follow certain rules of right conduct.	**UNBENDING** Being so principled that I don't yield, even on minor issues.
ANALYTICAL I dissect and digest whatever is going on.	**OBSESSED** Being so analytical that I get lost in concepts or details that don't matter.
METHODICAL I am orderly in action, thought, and expression.	**RIGID** Being so methodical that I am constrained and do not change my ways.
RESERVED I practice self-restraint in expressing thoughts and feelings.	**DISTANT** Being so reserved in expressing myself that I do not engage with people or issues.
CAUTIOUS I am careful to make sure of what is going on.	**SUSPICIOUS** Being so cautious that I start off with doubt, mistrust, and skepticism.

HUB

PRODUCTIVE STRENGTH	OVERDONE STRENGTH
OPTION-ORIENTED I look for and suggest different ways of doing things.	**INDECISIVE** Being so option-oriented that I do not have a clear aim or direction.
TOLERANT I respect differences, even when I don't agree.	**INDIFFERENT** Being so tolerant that I come across as having no opinion or preference.
ADAPTABLE I adjust readily to new or modified conditions.	**COMPLIANT** Being so adaptable that I let the situation dictate what I do.
INCLUSIVE I bring people together in order to reach consensus.	**INDISCRIMINATE** Being so inclusive that it decreases the value of each person's participation.
SOCIABLE I engage easily in group conversations and activities.	**INTRUSIVE** Being so sociable that I disrupt or distract others.
OPEN-TO-CHANGE I consider different perspectives, ideas, and opinions.	**INCONSISTENT** Being so open-to-change that my priorities and principles are not clear.
FLEXIBLE I act in whatever manner is appropriate at the moment.	**UNPREDICTABLE** Being so flexible that other people cannot be sure about what I will do.

LEADING TEAMS

Teams, and leaders of teams, benefit from visibility into the team's strengths, as well as the team's tendencies to overdo certain strengths. Most teams have more relationships than people. A four-person team would have six one-to-one relationships (3+2+1), as well as four configurations of three people. Team dynamics change when a person is missing - or when a new person is added. A ten-person team would have 45 one-to-one relationships and substantially more sub-groups of various sizes.

The Strengths (and Overdone) Portraits add rich, contextual details to the pictures of personalities created on the SDI Triangle. The portraits provide insight into the culture of a team, as well as insight into the deployment and perception of strengths in all the possible relationships and sub-groups that are possible within a team.

Figure 4.6 *Top Team Strengths*

		BLUE: PEOPLE							RED: PERFORMANCE						
NAMES	MVS	SUPPORTIVE	CARING	DEVOTED	MODEST	HELPFUL	LOYAL	TRUSTING	RISK-TAKING	COMPETITIVE	QUICK-TO-ACT	FORCEFUL	PERSUASIVE	AMBITIOUS	SELF-CONFIDENT
Amy Chang	BLUE	2	1	14	3	4	11	7	20	24	23	28	27	25	26
Chloe Davis	RED	27	10	5	28	11	8	12	4	9	6	19	15	1	3
Curtis Thompson	RED-BLUE	4	3	5	6	7	8	2	9	10	11	12	1	13	14
David Bailey	BLUE	6	1	2	9	3	4	5	25	27	18	28	26	17	16
Eric Lawrence	GREEN	20	23	13	10	15	4	9	19	24	14	25	16	21	27
Janice Lee	BLUE-GREEN	2	4	5	6	7	8	9	22	23	24	25	26	27	28
Kent Washington	RED-BLUE	24	7	19	13	25	17	26	28	3	21	27	14	5	15
Lance Lopez	GREEN	25	5	6	27	28	15	16	13	26	11	18	19	4	23
Mark Logan	GREEN	12	14	11	18	20	16	25	24	22	28	21	19	5	13
Susan Anderson	HUB	22	23	24	25	26	27	28	3	9	10	11	12	13	14

		GREEN: PROCESS							HUB: PERSPECTIVE						
NAMES	MVS	PERSEVERING	FAIR	PRINCIPLED	ANALYTICAL	METHODICAL	RESERVED	CAUTIOUS	OPTION-ORIENTED	TOLERANT	ADAPTABLE	INCLUSIVE	SOCIABLE	OPEN-TO-CHANGE	FLEXIBLE
Amy Chang	BLUE	12	8	15	21	22	6	18	13	10	17	5	16	9	19
Chloe Davis	RED	13	20	2	22	25	26	17	18	23	14	21	24	16	7
Curtis Thompson	RED-BLUE	15	16	17	18	19	20	21	22	23	24	25	26	27	28
David Bailey	BLUE	19	10	15	21	23	11	22	13	12	7	24	20	14	8
Eric Lawrence	GREEN	5	1	11	8	6	2	22	7	18	12	26	28	17	3
Janice Lee	BLUE-GREEN	16	17	18	19	20	21	1	10	11	12	13	3	14	15
Kent Washington	RED-BLUE	9	22	18	6	1	20	8	11	16	10	12	2	4	23
Lance Lopez	GREEN	7	8	14	1	9	22	17	3	12	10	21	24	2	20
Mark Logan	GREEN	23	8	7	6	1	10	3	9	2	15	4	26	27	17
Susan Anderson	HUB	15	16	17	18	19	20	21	4	5	2	1	7	8	6

Figure 4.6 shows the Strengths Portraits of all team members in a table. The top six strengths of each person are highlighted to facilitate discussion about how member's strengths can be used most effectively. Team coaches or team leaders can use this information to describe the current culture of the team, as well as to talk about future scenarios where different strengths may be needed and how the team will adjust.

Figure 4.7 shows the Overdone Strengths Portraits of all team members in a table. The top three and bottom three of each person are highlighted. This is intended to facilitate discussion about the most likely conflict triggers within the team. Top

Figure 4.7 *Team Overdone Strengths and Potential Conflict Triggers*

		BLUE: PEOPLE							RED: PERFORMANCE							GREEN: PROCESS							HUB: PERSPECTIVE						
NAMES	MVS	SUPPORTIVE (Self-Sacrificing)	CARING (Submissive)	DEVOTED (Subservient)	MODEST (Self-Effacing)	HELPFUL (Smothering)	LOYAL (Blind)	TRUSTING (Gullible)	RISK-TAKING (Reckless)	COMPETITIVE (Aggressive)	QUICK-TO-ACT (Rash)	FORCEFUL (Domineering)	PERSUASIVE (Abrasive)	AMBITIOUS (Ruthless)	SELF-CONFIDENT (Arrogant)	PERSEVERING (Stubborn)	FAIR (Cold)	PRINCIPLED (Unbending)	ANALYTICAL (Obsessed)	METHODICAL (Rigid)	RESERVED (Distant)	CAUTIOUS (Suspicious)	OPTION-ORIENTED (Indecisive)	TOLERANT (Indifferent)	ADAPTABLE (Compliant)	INCLUSIVE (Indiscriminate)	SOCIABLE (Intrusive)	OPEN-TO-CHANGE (Inconsistent)	FLEXIBLE (Unpredictable)
Amy Chang	BLUE	2	12	20	27	8	4	11	24	18	23	3	1	7	26	19	22	17	28	9	6	25	26	3	5	14	16	21	23
Chloe Davis	RED	5	21	23	11	14	18	25	7	27	12	22	20	19	10	8	15	2	3	9	4	13	16	6	26	28	1	17	24
Curtis Thompson	RED-BLUE	1	22	23	12	3	24	17	20	19	27	11	5	9	15	15	25	4	26	14	8	28	21	10	18	2	6	16	7
David Bailey	BLUE	4	17	18	8	20	28	6	25	1	14	2	21	19	9	13	22	10	5	27	11	7	3	12	26	23	16	24	15
Eric Lawrence	GREEN	5	21	23	11	14	18	25	7	27	2	22	20	19	10	8	15	12	13	9	4	3	16	6	26	28	1	17	24
Janice Lee	BLUE-GREEN	23	27	19	24	26	20	9	3	11	5	13	8	12	6	4	2	7	15	16	14	9	18	10	17	21	25	22	28
Kent Washington	RED-BLUE	15	13	6	4	20	3	16	8	28	11	25	26	9	7	1	10	22	5	2	18	19	24	27	23	14	21	12	17
Lance Lopez	GREEN	17	4	2	11	25	12	6	13	5	14	19	26	3	24	9	21	20	18	16	22	23	28	7	27	15	8	1	10
Mark Logan	GREEN	4	19	13	15	12	20	21	9	7	1	10	6	23	25	16	26	17	5	2	3	28	24	18	22	27	11	14	8
Susan Anderson	HUB	5	21	23	11	14	18	25	7	27	2	22	20	19	10	8	15	12	13	9	4	3	16	6	26	28	1	17	24

Top Overdone Strengths · Conflict Trigger (Behavior) · Bottom Overdone Strengths · Conflict Trigger (Perceived)

overdone strengths (positions 1-3) by some members are likely to cause conflict for members who have the same overdone strength near the bottom (positions 26-28). Team coaches or team leaders can use this information to process past conflicts or prevent future conflicts.

"The more a personality theory can be for a person, rather than about a person, the better it will serve that person."

— Elias Porter

5 THEORY AND STATISTICS

Part 5 presents three articles in a more scientific tone than the balance of the book.

THE SDI 2.0 VIEW OF PERSONALITY

This article explores four significant questions in personality theory and provides answers to the questions from the SDI 2.0 point of view.

HISTORY AND DEVELOPMENT OF THE SDI 2.0

This article provides a rich narrative of the SDI's roots, the involvement of key theorists, and its recent developments.

SDI 2.0 METHODOLOGY AND MEANING

This article describes the methods used to collect, summarize, and interpret data. It includes descriptive statistics and findings about the assessment's reliability and validity.

THE SDI 2.0 VIEW OF PERSONALITY

Tim Scudder, PhD

1. What is personality?
2. Is personality the result of nature or nurture?
3. Is the person or the situation responsible for behavior?
4. Does personality change?

These questions have inspired significant debate among academics for many years, and they continue to inspire conversations and personal reflection. Classic literature and more recent scientific findings, however, suggest that there are clear answers to them. And understanding those answers can provide insights for developing greater Relationship Intelligence.

This section provides a brief review of the academic literature for each of those questions, followed by practical implications from the SDI 2.0 point of view.

WHAT IS PERSONALITY?

Personality is "a stable set of tendencies and characteristics that determine those commonalities and differences in people's psychological behavior (thoughts, feelings, and actions) that have continuity in time and that may not be easily understood as the sole result of social and biological pressures of the moment" (Maddi, 1996, p. 6). The study of personality invites classification of persons into categories or types. As Kluckhohn and Murray (1948) noted, every person is like all other persons, like some other persons, and like no other person. Personality types are an attempt to explain this middle ground of how people are similar. The fact that people can be described as having the same personality type in no way invalidates their uniqueness; people of the same type still have significant differences from one another.

"Any representation of personality is a hypothetical formulation, not a record of facts" (Murray & Kluckhohn, 1948, p. 6). How, then, is the concept of personality to be described in ways that are meaningful and useful to individual people, yet still acceptable and useful for organizations and researchers? The underlying question here is: What should count as evidence of personality? There is philosophical tension between theorizing and measuring, between concepts and statistics, between subjective and objective data (Rosenberg, 2008).

While no one is arguing one side to the exclusion of the other, there are differences in emphasis. Some academicians recommend that personality theory be taught as science, rather than as history courses. They recommend that students of personality theory should know the grand theories of personality, as well as whether these theories are supported by measurement-based evidence (McCrae, 2011). Two of the grand theorists are Sigmund Freud and Carl Jung.

Freud's Typology

Sigmund Freud is best known for the development of psychoanalysis, and the character types he described, based on patients' successful development or fixation at a stage in development (Freud, 1923/1961). However, he was also interested in normal people. Near the end of his career, he modified his conception of normal adult personality types based on three innate libidinal drives and how they developed in early years. He named them Erotic, Narcissistic, and Obsessive.

He further explained that these drives rarely resulted in pure types in adults, and that blends of any two and an even mixture of all three could develop and be observed. This led him to describe seven normal personality types. In that article, he stated: "It is clear that the variety of individual human beings making up the general picture of mankind is almost infinite. Whoever undertakes the justifiable task of differentiating separate types within this multitude, from the beginning is free to select the distinguishing characteristics and principles which shall determine this classification" (Freud, 1932, p. 3).

Jung's Typology

Carl Jung, who had split from Freud by the time the above-referenced article was written, did select different characteristics for his classification. Jung (1923) did not include Freud's descriptions of drives as a basis for his typology; instead, he used mental processes, or functions and attitudes, that he believed were innate. Jung specifically identified eight types, beginning with the difference between the attitudes of introversion and extraversion. He claimed that introversion or extraversion, paired with one of four cognitive functions, could describe significant personality differences, depending on which of the four cognitive functions (thinking, feeling, sensing, or intuition) was dominant for each person.

Modification of Freud's and Jung's Typologies

Others subsequently modified Freud and Jung's typologies. The most well-known modification of Jung's work is the MBTI (Meyers Briggs Type Indicator), which made explicit the inferred dichotomy of judging and perceiving and increased the number of types from eight to 16 (Briggs Meyers, McCaulley, Quenk, & Hammer, 1998).

While Freud's psychoanalytic ideas gave rise to a movement, his character typology inspired less ongoing work. However, Erich Fromm (1947) advanced Freud's early typology; he described three non-productive orientations (receptive, exploitative, and hoarding) that were similar to Freud's and added a fourth, the marketing orientation. For Fromm, personality is "the totality of inherited and acquired psychic qualities which are characteristic of one individual and which make one individual unique" (1947, p. 50).

Fromm was also concerned with an ideal type, which he referred to as the productive orientation. Fromm's colleague, Michael Maccoby, subsequently modified Fromm's work; he described 16 personality types in a leadership context. The types were based on the four primary types and combinations of primary and secondary types (Maccoby, 2007; Maccoby & Scudder, 2010).

Elias Porter, who split from Carl Rogers over the ethical use of personality tests (Gordon, 1998), used Fromm's four types as the basis for several assessments. Near the end of his career, Porter (1976) stopped attempting to directly measure Fromm's marketing orientation and instead directly measured only the other three in the Strength Deployment Inventory (SDI). After a series of different typologies, Porter arrived at a set of seven personality types, based on three primary drives. Porter found that the personalities of people whose scores on the scales for these three primary motives were fairly close together were similar to Fromm's Marketing orientation. Porter's seven Motivational Value System (MVS) types align conceptually with Freud's (1932) seven types and are a "re-discovery" of these types; neither Porter nor Fromm ever referenced this late and little-known work of Freud.

Traits and Factors vs. Systems of Drives and Motives

The terms drives and motives, while often used interchangeably, are different. Drives tend to be more innate and less conscious than motives. Motives are pressure or energy toward action; they tend to be more learned and more conscious and purposive than drives are. Traits are characteristics that produce routine behavior, which is not necessarily motivated (Maddi, 1996). However, there is a debate about whether personality factors, such as extraversion, create multiple, discrete traits or whether traits combine to form factors (Wilt, Condon, Brown-Riddell, & Revelle, 2012).

Traits may also be confused with values. The same word may sometimes describe a trait and at other times describe a value. For example, fairness may be a trait if a person generally behaves without bias; fairness may be a value if fairness motivates (or gives energy and purpose to) a person's behavior (Parks & Guay, 2009). The interaction of traits and motives may also explain behavior in different contexts. For example, a person who is a risk-taker may drive cautiously when children are in the car if he or she is motivated to protect the children.

The Driven Personality

What drives are a part of personality? Freud (1905/1961, 1930/1961) identified sexual and aggressive drives. His earliest personality types resulted from the assumed fixation of energy in different stages of development.

Fromm (1947) focused primarily on the drive for relatedness to one's environment, to other people, and to oneself. Fromm's personality types result from the different, non-productive forms of relatedness: receptive, exploitative, hoarding, and marketing.

Maccoby's (1995) concept of drives is more dynamic, with a set of psychic drives that are assumed to be innate: survival, information, mastery, play, relatedness, dignity, and meaning. For Maccoby, the drives combine in different ways to form different personality types, the behavioral characteristics of which are similar to Fromm's and Freud's.

For Porter (1976), the universal drives are for relatedness and feelings of self-worth (akin to dignity in Maccoby's system).

Porter's personality types describe different ways of achieving feelings of self-worth in relationships with others. Porter proposed a dual-state view of personality. A set of seven types describes personality in the "going well" state, and a set of 13 types describes the state of conflict. As previously noted, the seven "going well" types had roots in Fromm's work and show a strong correlation to Freud's seven libidinal types.

The 13 conflict types in the SDI do not have a conceptual forebear and are Porter's original concept. However, Karen Horney (1950/1991) suggested three basic approaches to conflict: moving toward a person with compliance, moving against a person with aggression, and moving away from a person with aloofness. Each of these approaches can be idealized by the person using the approach. Compliance can be self-idealized as goodness or saintliness. Aggressiveness can be self-idealized as strength or heroism. Aloofness can be self-idealized as wisdom or independence.

The above referenced theoreticians made psychological drives an important part of their typologies. They suggest that types can be understood and explained, at least in part, by the way these drives are shaped during socialization. Jung, however, did not believe that drives had much influence on behavior (Maddi, 1996). Instead, he suggested that the focus of energy and mental processes could explain behavior. To risk oversimplification for the sake of clarity: Drive theorists would suggest that drives and motives give rise to decisions and actions; adherents to Jung's theory would suggest that drives and motives are the result of inherited mental processes. Either way, drives and cognitive processes are related.

The SDI View of Personality

In the SDI, personality is described as a dynamic system of motives that is expressed differently in different conditions. Porter (1976) claimed that affective states interact with motives to produce qualitatively different behaviors under two perceived conditions 1) things going well and 2) conflict situations. The SDI is a dual-state personality assessment; it offers two sets of types for two affective states.

Each person has one of seven Motivational Value System types and one of 13 Conflict Sequence types, which yield 91 possible combinations. Relationship Awareness Theory acknowledges that even these types are not sufficient to describe everything about people. Porter suggested that a full consideration of personality should account for people's concept formation, especially the self-concept. His early work in clinical and therapeutic settings enabled him to observe changes in behavior that followed changes in people's self-concept (Porter, 1950, 1976; Rogers, 1951).

Some of Porter's work with Rogers involved the use of Q-methodology, a technique developed by Stephenson (1935) that Porter applied to early versions of the Strengths Portrait and Overdone Strengths Portrait. In Q-sorts, the significance of personality traits is based on how those traits interact with other traits (Stephenson, 1950). People of the same personality type may have different strengths, or their similar strengths may have different meanings. But strengths are not the essence of personality, they are the expression of personality. Strength deployment is mediated by the demands of the environment and the free will of the person deploying the strengths. The SDI's Motivational Value System and Conflict Sequence types are based on why people do things; the focus is on the motive for behavior, not on the behavior itself.

One of the factors that distinguishes people from other animals is intentionality (Rosenberg, 2008); therefore, a personality typology that focuses on motives, rather than behavior, is a uniquely human typology. The SDI describes types, which have their origins in enduring motives. The Strengths Portrait and Overdone Strengths Portrait engage people in an exploration of the reasons they use their strengths and what their strengths mean to them.

IS PERSONALITY THE RESULT OF NATURE OR NURTURE?

The nature-nurture debate is based on a false dichotomy. The tabla rasa (blank slate) assumption of human potential is simply wrong (Funder, 2001), as is pure genetic determinism. People are not blank slates upon which society and the environment can write anything, nor is DNA destiny. From an evolutionary perspective, genetics and the environment are closely intertwined. "The only pertinent questions therefore are 1) which of the various genetic potentialities will be actualized as a consequence of a particular series of life events in a given physical, social, and cultural environment? and 2) what limits to the development of this personality are set by genetic constitution?" (Kluckhohn & Murray, 1948, p. 38).

Humans have fewer genetic instincts than other animals. People are not hard-wired for specific behaviors. However, the human genetic code appears to include epigenetic rules (Wilson, 2012). Epigenetic rules are predispositions for learning, phobias, attractions, language, and more that are based on many thousands, or millions, of years of evolution. The environment that people find themselves in may influence which of these genes are activated and how. But these rules are not beyond conscious control and therefore cannot be considered instincts.

Socialization can instill deep values in people, and people who are socialized in different ways can have different values. Erich Fromm (1947) described the results of these processes as social character. Social character is the set of values and attitudes shared by most people in a society. Fromm, who believed in the perfectibility of human nature (but within its genetic limits), described non-productive personality types as variations on the social character. His productive orientation was based on the ideal of loving productivity, which he believed could contribute to a better society (Fromm, 1955). For Fromm, the study of personality was a tool to critique the way society shaped people, to recommend ways to improve society, and to promote the productive development of people in society.

The SDI View of the Nature-Nurture Debate

Porter was deeply influenced by Fromm's writing while he was working closely with Carl Rogers at the University of Chicago's Counseling Center. In retrospect, this put him squarely in the center of a philosophical debate about human nature. Fromm and Rogers shared an interest in productive human development, but Fromm's vision of human perfectibility was different from Rogers' vision of human potential. Fromm argued that all people should develop toward a productive ideal, while Rogers (1961) argued that people should develop their individual potential.

Porter did not address the issue of innate vs. socialized personality types in his written work. However, in videotaped training programs, he expressed his opinion that at least some portion of the Motivational Value System was inborn. He cited his experience working with nurses, who could tell differences in personalities in newborn infants (Porter, c. 1980). Given Porter's academic and clinical experience and the views of those who influenced him, such as Fromm, Rogers, Kluckhohn, and Murray, it is reasonable to claim that the SDI view of personality is dialectical; it recognizes the interaction of nature and nurture.

The SDI concept of personality is consistent with Michael Maccoby's (2010), which claims that innate drives become values as people are socialized and that these values become a part of people's identities. In some ways, like Fromm's intent to improve society, the SDI explores personality with the implied promise of improving relationships and increasing productiveness. In some ways, like Rogers' intent to value and nurture the individual, the SDI is intended to increase self-awareness and contribute to the development of more congruent functioning.

IS THE PERSON OR THE SITUATION RESPONSIBLE FOR BEHAVIOR?

A Far Side cartoon by Gary Larson is titled, "The four basic personality types." In it, four different people approach the same table that has a glass of water on it. The first says, "The glass is half full!" The second says, "The glass is half empty." The third says, "Half full ... No! Wait! Half empty! ... No, half ... what was the question?" The fourth says, "Hey! I ordered a cheeseburger!"

Larson, perhaps unintentionally, has provided a useful illustration of Kurt Lewin's famous equation: B=f(PE). Behavior is a function of an interaction between a person and that person's environment (Lewin, 1935). In Larson's cartoon, the environment is the same for each person, and the behavior of each person is clearly different. The reader is left, then, to deduce the personalities of the four cartoon characters, which might be that they are, respectively, 1) optimistic, 2) pessimistic, 3) indecisive, and 4) demanding. Readers may find humor in the cartoon if they conclude that they could sort people they know into the four categories.

Lewin's equation suggests that behavior is a function of the person and the environment. However, some researchers and theorists have operated under the assumption that there are no meaningful differences among people; therefore, descriptions of personality types could serve no useful purpose (Weiner & Greene, 2008). If the person is removed from the equation or held constant, the environment alone can be used to predict and control behavior. The quest to explain behavior based on the environment led to schools of thought including radical behaviorism's pairing of stimulus and response, social learning theory's focus on changing the environment to affect a change in behavior, and interactionism's idea that role expectancies shape behavior (Barnouw, 1985; Goldhaber, 2000; Maddi, 1996).

The popularity of these mechanistic approaches led to a decrease in the perceived value of personality theory. Carl Rogers (1961) attacked mechanistic approaches, such as those advocated by B. F. Skinner. But he and other humanists also questioned the morality of personality assessments on the basis that personality tests were prejudicial and offered limited categories; they claimed that a person could only be understood as a unique individual (Weiner & Greene, 2008). These humanists minimized the role of the environment in Lewin's equation; they claimed that behavior was primarily a function of the person.

The interaction of a trait and an environment may produce a certain behavior, but this idea is incomplete. More complex models of behavior attempt to explain behavior as the dynamic interaction of cognition, affect, and motive in a given situation (Kammrath, Mendoza-Denton, & Mischel, 2005). Other models include behavior in the mix, rather than viewing behavior as an output of a system.

The ABCD model integrates these elements. Affect includes moods, emotions, and preferences. Behavior is motor activity such as walking and talking. Cognition is the process of making meaning, modes of thinking, and problem-solving. Desires are motivations or strivings (Wilt, Oehlberg, & Revelle, 2011). When behavior is viewed as a part of a human system, rather than just an output, more complex explanations are possible. For example, a valued behavior can improve a person's affective state, and this improved mood can contribute to another valued behavior or a change in the situation.

The person-situation debate has been declared over; the winner is both, and the loser is neither. The end of the debate has been signaled by two key recognitions in academic literature:

1) Behavior of individuals correlates between situations, and 2) the person-situation debate was based on a false dichotomy (Funder, 2001). More recently, even those who were strong proponents of the situational approach, such as Walter Mischel, have joined the integrative conversation, writing: "Over the past decade, however, this long-standing person-situation dichotomy has been challenged by a notable development in the personality literature that is just beginning to impact research and thinking in person perception. Namely, it has been discovered that interactive effects between dispositions and situations are common, everyday expressions of personality" (Kammrath et al., 2005, pp. 198-199).

The SDI View of the Person and Situation

The SDI's first contribution to the person-situation conversation is to split situations into two kinds: 1) situations when people feel good about themselves and 2) situations when people experience conflict. The natures of situations are determined by the perceptions of the people in the situations, not by any outside, objective criteria.

The second contribution is to simultaneously measure personality and behavior in the context of work. This is consistent with the way Lewin (1935) expressed the equation B=f(PE). The Motivational Value System and Conflict Sequence are elements of personality, they are stable and endure over time and across situations. But the Strengths Portrait and Overdone Strengths portrait reflect the person in the context of their work (the environment). People may deploy a wide range of strengths over time in pursuit of desirable goals in many different types of situations.

Lewin's equation was not intended to be subject to the rules of algebra (as the radical behaviorists attempted). The SDI view of behaviorism and manipulating an environment to produce desired actions is that these efforts sometimes succeed at producing desired actions. However, when they succeed, it may be at the expense of forcing people into inauthentic, incongruent behavior, which is stressful and unsustainable.

The SDI view is that the person interacting with the environment is a complex situation that must account for the whole person, for their motives, values, beliefs, feelings, cognitive processes, and perceptions. Clearly, the environment in which people interact includes other people; one person's behavior is part of the environment that another person perceives. Therefore, people cannot be fully understood without consideration of context, or environment.

The ABCD model should have an E added; ABCDE represents the interaction of Affect, Behavior, Cognition, Drive, and Environment. The SDI 2.0 addresses all five elements. The MVS and Conflict Sequence are two affective states. Strengths and Overdone Strengths are behaviors. The MVS and CS both act as filters that influence cognition. Motives as described by the SDI are drives. The environment of work is the required mindset for the strengths portion of the assessment.

The person and the situation both influence behavior.

DOES PERSONALITY CHANGE?

Some theorists (Fromm, 1947; Kluckhohn & Murray, 1948; Maddi, 1996) define personality as the unchanging psychological qualities of persons. But these definitions are generally meant to describe adults, and these theorists also talk about development. If personality develops at least in part through socialization, there must be some changes during this development, especially in youth. Developmental stage theorists, such as Erikson (1963), suggest a series of existential conflicts that must be resolved as a person grows and develops.

But does personality change in adulthood? One study of young adults in college found positive changes over a period of two-and-a-half years; participants in this study became more open, more conscientious, and less neurotic as measured by a five-factor assessment (Vaidya, Gray, Haig, & Watson, 2002). The researchers attributed part of this observed change in personality assessment results to a change in the environment; many students were free from parental control for the first time in their lives, and their environment required more self-direction. Stability in personality gradually increases until about age 30, after which personality factors remain relatively stable (Terracciano, McCrae, & Costa Jr., 2010). Other research indicates that values shaped during socialization change more in youth than in adulthood (Parks & Guay, 2009), and findings from research on twins suggest a strong genetic foundation for stability of personality factors in adulthood (Johnson, McGue, & Krueger, 2005).

Personality does appear to change as it develops, but the rate of change appears to decrease in adulthood. Different adults' rates of change seem to plateau at different levels. One possible explanation for this is that people who score high on openness to experience are more likely to change, as are people with a high degree of neuroticism, which has been linked to depression and other changes (Parks & Guay, 2009).

People may report that significant life experiences triggered changes in personality. However, in one telling study of adults who emigrated to the United States to escape persecution in Nazi Germany, the underlying characteristics of personality were found to remain essentially unchanged, despite the traumatic experiences (Allport, Bruner, & Jandorf, 1948). The researchers did describe changes in behaviors during the transition, but these were explained as temporary responses to the environment, rather than changes in personality. They were interpreted as changes in the way personality manifested itself in different situations.

Philosophically, the question of whether personality changes in adulthood can also raise questions of self-awareness. People who experience significant life changes may believe that their personality has changed as a result of these experiences. However, the possibility exists that the new environment simply was conducive to personality factors those people had previously repressed. Alternatively, a new situation may be conducive to the activation of a predisposition that was always a part of their potential. Hence, people's experience of change may, upon further analysis, actually represent an act of self-discovery or the development of an undeveloped part of their personalities.

Some theorists, such as Robert Kegan (1994), claim that development is characterized by progressive levels of consciousness. Kegan's subject-object theory holds that whatever is subject at one level of consciousness becomes the object at the next level. Therefore, as adults develop, they experience their self-concepts subjectively at first. They are who they are. Then at the next stage of development, they are able to intentionally alter their self-concepts, to engage in self-authorship. At a higher level of development, people are able to act on their self-concepts, instead of being limited to acting from their self-concepts.

Personality is not necessarily a result, nor is it a permanently fixed entity. Murray and Kluckhohn (1948) describe personality as a process, a dynamic and systemic concept that requires the understanding of the whole person as a prerequisite for explaining the parts of any person. Their concept of a whole personality suggests the integration of multiple drives at any given moment, as well as the consistent integration of drives during a long period of development. Development is characterized by the resolution of major life dilemmas. For them, "the chief overall function of personality, then, is to create a design for living which permits the periodic and harmonious appeasement of most of its needs as well as gradual progressions towards distant goals. At the highest level of integration, a design of this sort is equivalent to a philosophy of life" (Murray & Kluckhohn, 1948, p. 32).

The SDI View of Changes in Personality

Theoretically, the SDI is aligned with the idea that personality is relatively stable and unchanging in adults. However, this position is also compatible with the concept of continued adult development. Whether development is thought of as resolving existential conflicts (Erikson, 1963), moving through levels of consciousness (Kegan, 1994), becoming self-actualized (Maslow, 1954; Rogers, 1961), or the productive unfolding of one's powers (Fromm, 1947), the motivational or purposive aspects of personality are viewed as relatively stable, but they are expressed differently as people develop. This is consistent with Porter's (1976) view that behavior changes follow changes in self-concept. Changes in self-concept, however, do not require a change in the underlying motivational structure of personality.

Practically, the SDI measures personality, and people are often curious about whether their SDI results will change. SDI scores are reliable within +/- six points (Porter, 1985), and the results for most people are fairly consistent over time. However, significant changes in SDI results can be observed. Generally, these changes fall into two categories:

1) Different Mindsets: If the personality portion of the SDI is completed correctly (with a whole-life focus) on one occasion, then compared to an incorrectly completed SDI – for example, about a specific relationship on another occasion – there are likely to be differences in the results of the two SDIs. However, these differences do not represent a change in personality. Rather, one represents personality and the other represents behavior in a specific context.

2) Masks: In some cases, the SDI may be completed with the intent of using a whole-life focus, but people's responses may be influenced by situations in which they are consciously or unconsciously using a defensive mask. If on a later occasion people are free from the defensive mask, differences in SDI results are to be expected. This does not indicate that people's personalities have changed. Rather, their awareness of their personalities has changed – or their willingness

to respond honestly to the SDI items has changed. People who mask their true self may have self-concepts that include compliance with external demands, but when free from the masks, their self-concepts could include awareness of their true motives. People who have experiences of this nature may claim that their personalities have changed, and for them, those are valid experiences. However, further reflection may lead them to conclude that they shed false self-concepts and discovered truer self-concepts that were previously hidden behind the masks.

In summary, the SDI view of changes in personality is that it changes very little in adulthood. However, people continue to develop and are able to become more effective. Overtime, people learn more effective ways to interact and communicate, but they do not have to change their personality in order to do so.

CONCLUSION

This section began with four questions:

1. What is personality?
2. Is personality the result of nature or nurture?
3. Is the person or the situation responsible for behavior?
4. Does personality change?

While these questions may continue to generate debate and research, their answers, from an SDI point of view, can be simply stated:

1. What is personality?
Personality is a dynamic system of motives that are experienced under two conditions: when things are going well and when there is conflict. Types based on a purposive view of personality have great explanatory power; they help people to understand their own behavior and the behavior of others and to make more informed choices about behavior in relationships. The SDI 2.0 describes personality with the Motivational Value System and the Conflict Sequence.

2. Is personality the result of nature or nurture?
The Motivational Value System and Conflict Sequence are the result of both nature and nurture. Innate potential is developed in different ways in different contexts; the debate between nature and nurture represents, and always has represented, a false choice.

3. Is the person or the situation responsible for behavior?
Behavior, as Kurt Lewin originally stated, is a function of the person interacting with that person's environment. Because people have emotions, drives, consciousness, and purposes, understanding behavior requires an understanding of whole persons in their environment. The Strengths Portrait and Overdone Strengths Portrait show behavior of people in the context of work.

4. Does personality change?
Personality remains relatively stable in adulthood. However, people can develop without changing their personality. They can become more aware of their personality and more effective at expressing their motives in their relationships.

REFERENCES

Allport, G. W., Bruner, J. S., & Jandorf, E. M. (1948). Personality Under Social Catastrophe. In C. Kluckhohn & H. A. Murray (Eds.), Personality in Nature, Society, and Culture (pp. 347-366). New York, NY: Alfred A Knopf.

Barnouw, V. (1985). Culture and Personality (Fourth ed.). Belmont, CA: Wadsworth Publishing Company.

Briggs Meyers, I., McCaulley, M. H., Quenk, N. L., & Hammer, A. L. (1998). MBTI Manual. Palo Alto, CA: Consulting Psychologists Press.

Erikson, E. H. (1963). Childhood and Society (Second ed.). New York, NY: W.W. Norton & Company.

Freud, S. (1905/1961). Three Essays on the Theory of Sexuality. In J. Strachey (Ed.), The Standard Edition of the Complete Psychological Works of Sigmund Freud (Vol. VII (1901-5), pp. 125-243). London: Hogarth Press.

Freud, S. (1923/1961). The Ego and the Id. In J. Strachey (Ed.), The Standard Edition of the Complete Psychological Works of Sigmund Freud (Vol. XIX (1923-25)). London: Hogarth Press.

Freud, S. (1930/1961). Civilization and its Discontents. In J. Strachey (Ed.), The Standard Edition of the Complete Psychological Works of Sigmund Freud (Vol. XXI (1927-31), pp. 59-145). London: Hogarth Press.

Freud, S. (1932). Libidinal Types. Psychoanalytic Quarterly, 1(1), 3-6.

Fromm, E. (1947). Man for Himself: An inquiry into the psychology of ethics. New York, NY: Henry Holt and Company.

Fromm, E. (1955). The Sane Society. New York, NY: Henry Holt and Company.

Funder, D. C. (2001). Personality. Annual Review of Psychology, 52, 197-221.

Goldhaber, D. E. (2000). Theories of Human Development: Integrative perspectives. Mountain View, CA: Mayfield Publishing Company.

Gordon, T. (1998). [Interview conducted by Tim Scudder].

Horney, K. (1950/1991). Neurosis and Human Growth: The struggle toward self-realization. New York, NY: W. W. Norton & Company.

Johnson, W., McGue, M., & Krueger, R. F. (2005). Personality Stability in Late Adulthood: A behavioral genetic analysis. Journal of Personality, 73(2), 523-552.

Jung, C. G. (1923). Psychological Types. New York, NY: Harcourt Brace.

Kammrath, L. K., Mendoza-Denton, R., & Mischel, W. (2005). Incorporating If... Then... Personality Signatures in Person Perception: Beyond the person-situation dichotomy. Journal of Personality and Social Psychology, 88(4), 605-618.

Kegan, R. (1994). In Over Our Heads: The mental demands of modern life. Cambridge, MA: Harvard University Press.

Kluckhohn, C., & Murray, H. A. (1948). Personality Formation: The determinants. In C. Kluckhohn & H. A. Murray (Eds.), Personality in Nature, Society, and Culture (pp. 35-48). New York, NY: Alfred A Knopf.

Lewin, K. (1935). A Dynamic Theory of Personality. New York: McGraw-Hill.

Maccoby, M. (1995). Why Work? (2nd ed.). Alexandria, VA: Miles River Press.

Maccoby, M. (2007). Narcissistic Leaders. Boston, MA: Harvard Business School Press.

Maccoby, M., & Scudder, T. (2010). Becoming a Leader We Need with Strategic Intelligence. Carlsbad, CA: Personal Strengths Publishing.

Maddi, S. R. (1996). Personality Theories (Sixth ed.). Long Grove, IL: Waveland Press.

Maslow, A. H. (1954). Motivation and Personality. New York, NY: Harper & Brothers.

McCrae, R. R. (2011). Personality Theories for the 21st Century. Teaching of Psychology, 38(3), 209-214.

Murray, H. A., & Kluckhohn, C. (1948). Outline of a Conception of Personality. In C. Kluckhohn & H. A. Murray (Eds.), Personality in Nature, Society, and Culture (pp. 3-32). New York, NY: Alfred A Knopf.

Parks, L., & Guay, R. P. (2009). Personality, Values, and Motivation. Personality and Individual Differences, 47, 675-684.

Porter, E. H. (1950). Introduction to Therapeutic Counseling. Cambridge, MA: The Riverside Press.

Porter, E. H. (1976). On the Development of Relationship Awareness Theory: A personal note. Group & Organization Management, 1(3), 302-309.

Porter, E. H. (1985). Strength Deployment Inventory: Manual of administration and interpretation. Pacific Palisades, CA: Personal Strengths Publishing.

Porter, E. H. (c. 1980). Archival Video. Carlsbad, CA: Personal Strengths Publishing.

Rogers, C. R. (1951). Client-Centered Therapy. Boston: Houghton Mifflin.

Rogers, C. R. (1961). On Becoming a Person. New York, NY: Houghton Mifflin.

Rosenberg, A. (2008). Philosophy of Social Science (3rd ed.). Boulder, CO: Westview Press.

Stephenson, W. (1935). Correlating Persons Instead of Tests. Character and Personality, 4, 17-24.

Stephenson, W. (1950). The Significance of Q-technique for the Study of Personality. In M. L. Reymert (Ed.), Feelings and Emotions: The mooseheart symposium (pp. 552-570). New York, NY: McGraw-Hill.

Terracciano, A., McCrae, R. R., & Costa Jr., P. T. (2010). Intra-Individual Change in Personality Stability and Age. Journal of Research in Personality, 44, 31-37.

Vaidya, J. G., Gray, E. K., Haig, J., & Watson, D. (2002). On the Temporal Stability of Personality: Evidence for differential stability and the role of life experiences. Journal of Personality and Social Psychology, 83(6), 1469-1484.

Weiner, I. B., & Greene, R. L. (2008). Handbook of Personality Assessment. Hoboken, NJ: Wiley.

Wilson, E. O. (2012). The Social Conquest of Earth. New York, NY: Liveright Publishing Corporation.

Wilt, J., Condon, D. M., Brown-Riddell, A., & Revelle, W. (2012). Fundamental Questions in Personality. European Journal of Personality, 26, 629-631.

Wilt, J., Oehlberg, K., & Revelle, W. (2011). Anxiety in Personality. Personality and Individual Differences, 50(7), 987-993.

HISTORY AND DEVELOPMENT OF THE SDI 2.0

Tim Scudder, PhD

AUTHOR'S NOTE

I have been working full-time with the SDI since 1995 and have contributed to its development and utility through research, authorship, and application. Given my role, people often ask if I am the founder or creator. I am not. That distinction rightly belongs to Elias Porter, or "Port" as his friends called him. I have assumed the mantle of SDI development, and someday that mantle will pass to someone else. I never had the opportunity to meet Porter, but I do know one word that says a lot about him: Blue (shorthand for his Altruistic-Nurturing Motivational Value System). He wanted to help people and was not overly concerned about getting credit for his work. The more I learned about him, his Relationship Awareness Theory, and the SDI, the more I became convinced that his modesty and desire to help others succeed caused him to become an overlooked figure in psychology.

This is the story of the SDI 2.0, so named to reflect its evolution since Porter created it. The SDI 2.0 is now a single assessment that produces four interrelated views of a person:

1. Motivational Value System (MVS) – a personality type when things are going well.
2. Conflict Sequence – a personality type when experiencing conflict.
3. Strengths Portrait – a ranking of productive strengths used at work.
4. Overdone Strengths Portrait – a ranking of non-productive strengths used at work.

But this is not just a story of a product; it is a story of people interacting with each other and the social forces of their times. I am both the narrator and an actor in this story. I use the first person when I narrate my own involvement or add personal observations. I wrote this article because I realized that I was the sole keeper of an "oral history" of the SDI. I wanted to commit the facts to writing and hoped that the story would be interesting for anyone who uses the SDI 2.0. Let's rewind the clock a bit and get started.

ANCIENT HISTORY

The SDI 2.0, like all modern personality assessments, rests on the conceptual foundation laid by earlier societies and theorists. The idea of personality types is hardly new. Ancient Chinese society described personality types based on the year of birth. Mesopotamian society provided the 12 signs of the zodiac, which astrologists use to describe personality differences based on the day of birth. Various religious texts describe gifts from gods, many of which are like personality characteristics. In polytheistic traditions, the gods themselves have distinctly different personalities. Long-established caste and other hierarchical social systems describe differences in people based on birth circumstances, such as being an untouchable or having royal blood. The Greek philosopher Hippocrates ascribed four personality types to the effects of varying levels of different bodily fluids (blood, bile, etc.). His four temperaments are still used, albeit in revised or renamed versions, to describe differences among people despite the fact that his biological assumptions were incorrect.

Compared with those ancient practices, the idea of psychometrics — using standardized measurement techniques to describe differences in personality — is quite recent. Modern psychometrics still rely on human-created theories and concepts, but most are supported by rigorous scientific theory and methods. That is, they are evaluated against objective standards of reliability and validity, not solely by their face-validity or popularity.

EARLY INFLUENCES

Sigmund Freud's introduction of psychoanalysis was a monumental advancement in the science of understanding people. While Freud initially focused on biological drives as the explanation for behavior, he saw that these drives were shaped in the context of relationships, starting with the infant and the mother, and continuing through development and adult relationships. Freud is best known, and often justly criticized, for his early concepts, but he revised and advanced his thinking in later years. Toward the end of his life, Freud (1932) wrote a short article that described seven normal adult personality types. I will return to this article later because it has a surprising and important tie to the SDI.

Freud attracted some of the brightest minds of his time, such as Carl Jung, who went on to establish a contrary point of view regarding personality based not on interpersonal relatedness and drive, but on mental processes and preferences. The first SDI built on concepts from two people who advanced Freud's ideas, Erich Fromm and Karen Horney. Fromm (1947) departed from Freud by focusing on the relatedness of adults in society. He described four non-productive adult orientations (Receptive, Exploitative, Hoarding, and Marketing) that would later captivate Porter and prompt him to create psychometrics to attempt to validate Fromm's concepts. Horney (1950) brought a much-needed feminine perspective to psychoanalysis; her conceptualization of three conflict resolution strategies (compliance, aggression, and aloofness) linked to three types of responses to conflict: moving toward others, against others, or away from others.

Psychoanalytic theory, with its focus on discovering people's motives (or drives) – be they conscious or unconscious – behind their behaviors, represents core personality as a system of drives or strivings, which may be expressed in healthy, neurotic, or destructive ways. Psychoanalysis originated and found fertile ground in Europe in the early 1900s; the concept and practice spread widely through publication and the exodus from Germany and neighboring countries of renowned scientists and psychoanalysts in the 1930s during the rise of fascism. Fromm and Horney emigrated to New York where US-based psychologists, such as Harry Stack Sullivan (1953) were doing work that would result in other interpersonal theories. Another key immigrant to the US, as far as the SDI story goes, was Kurt Lewin (1935), whose field theory – behavior is the result of the person interacting in the environment – influenced Elias Porter's early education in the 1930s at the University of Oregon.

Fromm embraced and expanded on Freud's view of happiness – *lieben und arbeiten* – love and work. Fromm explored the idea of human relatedness in depth, with a focus not just on interpersonal relatedness, but also on the importance of being productively related to one's work. After some time in New York and Washington, DC, Fromm relocated to Mexico, where Michael Maccoby joined him for eight years, studying personality and social change (Fromm & Maccoby, 1970). When Maccoby returned to the United States, he built on Fromm's foundation and applied insights from the psychoanalytic method to the practice of leadership (Maccoby, 1976). I will return to this aspect of the story later because it is important to the development of the SDI 2.0. Maccoby and Porter did not have any contact; they developed Fromm's concepts in parallel. My own work includes the reintegration of these threads (Maccoby & Scudder, 2018).

PORTER'S RELATIONSHIP WITH ROGERS

In the 1940s, when Porter studied at Ohio State University, Rogers was his teacher and an advisor during Porter's (1942) doctoral research. Porter's pioneering study (1943) was the first to document the effectiveness of the client-centered methods (Suhd, 1996); he used audio recordings of Rogers' sessions with patients. After Rogers moved to Chicago in 1945, Porter and his best friend, Tom Gordon, joined him to help establish the University of Chicago's Counseling Center. At the time, one of the center's activities was to provide counseling to veterans returning from World War II (Kirschenbaum, 1979). Demand for counseling far outstripped capacity, and group therapy was invented by necessity. During this time, Porter, Gordon, Rogers, and others worked collaboratively. Their work contributed to a major re-focus for the entire field of psychology, from what is "wrong" with a person to what is "right." Up until then, the prevailing definition of mental health was freedom from pathology. People without pathologies were considered to be healthy; there was no positive definition of mental health. Porter's (1950) book, *An Introduction to Therapeutic Counseling,* influenced Rogers' (1951) landmark book, *Client-Centered Therapy.* Rogers wrote the foreword to Porter's book saying, "...the ingenuity which Dr. Porter has shown in developing devices which compel self-examination and facilitate attitudinal reorganization, incites

Client-centered therapy by Carl Rogers (1951) and An Introduction to Therapeutic Counseling by Elias Porter (1950)

my admiration. He has succeeded where to me failure seemed almost certain." Rogers referenced Porter several times.

I never had the opportunity to meet Porter or Rogers, but I did get to know their friend and colleague, Tom Gordon. He told me that Porter was as much of an influence on Rogers as Rogers was on Porter. Gordon (2001) is best known for his development of communication techniques, such as I-messages and active listening, which were used widely in many training and education programs.

The group at the Chicago Counseling Center initiated a revolution in humanistic, positive psychology and human potential, long before those terms became popular. Other notable concepts have roots in this time in Chicago (Kirschenbaum, 1979). Will Schutz (who introduced me to Tom Gordon) worked at the University of Chicago with Rogers and knew Porter. Schutz is the author of *Fundamental Interpersonal Relationship Orientation Theory* (Schutz, 1958) and an early psychometric, the FIRO-B. Paul Hersey was significantly influenced by Rogers. He told me, "You see further from the shoulders of giants, and Carl Rogers is one of my giants." Hersey created the Situational Leadership model of leader-follower interactions and a test to help people understand the leader-follower relationship, which was later revised by Ken Blanchard. Just one example of a modern interpretation is Stephen Covey's fifth habit – seek first to understand, then to be understood – which was inspired by therapeutic techniques first developed by Rogers, Porter, Gordon, and others.

Unfortunately, Porter's use of psychometrics led to a falling out with Rogers. At the time, Rogers was against any sort of personality test. He believed that the test itself would unduly influence the test-taker, who would see the test as an external authority and therefore fail to fully engage in the therapeutic relationship. But Porter persisted amid the high demand for counseling; he saw that psychometrics could do some of the work for the therapist, speed the self-discovery process, and allow the therapist to help more people. Years later, Porter and Rogers reconciled, and Rogers (1986/2005) would speak highly of Porter's work; he even used early versions of the SDI when he was at United States International University (now the California School of Professional Psychology within Alliant International University). I learned this when I gained access to Porter's personal correspondence, where I found a letter from Rogers to Porter, asking him to send some more SDIs.

PORTER'S EARLY WORK IN PSYCHOMETRICS

Porter's first experience in personality testing was to select public assistance workers at the Oregon State Public Welfare Commission in the 1930s. He created an 8-hour test to determine the ways that candidates interacted with people, placing them into one of five categories: moralistic, interpretive, reassurance-giving, probing, or empathic. During World War II he worked as a classification officer for the US Navy, where his job was to determine the most suitable roles for new recruits based on their skills, experience, and various test results.

In 1949, he read Fromm's (1947) *Man for Himself* and was so intrigued by Fromm's descriptions of personality types that he began constructing psychometrics to validate Fromm's concepts. Porter referred to two major insights from Fromm. First, the idea that a family of traits could form an entity. This was contrary to the prevailing research mindset at the time, which was based on physical science. Psychologists were trying to isolate traits, much as physical scientists were isolating elements or variables in order to show causal relationships. Porter saw that the interaction of traits, rather than isolated traits, was a more useful idea. Secondly, Porter credited Fromm with the idea that weaknesses in the context of relationships were often simply non-productive behaviors, which had productive counterparts. Porter's first published psychometric was the *Person Relatedness Test* (Porter, 1953). This was developed during his time working with Rogers, where he also learned to use Q-sorts – in which people sort cards printed with personality traits – as a method of measurement that reflected the human experience of multiple traits interacting simultaneously (Stephenson, 1935). He created an unpublished Q-sort that assessed a Freudian concept, the relative strength of the Id, Ego, and Superego within a person.

The *Person Relatedness Test* caught the attention of Stuart Atkins and Alan Katcher, who thought that a business could be built based on the assessment. They released a product called LIFO (Atkins, Katcher, Porter, 1967), which was a slightly revised version of the *Person Relatedness Test.* Porter was not satisfied with the assessment because the scale that was intended to measure Fromm's Marketing orientation did not have an acceptable level of reliability or validity. (The Marketing orientation refers to people who constantly change according to what others – the "market" – desire.) Despite Porter's concerns, Atkins and Katcher began selling the assessment, and the three soon dissolved their partnership.

I discovered (long after the fact when I read through Porter's old correspondence with Stuart Atkins) that one of Porter's oft-repeated conflict stories was about their break-up. I have an old video where Porter relayed the story of a business dealing with a partner (he never said Atkin's name when he told the story) who had a Red MVS and Red Stage 1 in conflict. Porter, as a Blue, felt he was not being listened to, and was being taken advantage of, both creatively and financially. In his Stage 1 Blue conflict, he responded, "Mustn't there be some type of misunderstanding?" but his "sweetness and light" approach did not get Atkins to listen to him. Then Porter went into a deep analysis (his Stage 2 Green), which Atkins dismissed. Finally, Porter was triggered into his third stage of Red, where he angrily confronted Atkins, who said in response, "Aha, now the real Porter comes out." Based on Porter's telling of the story, it seems that Atkins only respected people who used assertive behavior. But for Porter, it took the third stage of conflict to show assertive behavior, which caused him a great deal of stress. I had the opportunity to meet Atkins and Katcher and to interview Katcher at some length during a conference aboard the Queen Elizabeth II. I asked Katcher what caused the split with Porter. He said: “In retrospect, immaturity.” He would not say more, so I was left to make my own assumption about who was being immature.

SDI’S EARLY YEARS

After the split with Atkins and Katcher, Porter drafted a completely new assessment, this time eliminating everything related to Fromm’s Marketing orientation. He called it the *Strength Deployment Inventory* and founded Personal Strengths Assessment Service in 1971. At the time, he was teaching at the University of California, Los Angeles (UCLA) and serving patients in private practice. The assessment matured, and his business opportunities grew through the Los Angeles chapter of the American Society for Training and Development (since renamed the Association for Talent Development). Five years later, he incorporated his company in California as Personal Strengths Publishing. He and his wife, Sara Maloney Porter, then devoted their full-time efforts to the continued development of the SDI and to the business.

The first SDI was a simple, self-scorable form, printed on goldenrod-colored card stock; they were sold for $1 each. The results were presented on three scales, the altruistic-nurturing, assertive-directing, and analytic-conserving. A simple set of score totals described the results, and there was no interpretive information provided for the “conflict” results.

In 1972, based on a suggestion from a customer, Porter introduced the SDI triangle. The first SDI triangle delineated nine personality types, two of which have the same names in the current SDI. A second version later that same year also delineated nine types, but with different boundaries. Five of the nine type-names are the same in the current SDI.

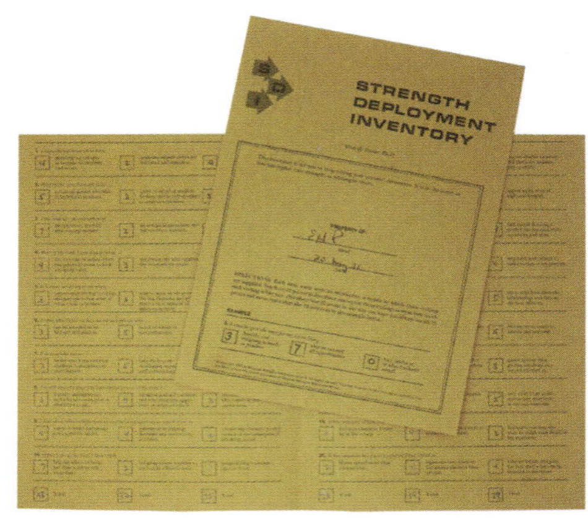
STRENGTH DEPLOYMENT INVENTORY

First printed SDI. Completed by Elias H. Porter, 1971

In 1973, having seen the benefits of drawing multiple people’s results on the triangle, he named it the Interpersonal Interaction Triangle and began producing it in color. The SDI was the first psychometric to use color-coded language for the results, a practice which is common today. Porter credited his wife Sara, who held a doctorate in social work, with the idea of using color-codes so people could speak about the results with ease and apply them to their daily relationships. The colors Blue, Red, and Green were chosen because Porter had noticed a slight correlation between personality type and people’s favorite color. Along with changes to the triangle, Porter made changes to the 60 assessment items to improve their reliability and validity. The 1973 version shows six personality types, the names of which all match

SDI TRIANGLES

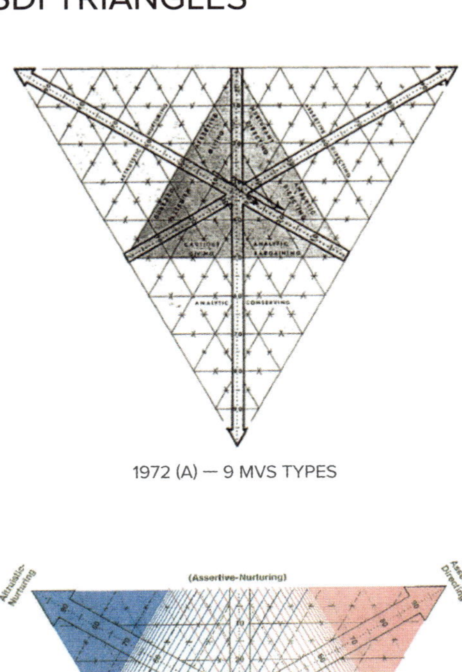

1972 (A) — 9 MVS TYPES

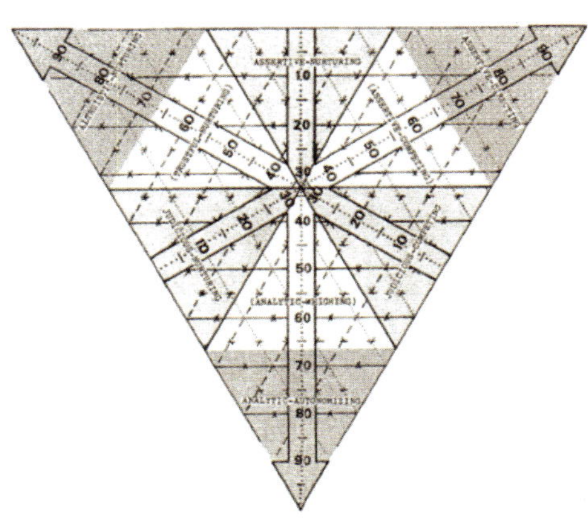

1972 (B) — 9 MVS TYPES

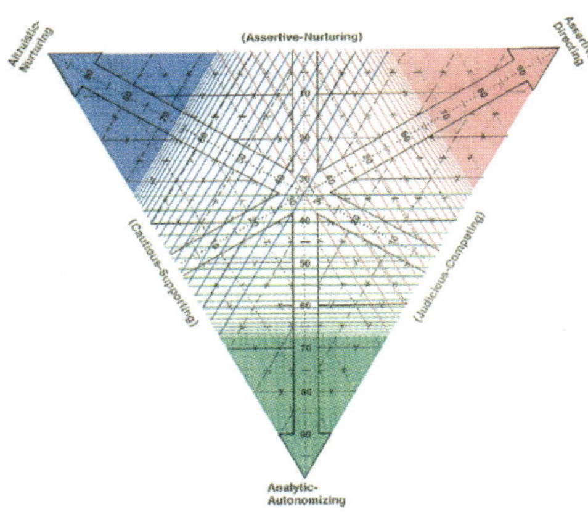

1973 — 6 MVS TYPES

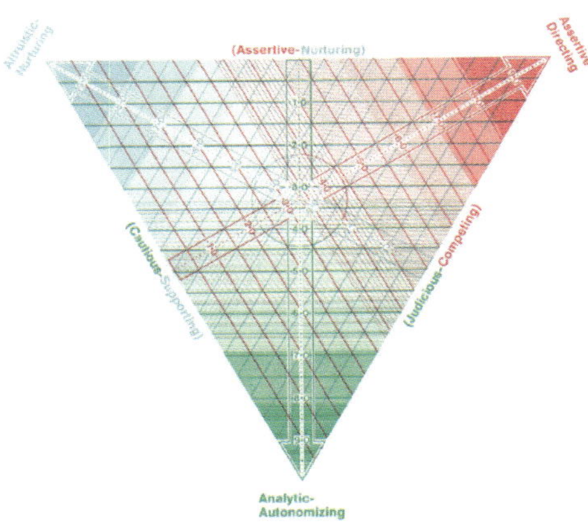

1977 — ADDITION OF HUB, 7 MVS TYPES

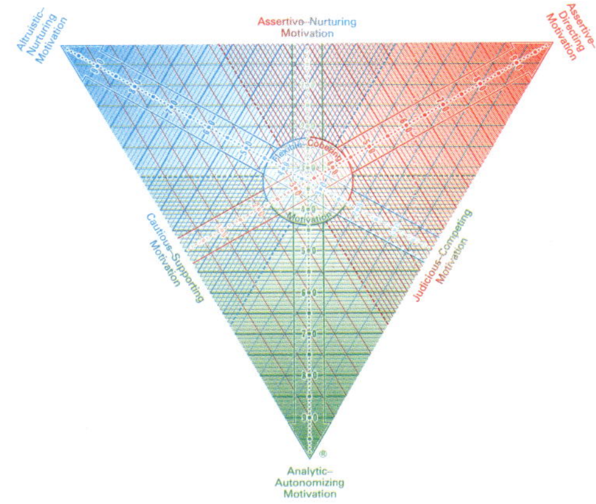

1996 — CIRCULAR HUB

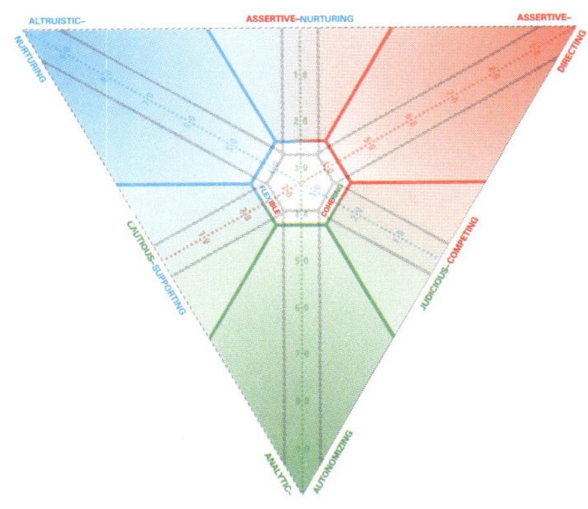

2015 — HEXAGONAL HUB

the current SDI. Notable by its absence is the Hub, Flexible-Cohering, type. This six-type iteration remained in production until 1977

Porter continued to help others, such as Ken Thomas, to develop their ideas. In Porter's files, I found correspondence from Thomas, thanking Porter for his assistance on what would become the Thomas-Kilmann Conflict Mode Instrument (TKI) – before Ralph Kilmann was involved. When I talked with Kilmann, he had no idea that Porter had contributed to the instrument that bore the Kilmann name. Here I discovered yet another example of Porter's Blue modesty and desire to help others, which had the unfortunate side effect of allowing his contributions to go unrecognized.

Elias Hull Porter, 1914-1987

Porter also tended to shy away from any reference that would link him to Freud. The 1970s were not the peak of Freud's popularity. In fact, many psychologists during this time tended to criticize Freud for ideas such as the Oedipus complex and preferred to focus on more linear, mechanistic methods such as the operant conditioning made popular by BF Skinner, Pavlov, and others. Porter was never a fan of behaviorism, saying that Skinner had "...done more to hold back the field of psychology than any person he could think of." I discovered that blistering critique in a video of a workshop where Porter was answering participants' questions. As a side note, early in his education, Porter conducted experimental research with rats in mazes. He documented that rats learned the mazes even without the presence of any rewards or punishments (Porter and Biehl, 1943), which is contrary to Skinnerian ideas.

The emergence of the Hub, or Flexible-Cohering type, was in some ways a happy accident. Porter experienced a high degree of face validity from people whose SDI results were charted in any of the regions near the six type names on the edges of the triangle, but people whose SDI results charted in the middle of the triangle did not identify with any of the six types; they did not feel that any of the descriptions fit them. In his first manual of administration (Porter, 1973), these people were described as having "undifferentiated motivations." As a skilled therapist and researcher, Porter began to notice a pattern in their responses. They wanted to be part of teams and wanted to adapt themselves to others' needs and the present situation. Porter noticed that many of these traits were similar to Fromm's Marketing orientation, which he had dismissed because his earlier psychometrics, the *Person-Relatedness Test and LIFO,* which attempted to directly measure the Marketing orientation, could not be properly validated.

The challenge of validating the Hub type is a persistent theme in the SDI story.

With the benefit of hindsight, I can see that Freud (1932) identified it first, but he did not describe it in any meaningful way. Fromm (1947) was next, but he did not connect it to Freud's idea. Fromm believed that the Marketing orientation was a new, emerging personality type due to a shift in social character; he described it great detail. Porter (1973) was not satisfied with the statistical evidence to clearly differentiate the Marketing orientation from other types. Fromm and Maccoby (1970) found evidence for all of Fromm's types except the Marketing orientation, however, this research was conducted in a farming culture where they did not expect to find the Marketing type. I have had the interesting experience of working with many people who have a Hub MVS who said that the SDI was the first personality assessment result they ever agreed with. I think this is true because Porter was astute enough to recognize that his early SDI was measuring something he did not intend to measure, then sophisticated enough to find another way to measure it, validate it, and describe it.

Porter was fond of saying "If something exists, it can be measured," so he set about determining whether something different existed for people whose results were in the center of the triangle. He returned to the lists of traits in Fromm's (1947) work that had inspired his initial work and created a card-sorting assessment of four different sets of productive behaviors. Those that we today call the Blue strengths (Caring, Helpful, etc.) correlated positively with the Blue (nurturant) motive. The Red strengths (Ambitious, Persuasive, etc.) correlated positively with the Red (directive) motive. The Green strengths (Cautious, Methodical, etc.) correlated positively with the Green (autonomous) motive. A new set of strengths, based on Fromm's Marketing orientation (Adaptable, Open-to-Change, etc.) did not have strong correlations with any of the three SDI scales. Instead, they correlated with sets of scores where all three scales were within one standard deviation of the mean. This was the foundational insight, backed by evidence, that led Porter to inscribe a circle with a radius of one standard deviation in the triangle and add a seventh personality type to the SDI and his theory. Later, Porter would introduce a card-sort of Overdone Strengths ("Gullible" for overdone Trusting, "Arrogant" for overdone Self-Confidence, etc.). I believe Porter coined the term "Overdone Strengths" in the early 1970s even though he credited Fromm with the concept. I have not seen a reference to that term in any earlier literature, although the term is widely used today.

Porter had determined that three primary motives interact to form seven distinct personality types. But Porter also saw that those seven types correlated with four categories of behavior, or strengths (as initially described by Fromm). This is the reason that the SDI 2.0 today has three motive scales and four categories of strengths. Porter introduced a revised SDI that included a triangle with seven regions in 1977 (45 years after Freud's publication of the same seven personality types). But this version of the SDI featured descriptions of only the four main personality types (Blue, Red, Green, and Hub) when things were going well. The SDI

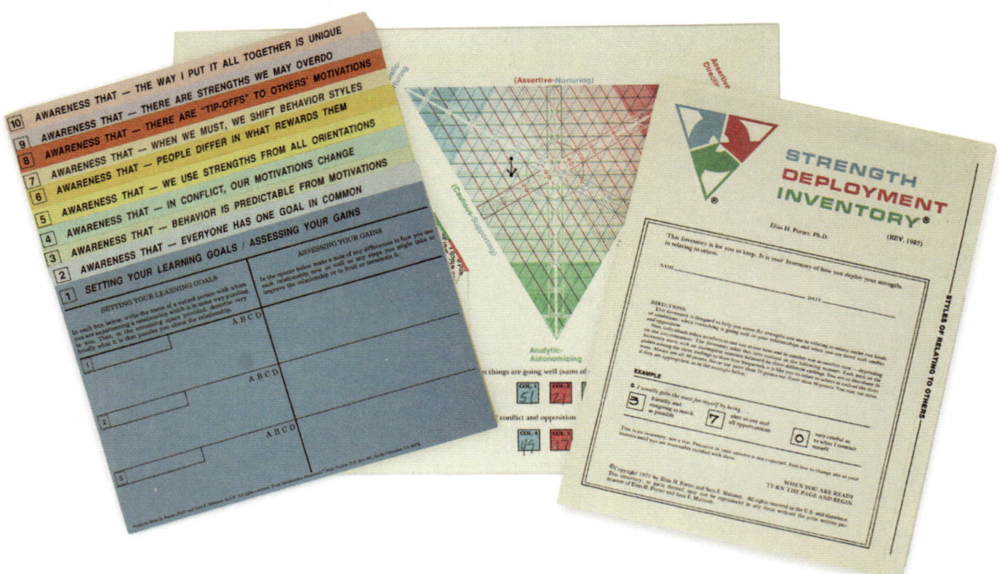

Relationship Awareness Basic Course, 1986

offered cursory descriptions of the three remaining types, which were often collectively referred to as "the blends" — Red-Blue, Red-Green, and Blue-Green. While the SDI offered instructions to the user about how to draw an arrow, with the dot representing the going-well state and the arrowhead representing the conflict state, no explanatory text regarding conflict was offered except for some short sentences in the SDI Manual of Administration (Porter, 1985). Unfortunately, Porter did not publish his ongoing research, and the only evidence I have been able to find is from recorded training programs that Porter led in the 1980s. During those sessions, he answered participants' questions and described the research he conducted.

From 1977 to 1987, the SDI itself remained essentially unchanged, although Porter revised the manual several times and introduced a structured training program called the Relationship Awareness Basic Course (Porter, 1986). This course included two card-sorts, one for strengths and one for overdone strengths. In his writing, and in video recordings, he indicated that Relationship Awareness Theory was not finished. He even contemplated renaming the theory to Theory V (for validation). I found this document in a draft book section; it was written in response to the Theory X and Theory Y that were popular at the time. Porter hinted at directions for further development such as the need to more clearly understand the Hub personality type. In 1987, Porter succumbed to oral cancer, which was undoubtedly linked to the pipe he enjoyed smoking. His widow, Sara Maloney Porter continued in the business until she sold it to Bob Tomkinson and me. She had been operating the business as a way to keep Porter's work alive and would not permit any changes to any product. It was exceedingly difficult to convince Sara that we would be true to Porter's original ideas as we developed the business, even though Tomkinson had been a long-time customer and trusted advisor of Porter's.

ADVANCING PORTER'S WORK

Prior to purchasing the business, I had been working as a CPA, then as a controller of a non-profit job-training organization in Los Angeles. Because the non-profit operated with federal grant funds from the US Department of Labor, I needed to document the return on investment of DOL's money in order to secure funding in subsequent years. I met Tomkinson when he operated one of the most successful training and job placement subcontractors that received funding through my organization. He claimed that the SDI was the secret to his success because it helped people understand their core motives and what they found personally meaningful at work.

On Tomkinson's recommendation, I took the SDI assessment, and he explained my results. Then I asked my girlfriend, Kim, to complete the SDI. I shared her results with Tomkinson, who then proceeded to give me two Feedback Editions of the SDI. Kim, who is now my wife, completed the Feedback Edition about how she saw me, and I completed it about how I saw her. Her view of me almost perfectly matched my view of myself. But my feedback to her was not even close. As it turned out, my feedback to her when things were going well exactly matched her conflict scores. There was a pattern in our relationship where she would say something was wrong, and I would dismiss it by saying everything seemed fine to me. The SDI and Feedback Edition results showed me that I was not seeing her accurately; this insight helped me to change my perception of her and improve our relationship.

When Tomkinson and I took over the business in 1995, I assumed the CEO role. On "day one" we had shelves full of SDIs that had not been updated since the early 1980s. We set a goal to make a new printed SDI live up to its potential. We clarified Porter's definitions and coined the terms Motivational Value System (MVS) and Conflict Sequence (CS). I mapped the MVS and CS boundaries on the triangle so people would not have to guess where the boundaries were or refer to other resources to know their MVS and CS results. We developed the card-sorts of strengths and overdone strengths from the *Basic Course* to make them independent assessments. We wrote a new manual of administration and posthumously gave Porter (1996) the authorship credit. With the help of Mike Gallon, the UK distributor at the time, we gave the two-color blended MVSs equal treatment in the SDI and released the first version of the SDI that represented the full personality typology: 7 Motivational Value Systems, 13 Conflict Sequences, and card-sorts of strengths and overdone strengths. We called it the Premier Edition of the SDI and listed Porter as the author.

I believe Elias Porter's most important and unique contribution to the field of psychology is the Conflict Sequence, although he characteristically did not publish it or promote it. He never even gave it a name, and he wrote very little about it, nothing

SDI Premier Edition, 1996

more than a few sentences about each of the 13 Conflict Sequences. These short descriptive statements were behavioral in nature and found only in a technical manual and in exercise 4 of his *Basic Course,* which was not widely used. When we added the Conflict Sequence results to every SDI, it fundamentally transformed the assessment and the training and development programs in which it was used. Understanding conflict and conflict management was a significant focus for me and the organization. We increased the emphasis on conflict identification and management in all our training programs and released the book *Have a Nice Conflict* (Scudder, Patterson, & Mitchell, 2012). I felt that the key to making Porter's concepts about conflict more useful was to focus on the motives and internal experience of conflict, which Porter alluded to, but did not fully develop. As I wrote various training programs, descriptive text for the SDI, and versions of our facilitator manuals, I focused on motives, not behavior. The essence of understanding personality in conflict is what people feel driven to do, not what they actually do. For example, a person who is experiencing a threat may feel compelled to fight with another person, but instead may choose to listen to that person. This choice is fostered by self-awareness, personal development, and self-management. The internal motive to fight may never change, but the decision to fight is up to the person in each situation. Thus, the motives that define personality are stable, and behavior is variable.

In retrospect, I think I was as fascinated with Porter's work as he was when he discovered Fromm's work in the late 1940s. I made it my personal mission to learn everything I could about the foundations of the theory and the assessment. I had access to Porter's working files and an archive of video tapes.

I collected all his published works and read all the books he indicated as significant influences. I went to meet people who worked with Porter and Carl Rogers at Chicago, such as Will Schutz and Tom Gordon.

I also met prominent authors who did not know Porter, such as Salvatore Maddi (1996), whose book on personality was in its sixth edition and was a standard in university courses. When I reviewed the SDI and Porter's work with Maddi in his University of California, Irvine office, he expressed regret for not knowing about Porter and said his work would have filled an important void in his text. Maddi criticized Fromm for a lack of empirical evidence for the Marketing orientation, criticized Rogers for failing to describe different personality types, and criticized Costa and McCrae's Five-Factor model for failure to integrate the "big five" factors into any useful typology that described whole persons and the interplay between the factors. Maddi said that Porter's Relationship Awareness Theory, and the evidence of reliability and validity that I presented, would have been a prime example of how a personality theory should be constructed; it followed and expanded on the excellent framework that Fromm had established, and it addressed the critiques he made of the other models. Sadly, there were no plans for a seventh edition of Personality Theories, a Comparative Analysis, and I added this to my mental tally of times that Porter was overlooked.

As the organization grew, we developed close relationships with customers around the world, translated products into over 20 languages, and created training programs to improve relationships in all types of organizations. During this time, we created an online platform to administer the assessments, increased the rigor of the facilitator certification experience, and continued to learn how our customers applied the SDI in real-world settings. Along with many successes, we noticed areas where the SDI could be improved.

GROWING AWARENESS THAT SDI NEEDED UPDATES

We found that the Strengths Portrait and Overdone Strengths Portrait were not generating the level of insight and application that we believed they could. The integration between strengths and motives was not as clear as it could be. We began noticing that some people did not trust their self-rankings of strengths, or overdone strengths, when they used the card-sort methodology. People said that since they could see the results taking shape in the card-sort, they were influenced by how they thought they should prioritize their strengths, not how they actually did. We also noticed consistent resistance to specific strengths and the way Porter worded them, such as "Experimenter." I would later eliminate that Hub strength from the Strengths Portrait and replace it with "Inclusive."

The more I worked with the SDI, the more I came to find value in a systems-thinking approach, exploring the connections between the results. Subtle but important distinctions began to emerge, which Porter had not clearly identified. Examples of these connections include: people find it

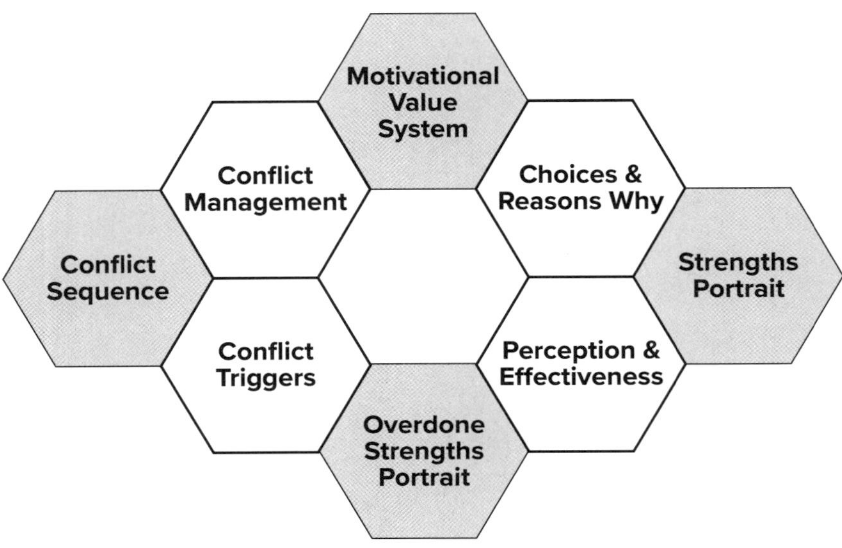

Summary Connections Between Four Views

easier to deploy strengths from the middle or bottom of their portrait if they do not restrict the use of higher strengths or if they can be connected to the MVS; the experience in Stage 1 conflict affects the experience in stages 2 and 3; the third stage of conflict acts as a filter that causes misperceptions in relationships; and overdone strengths near the bottom of the portraits tend to be conflict triggers for people. Understanding these connections between different results improved the quality of the individual and group experiences that I led. By integrating motives, conflict, and strengths, I was able to more accurately reflect people's experiences of themselves than when I limited my interpretations to the individual elements.

I collaborated with several students who were working on masters or doctoral degrees and supervised, sponsored, or advised them on research projects. During these projects, I found there was a paucity of published research that met current academic standards, which made it difficult for students to get faculty approval to use the SDI. Research often begets more research, and ironically, a lack of previous research can be an impediment to future research – at least in academic settings.

One day Cliff Norman, a customer with whom I enjoyed discussing theory and research, introduced me to Michael Maccoby. Norman knew my passion for Fromm's writing and had recently met Maccoby, who worked with Fromm in Mexico for eight years, co-authored *Social Character in a Mexican Village* with Fromm, and advised Fromm during the writing of The Anatomy of *Human Destructiveness.* Maccoby and I rapidly found that our respective work was compatible; we shared a common root and had similar philosophies about human development. We integrated the SDI and his work on leadership development and co-facilitated many programs for senior leaders in corporate and government organizations.

In about 2008, I decided to continue my education and enrolled in Fielding Graduate

Strength Deployment Inventory, 2015

University's Human and Organizational Systems PhD program. While I was working on a paper for one of my early classes, I visited Maccoby at his home and happened to ask where to find an article that he had mentioned. "Just a minute," he said as he headed toward his library. When he returned, he had Volume XXI of *The Complete Psychological Works of Sigmund Freud,* opened to a three-page article titled *Libidinal Types*. He handed it to me and said, "I think this is the beginning of SDI." I was amazed as I read it. Here was Sigmund Freud talking about normal adults and describing personality types based on motives. The Erotic (loving) type sounded like the Blue, Altruistic-Nurturing MVS by Porter, the Narcissistic type (dominated by the Ego) sounded like the Red, Assertive-Directing MVS type, and the Obsessional (or compulsive in some translations) type sounded like the Green, Analytic-Autonomizing MVS type. Freud went on to say that no person is a pure type and that everyone is actually a blend of types, with one or more being prominent. He also described three blends of two types, each of which matched the SDI, such as the Narcissistic-Obsessional type, which he personally identified with, and which has similar characteristics to the Red-Green, Judicious-Competing type in the SDI. Freud concluded by saying there was a seventh type, one characterized by an even mix of all three primary types (as is the case with the Hub MVS type).

What hit me in that moment was that Freud, at the end of his career, had created a personality typology that matched the typology Porter had created at the end of his career. Porter had spent the greater part of his life developing and refining psychometrics until he found a valid, reliable way to measure and describe personality types. Freud and Porter came to the same conclusion through vastly different methods. But Porter's conclusion came about 45 years after Freud's – with no awareness of Freud's (1932) conclusion. It seems Freud's libidinal types had been hiding in plain sight for a long time. The article was published in Volume 1, Issue 1 of *Psychoanalytic Quarterly.* But unlike Freud's well-known works from the same time, *Libidinal Types* was not widely known. A library search yielded less than 50 citations to this article; most were quite old. This insight sparked my own research and culminated in my dissertation (Scudder, 2013), where I used a large sample of SDI, Strengths Portrait, and Overdone Strengths Portrait results to provide the first empirical validation of Freud's libidinal types — along with support for all four of Fromm's non-productive orientations (including the Marketing orientation). Maccoby served on my dissertation committee, and the research gave me the data I needed to revise the assessment and improve the reporting of results.

One difference between Porter and Freud bears special attention. When Freud described the seventh type – what we know today as the Hub MVS type – he did not describe specific characteristics of this type. Freud said, somewhat enigmatically, that this type was not a type. Instead of describing it he called it the absolute norm. In my subsequent research, I found that the most consistent statistical pattern for the Hub MVS was that groups of Hubs did not show extreme mean scores on any measure, but instead showed central tendencies on every test I devised. This type cannot be easily isolated and directly measured. Fromm described it as the Marketing orientation, but Porter could not measure it reliably until he found, accidentally, that the Hub was actually the result of three motives working about equally – not a fourth, independent motive as he had attempted to measure in the *Person Relatedness Test*. While Porter did describe the Hub type in some detail, he struggled with capturing the essence of the type. He focused predominantly on the cohering part of the flexible-cohering (Hub) personality type, the desire to be a member of groups, to put the team before oneself, and to have a broad social circle. In my experience, people with Hub Motivational Value Systems describe themselves more frequently in terms of being interested in new ideas and perspectives, maintaining their future flexibility, and including other people in consensus-building efforts. Where Porter described a desire to be included by others, I saw a stronger drive to be the person who is inclusive of others. Some people who have worked with the SDI for a long time talk about the early versions having a "Blue bias," which makes sense because authors tend to put some of themselves into their work; Porter had a Blue MVS, and his first stage of conflict was Blue. I have a Red-Green MVS and my first stage of conflict is Green. While these differences were obviously not by design, I do like to think that a Red-Green filter has helped to remove some of the Blue bias, thereby improving the validity and utility of the SDI.

When our company introduced the revised SDI to the market under a new TotalSDI brand, my partners added my name to the product as an author. To be sure, by that time I had actually worked in the business longer than Porter did. My contributions resulted in a product that was different and better than what we started with in the mid 1990s, in some significant ways, including:

- New boundaries on the SDI triangle were supported by correlations between the motive scales and the strength rankings.

- The 7 Motivational Value System regions were revised; most notably the Hub MVS became a smaller region, with a hexagonal (rather than circular) shape.
- The 13 Conflict Sequence regions were also revised, most notably a larger area for the [BRG] Conflict Sequence in the middle.

- More explanatory text for the 7 MVS types and 13 CS types.
- The clarification of connections between the MVS and CS, such as conflict triggers and the path-back from conflict to resolution.
- Clear, memorable, keyword names for the three primary motives under two conditions. People, Performance, and Process when things are going well. Accommodate, Assert, and Analyze when experiencing conflict.
- Significant changes were made to the sets of 28 strengths and overdone strengths – and to their definitions. These were driven by data obtained in my research, then the new items were subject to further validation before publication.
- The connection between behavior and motive was made clearer by the introduction of the Strengths and Reasons content. I wrote example statements that connected each of the 28 strengths to each of 7 MVS types – offering users clarity about a concept that had not been fully developed in Porter's work. The strengths and reasons statements were one of the primary drivers of the development of the SDI 2.0.

THE SDI 2.0

As our business grew, and Bob Tomkinson retired, we expanded the ownership team and gave the CEO role to Kevin Small. With Small on the team we developed the Core Strengths brand and responded to our customers' demand for more digital assessments – and less paper. Our customers also wanted the assessment experience to be available to users on their mobile devices. The card-sort method is not suitable for mobile devices. This fact, along with some concerns that the card-sort was not accurate for people who failed to read the descriptions, or for people who consciously created a picture of an internalized ideal or role expectation, led us to seek a new method.

Q-sorts (card-sorts) originated at about the same time that Porter and Rogers were working together, and they used them to assess differences in people's ideal and actual selves (Rogers, 1961). But Q-sorts in the most recent versions of the Strengths Portrait and Overdone Strengths Portrait instructed people to choose a frame of reference before beginning the Q-sort. Some people chose a

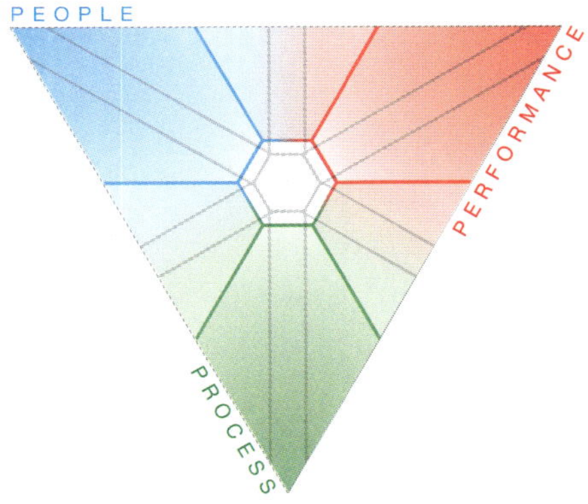

SDI 2.0 Triangle, 2018

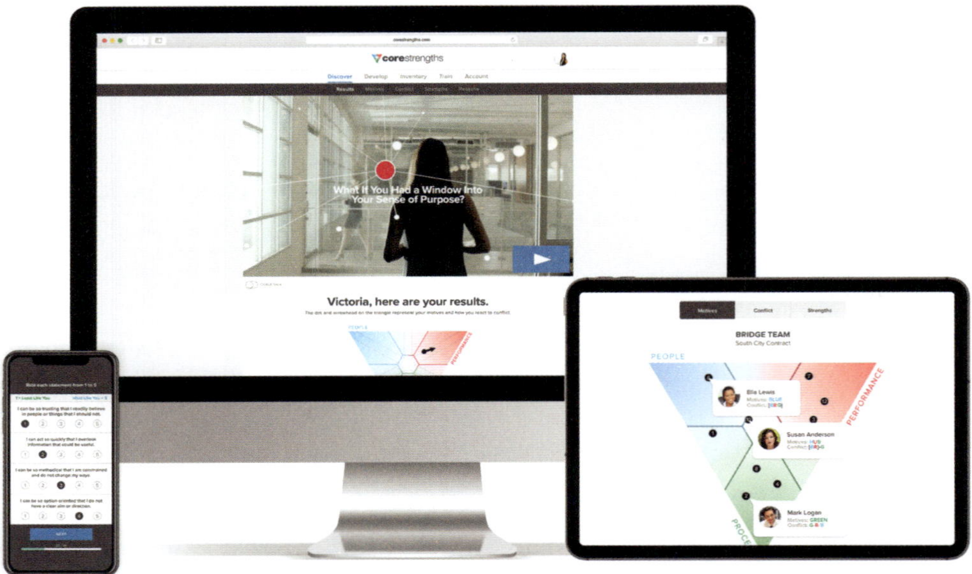

SDI 2.0 and the Core Strengths Platform

broad focus, while others focused on a specific role or situation. We noticed that the greatest utility for our customers was in comparing the core personality of people to the way they deployed, and sometimes overused, their strengths in their work.

I reworked the assessment methodology to produce results that resemble the Q-sort, but which did not present the final result until all the items had been responded to. This differs from Q-methodology, where respondents place strengths directly in the Q-sort template to indicate their relative value. My first version generated too much resistance: about 30% of respondents disagreed with their results (only 70% face validity). I restructured the assessment again, this time presenting sets of four statements that required independent ratings on a 1 to 5 scale, and tie-breaker responses in cases where two or more items were rated equally high or low. In this way, I forced each set of items into a Q-sort where one of the four must be most like the respondent, and one must be least like the respondent, even if all four received the same numerical rating on a Likert scale. From there, I developed an algorithm to produce the ordinal ranking of all 28 strengths and overdone strengths.

Statistics and practical experience convinced me that we now had a better assessment, truly a next generation of the SDI: the SDI 2.0. The SDI 2.0 is now a single assessment that produces the four interrelated views of a person that I referred to in the Author's Note at the beginning: (1) Motivational Value System; (2) Conflict Sequence; (3) Strengths Portrait; and (4) Overdone Strengths Portrait.

The SDI 2.0 requires that people complete all items in the assessment in one sitting. This enables the production of reports that reflect the systemic nature of personality and the dynamic connections between motives and behaviors. Previously, users of the SDI and portraits were left to make their own connections between independent assessments. The SDI 2.0 is a better guide to self-discovery and to personal effectiveness because it helps

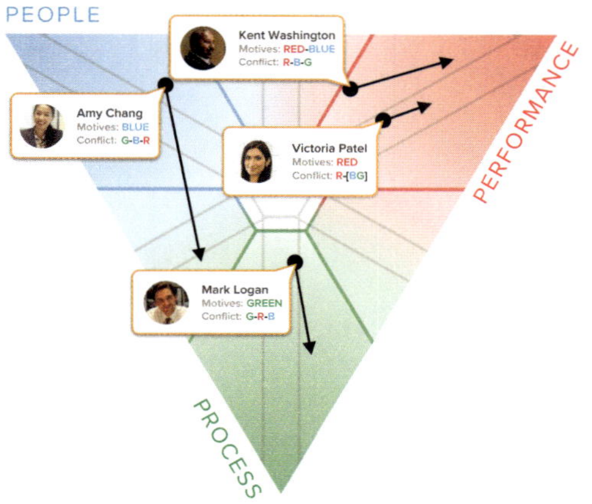

SDI 2.0 Team Triangle, 2018

people to understand themselves more fully and how they apply (or misapply) their strengths at work. In addition to the strengths and reasons content, I wrote longer, narrative descriptions for all 28 strengths and overdone strengths, which help people understand what drives them to deploy their strengths (or overdo them) at work.

The SDI 2.0 also takes advantage of technology to make the results more readily applicable to relationships. The assessment has roots in Porter's Relationship Awareness Theory, but awareness alone doesn't improve relationships. Relationship Intelligence (which we call RQ) is the application of insight to improve interactions and develop authentic interpersonal relationships. The SDI 2.0 is purely a digital assessment scored by algorithm (there is no paper, self-scorable version). Its digital nature means the assessment can serve as the foundation and common language for the digital platform we have created. Not only does the platform empower users to discover their own results, but it also allows users to compare or combine their results with other people's results, for example those of their team members. With the digital platform, the SDI 2.0 finally fulfills the need I have heard from so many customers for so many years: "Help us build an organizational culture where positive relationships flourish, conflict is managed respectfully, and people engage their strengths most productively". The SDI 2.0 satisfies all three of those goals.

As for my role, I still get asked if I am the founder or originator of the SDI. I say "No, but I am the current author." And I like to playfully point out that I was just six years old when the SDI was first introduced, so I would have had to be quite the boy-genius (I was not). As I write this, I am still smiling about what I heard as a customer's accidental word creation. He asked if I was the originator of the SDI. I said "No" with the above explanation. He responded, "So you're not the originator, you're the continuator?" "Yes," I agreed, "I think I am." I didn't think that was a real word. But I liked it – so I checked the dictionary. It's a real word. A "continuator" is a writer who creates new work based on a prior writer's work. That is exactly how I see my role in the development of the SDI 2.0.

REFERENCES

Atkins, S., Katcher, A., & Porter, E. H. (1967). *LIFO: Life Orientations and Strength Excess Profile.* Los Angeles, CA: Atkins-Katcher Associates.

Freud, S. (1932). Libidinal Types. *Psychoanalytic Quarterly,* 1(1), 3-6.

Fromm, E. (1947). *Man for Himself: An inquiry into the psychology of ethics.* New York, NY: Henry Holt and Company.

Fromm, E., & Maccoby, M. (1970). *Social Character in a Mexican Village.* Englewood Cliffs, NJ: Prentice-Hall.

Gordon, T. (2001). *Leader Effectiveness Training.* New York, NY: Berkley Publishing Group.

Horney, K. (1950). *Neurosis and Human Growth: The struggle toward self-realization.* New York, NY: W. W. Norton & Company.

Kirschenbaum, H. (1979). *On Becoming Carl Rogers.* New York, NY: Delacorte Press.

Lewin, K. (1935). *A Dynamic Theory of Personality.* New York: McGraw-Hill.

Maccoby, M. (1976). *The Gamesman.* New York, NY: Simon and Schuster.

Maccoby, M., & Scudder, T. (2018). *The Leaders We Need, and what makes us follow* (Second ed.). Carlsbad, CA: Personal Strengths.

Maddi, S. R. (1996). *Personality Theories* (Sixth ed.). Long Grove, IL: Waveland Press.

Porter, E. H. (1942). *The Development and Evaluation of a Measure of Counseling Interview Procedures.* (Ph.D.), The Ohio State University, Columbus, OH. (0155823)

Porter, E. H. (1943). The Development and Evaluation of a Measure of Counseling Interview Procedures: Part I the development. *Educational and Psychological Measurement,* 3, 105-126.

Porter, E. H. (1950). *An Introduction to Therapeutic Counseling.* Cambridge, MA: The Riverside Press.

Porter, E. H. (1953). *The Person Relatedness Test.* Chicago, IL: Science Research Associates.

Porter, E. H. (1973). *Strength Deployment Inventory: First manual of administration and interpretation.* Pacific Palisades, CA: Personal Strengths Assessment Service.

Porter, E. H. (1985). *Strength Deployment Inventory: Manual of administration and interpretation.* Pacific Palisades, CA: Personal Strengths Publishing.

Porter, E. H. (1986). *Relationship Awareness Basic Course: Facilitator's guide.* Pacific Palisades, CA: Personal Strengths Publishing.

Porter, E. H. (1996). *Relationship Awareness Theory* (Ninth ed.). Carlsbad, CA: Personal Strengths Publishing.

Porter, E. H., & Biel, W. C. (1943). Alleged Regressive Behavior in a Two-Unit Maze. *Journal of Comparative Psychology, 35,* 187-195.

Rogers, C. R. (1951). *Client Centered Therapy.* Boston: Houghton Mifflin.

Rogers, C. R. (1961). *On Becoming a Person.* New York, NY: Houghton Mifflin.

Rogers, C. R., Cornelius-White, J. H. D., & Cornelius-White, C. F. (1986/2005). Reminiscing and Predicting: Rogers' Beyond Words Speech and Commentary. *Journal of Humanistic Psychology, 45.*

Schutz, W. (1958). *FIRO: a Three-Dimensional Theory of Interpersonal Behavior.* New York, NY: Holt, Rinehart and Winston.

Scudder, T. (2013). *Personality Types in Relationship Awareness Theory: The validation of Freud's libidinal types and explication of Porter's motivational typology.* (Doctor of Philosophy Dissertation), Fielding Graduate University, Santa Barbara.

Scudder, T., Patterson, M., & Mitchell, K. (2012). *Have a Nice Conflict.* Jossey Bass: San Francisco, CA.

Stephenson, W. (1935). Correlating Persons Instead of Tests. *Character and Personality,* 4, 17-24.

Suhd, M. (1996). *Positive Regard: Carl Rogers and other notables he influenced.* Palo Alto, CA: Science & Behavior Books.

Sullivan, H. S. (1953). *The Interpersonal Theory of Psychiatry.* New York, NY: W.W. Norton & Company

SDI 2.0 METHODOLOGY AND MEANING

Tim Scudder, PhD

The Strength Deployment Inventory 2.0 (SDI 2.0) is an assessment of human motives and strengths. It stands on the foundation of practical application, scholarship, and research that began with Elias Porter's introduction of the SDI in 1971 and publication of Relationship Awareness Theory (Porter, 1976). The theory has roots in psychoanalysis (Fromm, 1947) and client-centered therapy (Porter, 1950; Rogers, 1951, 1961).

Today the SDI 2.0 offers four views of a person: a Motivational Value System, a Conflict Sequence, a Strengths Portrait, and an Overdone Strengths Portrait. These four views form a systems view of personality and productiveness at work. When personality is considered in the context of relationships, and viewed as a dynamic system, greater explanatory power is available than when personality is viewed as independent variables or dichotomies (Lewin, 1935; Piers, 2000; Sullivan, 1953). In a systems view, the conscious interaction of emotional states, behavior, and motives is an advancement from classic psychoanalytic theory, which holds that motives and drives are largely relegated to the unconscious (Meissner, 2009).

PURPOSE AND FOUNDATIONAL CONCEPTS

To fully understand the methodology and meaning of the SDI 2.0 assessment, the purpose of the assessment must be considered. The SDI 2.0 is based on foundational concepts that lead to specific types of measurement (data collection), scoring, reporting, validity and reliability testing, and the application of assessment results.

The purpose of the SDI 2.0 is to improve the quality of working relationships. People have relationships within themselves, with each other, and with their work. Relationships are psychological connections over time; they have history, the present moment, and expectations for the future (Figure 1). Improving relationships requires beginning with self-awareness. Increased self-awareness results from greater conscious understanding of the true self, and the reduction or removal of defenses against self-understanding. Greater self-awareness enables more clear and accurate understanding of others.

Figure 1 *Relationship Intelligence Model*

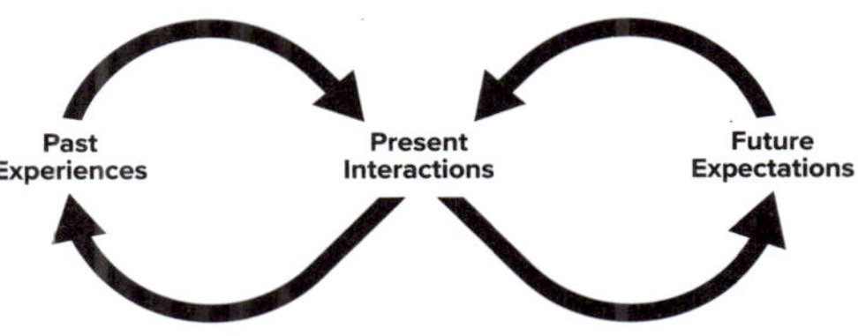

Relationship Intelligence is the application of knowledge in specific settings or contexts to produce results that are meaningful to people in relationships. Relationship Intelligence helps people to:

- better understand past interactions, enabling a deeper understanding and appreciation of self and others
- manage choices and perceptions in the present moment, enabling more

effective behavior and communication in relationships

- anticipate the thoughts, feelings, and actions of others, giving them greater control over the future outcomes of their relationships

These skills are essential to creating collaborative communities that foster learning, development, and authentic connections to others and to work.

Personality Type and Traits

Personality is broadly defined as the set of stable tendencies and characteristics that influence people's thoughts, feelings, and actions across all types of situations (Maddi, 1996; Weiner & Greene, 2008). Personality is not easy to classify. As Kluckhohn and Murray (1948) noted, every person is like every other person in some regards; every person is like some other persons in some regards; and every person is unique in some ways. Personality types are the result of theory and analysis that describe that middle ground, the way that people share characteristics with some, but not all, other people. The assignment of a type to a person as the result of a personality assessment in no way invalidates the uniqueness of a person. Instead, it helps to provide a frame of reference to anticipate people's thoughts, feelings, and actions. People with the same personality type may still have uniquely personal traits.

Motives

Motives are the primary determinants of personality types described by SDI 2.0 results. There are three primary motives, which are experienced differently in two emotional states: 1) when things are going well and 2) when there is conflict. Motives are purposive in nature; they are the underlying drives or reasons that energize a person to think, feel, or act in various ways as they relate to others.

Three primary motives are present in every person in both conditions, but in varying degrees. When things are going well, three primary motives work together in each person to form a Motivational Value System. When people experience conflict, these motives take on a different quality and are accessed in a predictable pattern, termed a

Table 1 *Motives in Two Conditions*

Motive	Color	Well State Keyword and Meaning of Motive	Conflict State Keyword and Meaning of Motive
Nurturant	Blue	People Actively seeking to help others	Accommodate Drive to preserve or restore harmony
Directive	Red	Performance Actively seeking opportunities to achieve results	Assert Drive to prevail over another person or obstacle
Autonomous	Green	Process Actively seeking logical orderliness and self-reliance	Analyze Drive to conserve resources and assure independence

Conflict Sequence. Table 1 shows the three motives under two conditions, along with the color-codes and keywords that are used in SDI 2.0 assessment results.

Fulfilling a motive in a well-state contributes to feelings of self-worth, while the restriction of a motive in a well-state may trigger a shift to the conflict state. Fulfilling a motive in the conflict state can trigger a return to the well state, but the restriction of a motive in the conflict state may trigger a shift to another stage of conflict. The connections between these two independent states create a large number of dynamic types, which are further explained in the report generation section.

Strengths

The SDI 2.0 presents a prioritized set of 28 strengths to each respondent. Strengths are behaviors that are driven by underlying motives and productive intentions. Strengths are generally valued and appreciated in the context of relationships. The 28 strengths (and their overdone counterparts) in the SDI 2.0 should be viewed as part of an overall personality theory. Elias Porter's initial work with strengths was inspired by Erich Fromm's (1947) lists of positive and negative aspects of personality types. Porter refined the lists of strengths through his own research and practical application. More recent research (Scudder, 2013) drove further changes to the 28 strengths that improved their validity, reliability, and usefulness in the present version, the SDI 2.0.

Strengths may also be viewed as traits. Each strength has a connection with motives and personality type. But strengths, because they are behaviors, are freely chosen by people as they consider their situations, goals, and relationships. Desires and beliefs help to explain action and give it meaning (Rosenberg, 2008). The application of strengths is variable across situations. There are correlations with personality, but strengths alone are not the essence of personality. Instead, strengths are the ways that individuals express their core motives through action.

Overdone Strengths

The SDI 2.0 also presents a prioritized set of 28 overdone strengths, which are the nonproductive counterparts to the strengths (Fromm, 1947). Because strengths are driven by motives, and motives are purposive, people expect their strengths to produce desired results. When desired results are not achieved, people may try a little harder, with the expectation that more effort with the same strength will produce the desired result. This is how people can sometimes get over-invested in their strengths, to the point that an overdone strength can limit their effectiveness or create tension or conflict in relationships.

Bringing awareness of the implications, or effects, of overdone strengths to people helps them manage the frequency, duration, intensity, or context (Livson & Nichols, 1957) of the behavior for greater effectiveness. It also helps them make more informed decisions about what other strengths they could use in various situations and relationships. SDI 2.0 results bring overdone strengths into conscious awareness and gives people the power to improve their relationships and their effectiveness.

The Present Study

In addition to reviewing the methodology and summarizing relevant past research, the present study reports the results of 12,565 SDI 2.0 assessments. The population is comprised of working adults, predominantly from large, multinational, US-based corporations, who participated in Core Strengths Results through Relationships training programs in late 2018 and early 2019. No data regarding age, gender, ethnicity, or other demographics were collected, and no effort was made to control for other mediating variables such as role or industry.

DATA COLLECTION AND SCORING

The methods of collecting data are influenced by the underlying phenomena to be measured and the application to which the results are to be used. Given the focus on motives as the primary determinants of personality, and that personality is stable across all types of situations, the motives section of the SDI 2.0 asks people to assume a whole-life perspective and think about themselves in all types of situations as they complete the assessment. The strengths section requires that the respondent adopt a change in mindset. Given that strengths are behaviors, and therefore not necessarily consistent across situations, respondents are directed to think about workplace situations when they complete the strengths section of SDI 2.0. This is because the results from the strengths section of the assessment are used primarily in work situations, but need to be connected to the underlying personality and motives of the person doing the work.

Motives: Whole-Life Perspective

The motives section of the SDI 2.0 is a 60-item, dual-state, ipsative assessment. Respondents assume a whole-life perspective as they respond to two groups of items, one for each state: 1) when things are going well, and 2) the experience of conflict. Each state has three scales and the sum of scale scores for each state must be 100. Items are presented in sets of three via sentence stems that require respondents to allocate 10 points among three different sentence endings to show how frequently the different endings describe them. The range of possible responses for each item is zero to 10. The range of possible scores on each scale is from zero to 100.

The scale scores from the going well section of the SDI are used to identify one of seven personality types called Motivational Value Systems (MVS). The scale scores from the conflict section of the SDI are used to identify one of 13 personality types called Conflict Sequences (CS). Each respondent's scores are associated with two types, an MVS and a CS. There are 91 (7 x 13) possible dynamic types.

The ipsative data collection method mirrors the underlying phenomena that it measures. Each person is assumed to have all three core motives in varying degrees. The ipsative items force respondents to allocate points in a manner that represents the interplay between the three motives. The 100 point totals, allocated among three scale scores, facilitate the presentation of results in familiar manners, such as percentages. The fact that every respondent must have the same total score also facilitates comparison between many individuals. It removes the discrepancies often associated with other methods, such as Likert scales, where some people frequently give maximum scores, but others rarely give maximum scores.

Strengths: Work Perspective

In the strengths section of the SDI 2.0 respondents assume a mindset based on their current work role and environment. The intent is to focus the respondent on the work environment, where they are most likely to apply the results of the assessment. There are 56 strengths statements, which respondents rate using a five-point Likert scale. Statements are presented in sets of four; each set has a strength that correlates to the Blue, Red, Green, and Hub MVS types. There are 14 sets of four statements, seven of which are productive statements of strength, and seven of which contain non-productive, overdone statements. Within each set, respondents must first choose 1 through 5 from Likert scales. Then, if two or more items are rated equally high or equally low, forced-choice tiebreakers are presented. This method ensures that respondents must choose one statement that is most like them and one statement that is least like them from every set of four. Each set of four statements yields six data elements, the four Likert-scale responses, and an ipsative component that identifies the in-set statements that are most-like, and least-like the respondent. A proprietary scoring algorithm is applied to the responses, which yields an ordinal ranking of 28 strengths, and 28 overdone strengths.

Analysis of Ordinal Data

Ipsative, Likert-scale, and forced-choice data collection methods produce ordinal, not interval, data. Respondents' scores indicate preferences or relative weightings among possible responses, but the preferences (even on Likert scales) do not have fixed intervals. For example the difference between 2 and 3 on a Likert scale is not exactly the same as the distance between 3 and 4. In fact two items could have a response of 3, but on one the respondent could have wavered between 2 and 3, while they wavered between 3 and 4 on the other. In this case, the two responses of 3 are not equal from a psychological perspective. However, research conducted with a Likert scale version of the SDI demonstrated a strong positive correlation with the ipsative version's scales (Barney, 1996).

Parametric methods are meant to be applied to interval data, and non-parametric methods applied to ordinal data. But parametric methods yield similar results to non-parametric methods when applied to ordinal data, especially with large populations and when data are distributed roughly normally (Rust & Golombok, 2008; Warner, 2008). Analysis of SDI 2.0 data shows normal distributions with large population samples, therefore, parametric methods, such as the calculation of means and standard deviations, are appropriately applied to SDI 2.0 data.

REPORT GENERATION

The SDI 2.0 gives four interrelated views of a person that are informed by numerical results.

1. Motivational Value System
2. Conflict Sequence
3. Strengths Portrait, and
4. Overdone Strengths Portrait

Motivational Value System

The three scores from the going-well section indicate a Motivational Value System type as defined by the criteria in Table 2. These mathematical definitions correspond with regions on the SDI Triangle (Figure 2). The triangle is comprised of three scales, from 0 to 100, that intersect at 33⅓. The MVS boundaries on the triangle are set at decimal locations, which ensure that no set of scores can be on a border, because all scores must be whole numbers.

Each individual set of three going-well scores is represented by a dot on the triangle. The location of the dot's center is determined by the intersection of all three scores. Every point on the triangle represents a unique set of three numbers that add to 100. There are 5,151 possible locations for an MVS dot on the triangle (which is the sum of all integers between 1 and 101). If an MVS dot is within 6 points of any border (which is the test-retest reliability of the scales), additional guidance regarding the neighboring MVS region is reported. Figure 3 shows a dot in the Blue MVS with a test-retest reliability circle that crosses into the Blue-Green MVS.

Conflict Sequence

The three scores from the conflict section indicate a Conflict Sequence type as defined by the criteria in Table 3.

The triangle has two sets of boundaries, but uses the same three scales to determine the location of an arrowhead's point, which represents the Conflict Sequence. The mathematical definitions correspond with 13 regions on the SDI Triangle (Figure 4). There are also 5,151 possible locations for the arrowhead.

Figure 2
SDI Triangle with Three Scales and Seven MVS Types

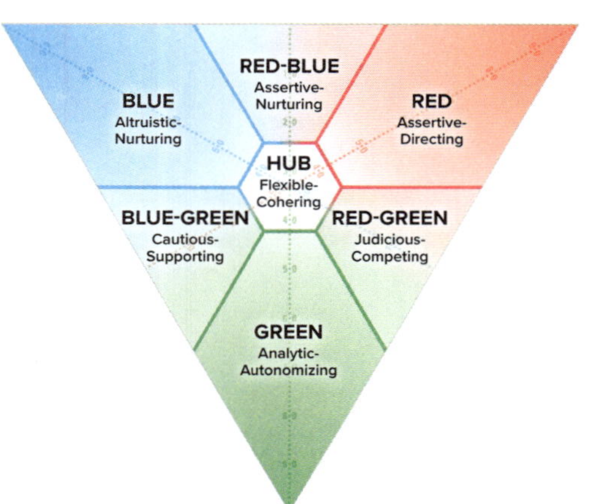

Figure 3
Visual Example of Test Retest Reliability

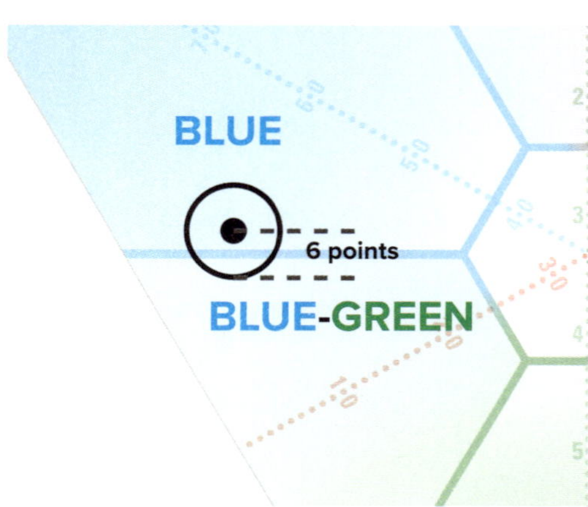

Table 2 *Mathematical Definitions of MVS Types*

MVS Type	Well Blue	Well Red	Well Green
Blue / Altruistic-Nurturing	WB > 42.3	WR < 33.3	WG < 33.3
Red / Assertive-Directing	WB < 33.3	WR > 42.3	WG < 33.3
Green / Analytic-Autonomizing	WB < 33.3	WR < 33.3	WG > 42.3
Red-Blue / Assertive-Nurturing	WB > 33.3	WR > 33.3	WG < 24.3
Red-Green / Judicious-Competing	WB < 24.3	WR > 33.3	WG > 33.3
Blue-Green / Cautious-Supporting	WB > 33.3	WR < 24.3	WG > 33.3
Hub / Flexible-Cohering	24.3 < WB < 42.3	24.3 < WR < 42.3	24.3 < WG < 42.3

Each bounded region of the triangle delineates an area where scores have the same pattern. Six regions show clear, three-stage Conflict Sequences with a different color at each stage. Three regions have a bracketed Stage 1 and 2, with a clear Stage 3. Three regions have a clear Stage 1 with brackets for Stages 2 and 3. One region, the small hexagon in the center, has a bracket including all three colors in all three stages. The brackets indicate scores that are close together. The practical significance of brackets in a Conflict Sequence is that brackets indicate a personal choice between two or more alternatives at the indicated stage(s) of conflict.

When the Motivational Value System and Conflict Sequence are presented on the SDI triangle together, the dot and arrowhead are joined by a line to indicate that the two results are associated with one person. Several individuals may be presented together on the same triangle. (Figure 5). The three scores for the going-well scales must equal 100, as must the

Figure 4
SDI Triangle with Three Scales and Conflict Sequence Regions

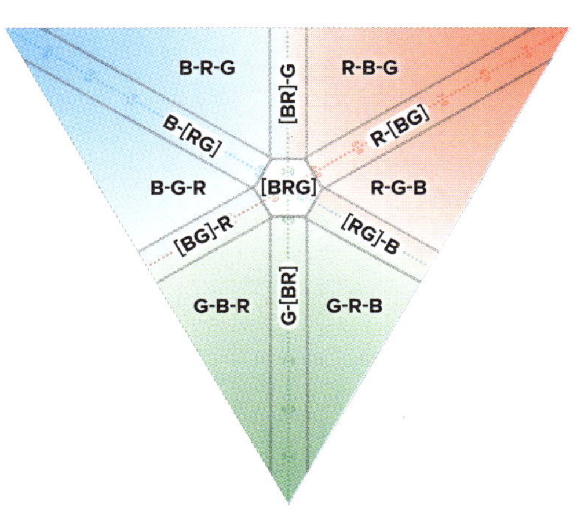

Figure 5
SDI Triangle with Three Example Arrows

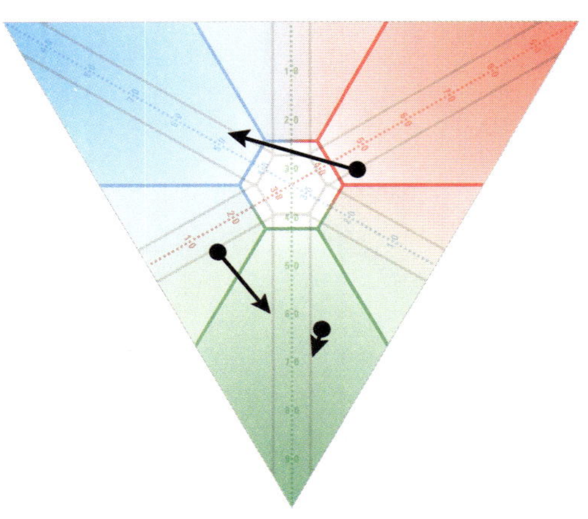

Table 3 *Mathematical Definitions of CS Types*

CS Type	Conflict Blue	Conflict Red	Conflict Green	Other TEST(s)
B-R-G	CB > 39.3	-	CG < 27.3	CB-CR > 6.3 CR-CG > 6.3
B-G-R	CB > 39.3	CR < 27.3	-	CB-CG > 6.3 CG-CR > 6.3
B-[RG]	CB > 39.3	-	-	ABS(CR-CG) < 6.3
R-B-G	-	CR > 39.3	CG < 27.3	CR-CB > 6.3 CB-CG > 6.3
R-G-B	CB < 27.3	CR > 39.3	-	CR-CG > 6.3 CG-CB > 6.3
R-[BG]	-	CR > 39.3	-	ABS(CB-CG) < 6.3
G-B-R	-	CR < 27.3	CG > 39.3	CG-CB > 6.3 CB-CR > 6.3
G-R-B	CB < 27.3	-	CG > 39.3	CG-CR > 6.3 CR-CB > 6.3
G-[BR]	-	-	CG > 39.3	ABS(CB-CR) < 6.3
[RB]-G	-	-	CG < 27.3	ABS(CB-CR) < 6.3
[RG]-B	CB < 27.3	-	-	ABS(CR-CG) < 6.3
[BG]-R	-	CR < 27.3	-	ABS(CB-CG) < 6.3
[BRG]	27.3 < CB < 39.3	27.3 < CR < 39.3	27.3 < CG < 39.3	-

Table 4 *Cross-Tabulation of MVS and CS Types: Percentages*

CS Type	Blue	Red	Green	Red-Blue	Red-Green	Blue-Green	Hub	Total
B-R-G	0.26	0.04	0.01	0.32	0.00	0.04	0.09	0.76
B-G-R	4.60	0.16	0.19	1.39	0.01	1.69	1.13	9.19
B-[RG]	1.20	0.13	0.02	0.81	0.03	0.29	0.56	3.04
R-B-G	0.14	0.21	0.01	0.37	0.01	0.00	0.11	0.86
R-G-B	0.31	2.16	0.44	0.81	0.70	0.22	1.59	6.24
R-[BG]	0.34	0.84	0.07	0.78	0.11	0.09	0.70	2.93
G-B-R	4.67	0.75	1.77	1.80	0.28	3.81	5.10	18.17
G-R-B	0.83	1.78	2.11	1.04	1.00	1.08	3.67	11.51
G-[BR]	2.17	1.00	1.93	1.83	0.62	2.04	5.86	15.45
[BR]-G	0.31	0.09	0.02	0.56	0.00	0.05	0.22	1.26
[RG]-B	0.49	1.79	0.66	1.28	0.69	0.45	2.70	8.06
[BG]-R	3.92	0.43	0.52	1.61	0.08	1.93	3.16	11.66
[BRG]	1.72	1.18	0.39	2.16	0.08	0.73	4.61	10.89
Total	20.96	10.56	8.14	14.74	3.62	12.43	29.54	100.00

n=9,798

Table 5 *Line Length and Practical Significance*

Line Length		Change in Motives from MVS to Stage 1 Conflict
From	*To*	
0	10	Can be difficult to detect by self and others
> 10	25	Somewhat noticeable by self and others
> 25	-	Usually obvious to self and others

three scores for the conflict scales. But the two sets of scales are independent; one set does not predict or control the other. The MVS dot can be anywhere on the triangle, and the CS arrowhead can be anywhere on the triangle. Therefore, from a typology perspective, 91 dynamic types are possible (7 MVS x 13 CS). But there are many more possible arrows, because there are 5,151 points on the triangle, each of which are used twice for one arrow. This results in 26,531,801 (5,1312) possible unique arrows based on the interplay of three core motives in two affective states.

Table 4 (Scudder, 2013) shows the distribution of all 7 MVS types, all 13 CS types and the 91 possible combinations thereof. The data in this table are assumed to be roughly representative of working adults in the United States because the sample represents a broad cross section of organizations and a wide variety of applications.

A systems view of personality enables explanation of phenomena that are due to the interaction between independent results, as opposed to the static-state views that are most common in personality theory and testing. The connections between the MVS and the CS are used in report generation to provide additional information to respondents, such as the length of the line and ideas about how to resolve conflict. Each respondent receives one of 49 descriptions that connect the motives in one of seven Stage 1 conflict states to one of 7 MVS types as an example of conflict resolution. Each respondent also receives information about the length of the line connecting the MVS dot and the CS arrowhead, per Table 5.

Summary of Report Generation or Motive Scales

Each respondent receives their individual scale scores, along with an arrow drawn on the SDI triangle, which is a graphic representation of the scale scores. Explanatory text for the Motivational Value System is offered based on one of seven possibilities. Explanatory text for the Conflict Sequence is offered based on one of 13 possibilities. There are 91 permutations of explanatory text for the MVS and CS. Additional explanatory text is offered based on the whether results are close to another type, and connections between the results. All of these variables work together to inform a report generation process that describes personality as a system of motives under two conditions.

Strengths and Overdone Strengths

The results from the work-focused, strengths section of the SDI 2.0 are used to produce two portraits of the way respondents deploy their strengths. The Strengths Portrait, and variations of it, present the positive, productive strengths in an array from most likely to deploy to least likely to deploy. The Overdone Strengths Portrait, and its variations, similarly display the overdone strengths that may limit respondents' effectiveness at work or cause difficulty in working relationships. Respondents' work roles are identified on the strengths reports, but the roles are omitted from the reports that describe personality, because personality applies across multiple situations and the strengths reports are based on the work environment.

The SDI 2.0 reports 28 strengths, and 28 overdone strengths, in rank order. The data are normally distributed, and are presented to respondents in a graphical format that resembles a normal curve. The display format is derived from Q-methodology (Stephenson, 1953/1975). It shows the items of most significance in the two tails of the normal curve. Strengths (or Overdone Strengths) near the top of the portrait are most like respondents to deploy at work, and those at the bottom are least like them to deploy at work. Strengths on the same line have underlying scores that are close to each other, which suggests that respondents deploy those strengths at about equal levels. Figure 6 presents the standard portrait template, along with a transformation of the template under the normal curve.

The top strengths, and overdone strengths, are most significant. Detailed interpretive text is provided for the top strengths, while limited interpretive text is provided for the remaining strengths.

Strengths and Reasons

Behavior is the result of purposive striving towards personally meaningful goals. In simpler terms, motives drive behavior. Therefore, the work-focused, strengths results of the SDI 2.0 have greater explanatory power when combined with personality results. Each of the 28 strengths may be connected to any of the seven Motivational Value Systems. People with different personality types can deploy the same strength at work, but for different reasons.

SDI 2.0 results take this into account by presenting a view of strengths informed by the most likely reasons to use those strengths,

Figure 6 *Portrait Template and the Normal Curve*

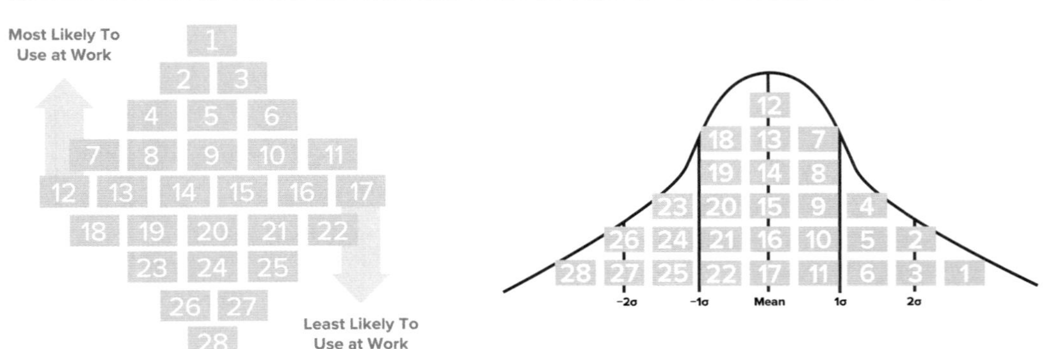

Table 6 *The Methodical Strength and Example Reasons to Deploy It*

Strength	Blue MVS Reason	Red MVS Reason	Green MVS Reason	Hub MVS Reason
Methodical I am orderly in action, thought, and expression...	...to create a structure that will benefit people.	...to establish a standard to evaluate performance.	...to give the process a chance to work as intended.	...to be sure we have considered all perspectives.

Table 7 *SDI 2.0 Motive Scales Descriptive Statistics*

Test	Well Blue	Well Red	Well Green	Conflict Blue	Conflict Red	Conflict Green
Mean	36.6	31.6	31.8	29.0	27.0	44.0
Std. Dev	10.4	11.3	10.9	11.9	12.4	11.3
Min	0	0	0	0	0	0
Max	100	100	93	100	100	100
Skew	.397	.150	.475	.468	.431	.382
Kurtosis	1.437	.762	1.232	1.074	.721	.862

n=9,798

based on respondents' MVS. Table 6 shows four sample reasons to use one strength.

The number of possible variations of the Strengths Portrait and Overdone Strengths Portrait is so large that for practical purposes, the number is almost infinite. There are 28-factorial possible ordinal rankings, with 7 MVS overlays. The formula for possible permutations is therefore 7(28!). This method and systems view of personality situated in a work context ensures a truly personalized report for each respondent.

DESCRIPTIVE STATISTICS

SDI 2.0 data are roughly normally distributed on all scales. Descriptive statistics for scales or results are presented in Tables 7, 8, and 9.

The motives scales descriptive statistics show that the data are roughly normally distributed and have similar patterns to prior studies (Barney, 1998; Cunningham, 2004; Porter, 1973; Scudder, 2013).

Tables 8 and 9 show the descriptive statistics for strength and overdone strength rankings. 1 represents the strength most likely to be deployed at work and 28 represents the strength least likely to be deployed at work. Both tables demonstrate that the strengths are about normally distributed across a large population.

As shown by the descriptive statistics. Large populations of SDI 2.0 data are roughly normally distributed and it is therefore appropriate to apply parametric methods to evaluate the validity and reliability of the assessment (Rust & Golombok, 2008; Warner, 2008).

VALIDITY AND RELIABILITY

In personality assessment, validity is about whether the results are true and accurate, while reliability is about consistency, or repeatability of the findings. Statistically speaking, the least important form of validity is face-validity, whether the respondent agrees with the results. However, face-validity is the most important aspect for users of the results. If the results are not presented in a way that rings true for the users, they will not accept or apply the results, and the assessment effort will be wasted.

Achieving face validity is an art with a scientific foundation. The SDI 2.0 uses valid and reliable data, along with grounded theory, to inform internally consistent descriptions of results that resonate for the users. The SDI 2.0

Table 8 *Strengths Portrait Ranking Descriptive Statistics*

ID	Strength	Mean	Std. Dev.	Min	Max	Skew	Kurtosis
B1	Supportive	9.9	6.5	1	28	0.586	-0.426
B2	Caring	11.1	7.1	1	28	0.456	-0.754
B3	Devoted	15.9	7.6	1	28	-0.196	-1.058
B4	Modest	13.5	8.4	1	28	0.131	-1.179
B5	Helpful	11.6	7.0	1	28	0.320	-0.921
B6	Loyal	12.1	6.6	1	28	0.227	-0.784
B7	Trusting	17.0	7.5	1	28	-0.331	-0.900
R1	Risk-Taking	20.9	7.2	1	28	-1.138	0.271
R2	Competitive	19.4	8.1	1	28	-0.804	-0.582
R3	Quick-to-Act	16.1	7.9	1	28	-0.335	-1.100
R4	Forceful	20.1	7.4	1	28	-0.994	-0.112
R5	Persuasive	17.7	8.1	1	28	-0.513	-0.962
R6	Ambitious	18.2	7.9	1	28	-0.628	-0.830
R7	Self-Confident	13.9	8.0	1	28	-0.022	-1.235
G1	Persevering	15.2	7.3	1	28	-0.227	-1.000
G2	Fair	11.7	6.5	1	28	-0.288	-0.731
G3	Principled	14.0	7.4	1	28	0.001	-1.084
G4	Analytical	14.0	8.4	1	28	0.035	-1.300
G5	Methodical	13.4	8.1	1	28	0.053	-1.202
G6	Reserved	16.8	9.0	1	28	-0.353	-1.274
G7	Cautious	14.9	7.6	1	28	-0.074	-1.061
H1	Option-Oriented	12.7	7.1	1	28	0.154	-1.045
H2	Tolerant	11.7	6.7	1	28	0.387	-0.722
H3	Adaptable	11.4	7.1	1	28	0.320	-0.900
H4	Inclusive	12.6	7.2	1	28	0.183	-0.979
H5	Sociable	13.7	8.9	1	28	0.088	-1.410
H6	Open-to-Change	12.2	7.4	1	28	0.243	-1.107
H7	Flexible	14.1	7.3	1	28	0.040	-1.045

n=12,565

has extremely high face-validity. Respondents have a near universal acceptance of their results; it is rare to encounter a person who disagrees strongly with their SDI 2.0 results.

Validity

In addition to high face validity, the motives and strengths results exhibit construct validity, concurrent validity and differential validity. See Scudder (2013) for support for these claims, which are summarized below.

- Construct Validity: The results are conceptually consistent with the underlying theories and descriptions of personality types found in the work of Freud (1932), Fromm (1947) and Porter (1976). In other words, the SDI measures what it claims to measure.
- Concurrent Validity: Independent measures of motives and strengths have strong and statistically significant correlations that are consistent with the underlying typologies. Extensive factor analysis further confirmed the

Table 9 *Overdone Strengths Portrait Ranking Descriptive Statistics*

ID	Overdone Strength	Mean	Std. Dev.	Min	Max	Skew	Kurtosis
B1	Self-Sacrificing	9.4	7.4	1	28	0.691	-0.610
B2	Submissive	14.1	7.6	1	28	0.033	-1.191
B3	Subservient	16.2	7.8	1	28	-0.226	-1.101
B4	Self-Effacing	8.9	7.5	1	28	0.882	-0.271
B5	Smothering	14.8	7.5	1	28	-0.110	-1.115
B6	Blind	12.7	6.8	1	28	0.202	-0.859
B7	Gullible	15.2	8.1	1	28	-0.038	-1.247
R1	Reckless	18.6	7.8	1	28	-0.565	-0.845
R2	Aggressive	18.3	8.8	1	28	-0.536	-1.166
R3	Rash	12.4	7.6	1	28	0.285	-1.086
R4	Domineering	17.4	8.3	1	28	-0.339	-1.185
R5	Abrasive	16.6	8.1	1	28	-0.326	-1.210
R6	Ruthless	19.9	7.4	1	28	-0.888	-0.279
R7	Arrogant	11.3	8.0	1	28	0.439	-1.083
G1	Stubborn	11.2	7.0	1	28	0.384	-0.922
G2	Cold	15.0	7.3	1	28	-0.206	-0.988
G3	Unbending	14.2	7.4	1	28	-0.019	-1.064
G4	Obsessed	13.5	7.9	1	28	0.103	-1.102
G5	Rigid	13.9	7.8	1	28	0.030	-1.174
G6	Distant	15.8	8.8	1	28	-0.115	-1.366
G7	Suspicious	15.3	8.3	1	28	-0.117	-1.286
H1	Indecisive	15.5	7.1	1	28	-0.130	-0.990
H2	Indifferent	14.6	7.6	1	28	0.009	-1.167
H3	Compliant	11.4	7.0	1	28	0.393	-0.880
H4	Indiscriminate	15.6	6.5	1	28	-0.177	-0.684
H5	Intrusive	15.9	8.2	1	28	-0.264	-1.129
H6	Inconsistent	13.8	7.1	1	28	0.042	-0.955
H7	Unpredictable	14.7	7.2	1	28	-0.069	-0.970

n=12,565

relationships between the concurrent measures.

- Differential Validity: Members of each MVS type deploy strengths in a pattern that is more like their type than the strength deployment patterns of other types. The differences between types were identified by comparing mean strength scores for each MVS type against the population and validated by t-tests showing statistically significant differences in population means.

Differential Validity is also useful in practical application, because it helps to clarify the differences between types of people and to identify patterns that explain types. Tables 10 and 11 present the ordinal rankings of strengths and overdone strengths, by each MVS type. The ordinal rankings go from 1 (most typical) to 28 (least typical). The mean rankings were calculated by averaging the ordinal rankings of all portrait results of people in each MVS type.

Given that the MVS is a measure of personality, and the Strengths Portrait and Overdone Strengths Portrait reflect the deployment of strengths in specific roles, the work context is a mediating variable between motive and behavior. No attempt has been made to control for this mediating variable in the descriptive differential analysis in Tables 10 and 11. However, clear patterns are identifiable in the data that differentiate MVS types by the patterns of strengths that are most and least likely to be deployed in working relationships. As indicated by Tables 10 and 11, Strengths of each color are generally most likely to be deployed (lowest numbers in bold) by people with that color MVS, and least likely to be deployed (highest numbers in bold italics) by people with the two-color blended MVS on the opposite side of the triangle. For example, people with a Blue MVS are most likely to deploy the Blue strength Caring at work (mean of 6.9), while people with a Red-Green MVS are least likely to deploy Caring at work (mean of 18.1). People with a Hub MVS do not show clear preferences or patterns, which is one of the defining characteristics of the Hub MVS.

Reliability

The test-retest, or repeated measures, reliability of the SDI's motives scales is +/- 6 points. This means that the majority of scale scores do not change enough to alter the basic understanding or interpretation of the results. However, there are some sets of scores that change on retest more than the stated metric. This is normal for test-retest calculations. Table 12 reports the retest reliability measures from three studies. Porter's (1973) study used the Pearsonian coefficient, while Barney's (1998) and Cunningham's (2004) studies reported Cronbach's alpha.

The internal reliability of the motive scales is presented in Table 13, along with comparable data from an earlier study (Scudder, 2013). Both studies report the Cronbach's Alpha values. Each item comprising the SDI scales was evaluated to determine the effect on the internal reliability of the scales if the item were deleted.

Table 10 *Strength Means by MVS*

ID	Strength	Blue MVS	Red-Blue MVS	Red MVS	Red-Green MVS	Green MVS	Blue-Green MVS	HUB MVS
B1	Supportive	6.6	8.4	12.9	15.2	12.9	8.9	10.2
B2	Caring	6.9	8.7	14.6	18.1	15.1	9.7	11.5
B3	Devoted	12.7	15.7	18.7	18.9	17.5	14.2	16.5
B4	Modest	11.2	15.4	18.2	16.3	12.1	10.1	13.7
B5	Helpful	8.0	10.9	15.8	16.7	14.1	9.6	11.9
B6	Loyal	10.3	12.0	14.2	14.9	12.6	10.7	12.4
B7	Trusting	13.5	15.3	19.3	21.9	20.5	15.8	17.6
R1	Risk-Taking	22.9	19.0	15.8	17.4	22.2	23.8	21.0
R2	Competitive	22.7	18.3	13.9	14.1	19.6	23.2	19.1
R3	Quick-to-Act	16.4	14.3	13.1	14.9	17.6	18.0	16.5
R4	Forceful	23.1	19.3	14.0	14.5	20.2	23.6	20.1
R5	Persuasive	20.9	14.3	10.7	13.5	19.5	22.7	17.6
R6	Ambitious	20.9	17.6	12.6	13.2	18.5	21.5	17.9
R7	Self-Confident	17.5	12.9	8.6	9.3	13.0	17.8	13.5
G1	Persevering	17.3	16.0	13.6	12.4	13.3	15.4	15.1
G2	Fair	12.3	13.2	13.2	11.4	9.5	10.8	11.3
G3	Principled	14.5	15.8	15.1	12.7	11.5	12.8	13.9
G4	Analytical	16.8	18.0	15.5	10.1	8.8	11.9	13.4
G5	Methodical	15.7	17.2	14.4	8.9	8.8	11.8	13.0
G6	Reserved	16.4	22.0	22.5	17.1	11.4	11.3	16.9
G7	Cautious	15.5	20.2	20.2	13.5	9.6	10.7	14.5
H1	Option-Oriented	13.7	12.7	12.2	11.9	11.9	13.3	12.6
H2	Tolerant	10.8	12.7	14.0	14.2	11.6	9.8	11.7
H3	Adaptable	11.9	11.2	10.9	11.6	11.6	12.2	11.1
H4	Inclusive	11.2	10.0	12.8	15.6	15.5	14.2	12.5
H5	Sociable	12.4	9.4	10.6	16.8	18.4	17.2	14.0
H6	Open-to-Change	11.3	11.3	13.0	14.5	13.5	12.2	12.3
H7	Flexible	12.8	14.2	15.7	16.4	15.2	12.9	14.2

n=12,565

Table 11 *Overdone Strength Means by MVS*

ID	Overdone Strength	Blue MVS	Red-Blue MVS	Red MVS	Red-Green MVS	Green MVS	Blue-Green MVS	HUB MVS
B1	Self-Sacrificing	5.8	8.1	13.4	15.3	12.5	7.6	9.5
B2	Submissive	9.9	13.7	18.1	19.8	16.9	11.5	14.7
B3	Subservient	12.8	15.7	18.9	20.1	18.5	14.0	16.8
B4	Self-Effacing	7.1	10.3	12.8	11.5	8.3	6.6	8.9
B5	Smothering	11.9	13.3	17.2	18.5	17.5	13.8	15.3
B6	Blind	10.9	11.9	14.1	15.6	13.9	11.9	13.1
B7	Gullible	11.8	13.0	17.2	19.8	18.9	14.7	15.6
R1	Reckless	20.5	16.8	14.1	15.6	19.7	21.8	18.6
R2	Aggressive	22.2	17.1	12.4	12.6	18.4	22.8	17.7
R3	Rash	12.2	9.8	9.7	13.0	14.8	14.8	12.6
R4	Domineering	21.6	16.1	11.1	11.4	16.9	21.9	17.0
R5	Abrasive	20.3	13.8	9.9	11.4	17.6	21.7	16.4
R6	Ruthless	23.0	19.8	14.0	14.3	19.5	23.0	19.8
R7	Arrogant	15.0	9.5	6.0	7.8	10.9	15.7	10.6
G1	Stubborn	14.2	11.6	8.7	7.8	9.8	12.8	10.6
G2	Cold	17.4	16.6	14.0	11.1	12.0	15.4	14.7
G3	Unbending	15.8	15.8	13.8	11.6	11.6	14.4	13.8
G4	Obsessed	14.9	16.7	15.1	11.8	9.8	11.4	13.2
G5	Rigid	16.2	17.6	15.0	10.0	9.3	12.3	13.5
G6	Distant	14.7	20.7	21.6	17.0	11.0	10.3	15.9
G7	Suspicious	15.8	19.7	19.4	13.7	10.6	11.4	15.1
H1	Indecisive	15.1	15.8	16.1	15.5	15.0	14.5	15.8
H2	Indifferent	11.9	16.3	18.7	18.4	14.1	11.0	14.9
H3	Compliant	10.3	11.2	13.2	13.7	11.8	10.4	11.4
H4	Indiscriminate	14.9	14.0	15.6	17.1	17.1	16.1	15.7
H5	Intrusive	14.3	12.3	14.5	18.6	19.1	17.8	16.3
H6	Inconsistent	12.3	13.0	14.5	15.9	15.2	13.4	14.0
H7	Unpredictable	13.5	15.4	16.8	17.0	15.5	13.1	14.5

n=12,565

Table 12 *SDI Motive Scales Test-Retest Reliability*

Test	n	Well Blue	Well Red	Well Green	Conflict Blue	Conflict Red	Conflict Green
Porter (1973)	100	.78	.78	.76	n/a	n/a	n/a
Barney (1998)	106	.85	.84	.83	.87	.81	.82
Cunningham (2004)	322	.90	.91	.89	.89	.90	.86

Table 13 *Motive Scales Internal Reliability*

Test	Well Blue	Well Red	Well Green	Conflict Blue	Conflict Red	Conflict Green
Scudder, (2013) n=9,798	.796	.846	.781	.806	.826	.710
Present Study n=12,565	.794	.818	.759	.766	.797	.678

As shown in Table 14, the internal reliability of the scales would be reduced if any set of items was removed from the assessment. This indicates that every set increases the internal reliability. Two items (C16 Green and C20 Blue) would slightly raise the internal reliability if deleted. However, to do so would require the removal of the other in-set responses, which would decrease the overall internal reliability of the assessment.

Table 14 *Motive Scales: Alpha Values if Items Deleted*

	Well-Scales: Items 1 to 10			Conflict-Scales: Items 11 to 20		
Well/Conflict Item	**Well Blue**	**Well Red**	**Well Green**	**Conflict Blue**	**Conflict Red**	**Conflict Green**
W1/C11	.748	.817	.735	.739	.771	.646
W2/C12	.720	.796	.715	.739	.779	.650
W3/C13	.743	.822	.747	.735	.794	.651
W4/C14	.707	.792	.717	.725	.760	.627
W5/C15	.728	.794	.731	.721	.766	.656
W6/C16	.726	.811	.745	.746	.786	**.679**
W7/C17	.730	.784	.725	.746	.780	.658
W8/C18	.714	.793	.723	.724	.777	.633
W9/C19	.735	.798	.739	.745	.781	.636
W10/C20	.735	.808	.731	**.779**	.794	.669

n=12,565

CONCLUSION

Relationship Intelligence and the SDI 2.0 take a whole-life, systems view of personality, and situate the deployment of strengths in a workplace context, based on respondents' roles. The essence of a systems view is that the interaction between elements, such as motives and strengths, is just as important, if not more important, than the elements themselves. The systems view sharply contrasts with approaches to understanding people that isolate variables, and identify traits or types without accounting for emotional states or contexts in which respondents have self-determination. These reductionist approaches result in limiting, impractical measures that may have statistical validity, but lack real-world utility because they do not reflect the true complexity of human experience.

Each of the four views: Motivational Value System, Conflict Sequence, Strengths, and Overdone Strengths, connects with the other three. Figure 7 identifies four of the clearest connections, which are often used in training and development efforts that include the SDI 2.0. The MVS is part of core personality. People's drives, motives, and values influence the way they choose to deploy their strengths at work. The use of strengths at work is most authentic when people deploy their strengths for an underlying reason that resonates with their MVS.

Strengths deployed in relationships at work do not always have the intended effect. This opens up connections with the concept of overdone strengths and consideration of whether the strength was appropriately applied to the task or relationship.

Figure 7
Summary Connections Between Four Views Provided by SDI 2.0

The focus on relationships includes consideration of how strengths are perceived by others. When perceived as overdone, it may trigger conflict in the relationship. Conflict Triggers may also originate with the MVS as events restrict people's motives or go against their values.

The Conflict Sequence is part of core personality, but under a different emotional state than the MVS. Motives during conflict are directed toward addressing the issue at hand in a way that results in resolution and a change to people's emotional states, such that they are working from their MVS again once the conflict is resolved.

The independent variables within the SDI 2.0 produce virtually limitless combinations, which in turn produce deeply personalized reports for respondents. Sound academic theory, coupled with a long history of empirical support, enable the reporting and application of SDI 2.0 results to blend art and science. The methodology of the SDI 2.0 ensures that users receive rich, textured descriptions of personality and strengths at work, which can be applied with confidence to improve the quality of working relationships.

REFERENCES

Barney, A. (1998). *An Examination of the Theoretical Roots and Psychometric Properties of the Strength Deployment Inventory.* (Masters of Philosophy Thesis), Aukland University, Aukland, NZ.

Cunningham, D. (2004). *Strength Deployment Inventory: Reliability and validity executive summary.* California School of Professional Psychology. Alliant International University. San Diego, CA.

Freud, S. (1932). Libidinal Types. *Psychoanalytic Quarterly,* 1(1), 3-6.

Fromm, E. (1947). *Man for Himself: An inquiry into the psychology of ethics.* New York, NY: Henry Holt and Company.

Lewin, K. (1935). *A Dynamic Theory of Personality.* New York: McGraw-Hill.

Livson, N. H., & Nichols, T. F. (1957). Discrimination and Reliability in Q-sort Personality Descriptions. *The Journal of Abnormal and Social Psychology,* 52(2), 159-165.

Murray, H. A., & Kluckhohn, C. (1948). Outline of a Conception of Personality. In C. Kluckhohn & H. A. Murray (Eds.), *Personality in Nature, Society, and Culture* (pp. 3-32). New York, NY: Alfred A Knopf.

Maddi, S. R. (1996). *Personality Theories (Sixth ed.).* Long Grove, IL: Waveland Press.

Meissner, W. W. (2009). The Questions of Drive vs. Motive in Psychoanalysis: A modest proposal. *Journal of the American Psychoanalytic Association,* 57(4), 807-845.

Piers, C. (2000). Character as Self-Organizing Complexity. *Psychoanalysis and Contemporary Thought,* 23, 3-34.

Porter, E. H. (1950). *An Introduction to Therapeutic Counseling.* Cambridge, MA: The Riverside Press.

Porter, E. H. (1973). *Strength Deployment Inventory: First manual of administration and interpretation.* Pacific Palisades, CA: Personal Strengths Assessment Service.

Porter, E. H. (1976). On the Development of Relationship Awareness Theory: A personal note. *Group & Organization Management,* 1(3), 302-309.

Rogers, C. R. (1951). *Client Centered Therapy.* Boston: Houghton Mifflin.

Rogers, C. R. (1961). *On Becoming a Person.* New York, NY: Houghton Mifflin.

Rosenberg, A. (2008). *Philosophy of Social Science* (3rd ed.). Boulder, CO: Westview Press.

Rust, J., & Golombok, S. (2008). *Modern Psychometrics* (Third ed.): Routledge.

Scudder, T. (2013). *Personality Types in Relationship Awareness Theory: The validation of Freud's libidinal types and explication of Porter's motivational typology.* (Doctor of Philosophy Dissertation), Fielding Graduate University, Santa Barbara.

Scudder, T., Porter, E.H. (2018). *SDI 2.0 Strength Deployment Inventory 2.0.* Carlsbad, CA: Personal Strengths Publishing.

Stephenson, W. (1953/1975). *The Study of Behavior: Q-technique and its methodology* (Midway reprint ed.). Chicago, IL: The University of Chicago Press.

Sullivan, H. S. (1953). *The Interpersonal Theory of Psychiatry.* New York, NY: W.W. Norton & Company.

Warner, R. M. (2008). *Applied Statistics: From bivariate through multivariate techniques.* Thousand Oaks, CA: Sage.

Weiner, I. B., & Greene, R. L. (2008). *Handbook of Personality Assessment.* Hoboken, NJ: Wiley.

Notes

Part 1: Introduction

1. The text in this table is slightly modified from Porter's original statement: "When an individual is free to pursue his gratifications, the nurturant motivation takes the form of actively seeking to be helpful to others, the directive motivation takes the form of self-assertion and seeking opportunities to provide leadership (in the conventional sense of leadership), and the autonomizing motivation takes the form of actively seeking logical orderliness and self-reliance. In the face of conflict and opposition, the nurturant motivation is expressed in efforts to preserve and restore harmony, the directive motivation is expressed in efforts to prevail over the other person, and the autonomizing motivation is expressed in efforts to conserve resources and assure independence." Elias H. Porter, "On the Development of Relationship Awareness Theory: A Personal Note," Group & Organization Management 1, no. 3 (1976), 306.

2. This process is consistent with the statement B=f(PE); behavior is a function of the person interacting with that person's environment. Kurt Lewin, A Dynamic Theory of Personality (New York: McGraw-Hill, 1935).

3. Most personality and behavior assessments are based on theories of the individual and base their typologies on behavioral traits, preferences, or factors that have a genetic component. Relationship Awareness Theory defines personality types based on motives in the context of interpersonal relationships. Elias H. Porter, "On the Development of Relationship Awareness Theory: A Personal Note," Group & Organization Management 1, no. 3 (1976), 306.

4. The quote from Goleman was edited for readability and context. The full quote is: "But as I've come to see, simply lumping social intelligence in with the emotional sort stunts fresh thinking about the human aptitude for relationship, ignoring what transpires as we interact. This myopia leaves the "social" part out of intelligence." Daniel Goleman, Social Intelligence, (New York, Bantam Dell, 2007), 83.

5. Definitions of the terms shown in the iceberg model were informed by several sources. New Oxford American Dictionary, Third ed., (New York: Oxford University Press, 2010); Laura Parks and Russell P. Guay, "Personality, Values, and Motivation," Personality and Individual Differences 47 (2009); Salvatore R. Maddi, Personality Theories, Sixth ed., (Long Grove, IL: Waveland Press, 1996); Elias H. Porter, Relationship Awareness Theory, (Carlsbad, CA: Personal Strengths Publishing, 1996); Tim Scudder, ed.

6. Porter credited Erich Fromm with the concept of positive and negative aspects of the same traits for people of different personality types. While Fromm critiqued the non-productive orientations, Porter reframed this concept to begin with strengths. Erich Fromm, Man for Himself: An Inquiry into the Psychology of Ethics, (New York: Henry Holt and Company, 1947); Elias H. Porter, "On the Development of Relationship Awareness Theory: A Personal Note," Group & Organization Management 1, no. 3 (1976), 306.

7. Some authors and assessments define a strength as a theme of talent, skill, or competency. In these schemas, individuals are advised to find situations that fit their strengths - and not be concerned about developing lesser talents. The idea is for people to concentrate on what they do best. While this is good advice for using skills at work, it does not apply to the deployment of strengths in relationships. To be effective in relationships, people need to be able to consciously choose to use strengths that will be effective in various situations and with all different types of other people. For examples of strengths as talents, refer to: Tom Rath, Strengths Finder 2.0 (New York, Gallup, 2007); and Marcus Buckingham, StandOut 2.0 (Harvard Business Review Press, 2015).

8. The attributes of frequency, duration, intensity, and context are often used in training and developmental efforts to describe the manner in which strengths are overdone. This is typically linked to the use of the Overdone Strengths Portrait, but the attributes may also be used to describe expectations of future behavior. For the earliest known reference to this schema see Norman H. Livson and Thomas F. Nichols, "Discrimination and Reliability in Q-Sort Personality Descriptions," The Journal of Abnormal and Social Psychology 52, no. 2 (1957), 159.

9. These terms are all unique to Relationship Awareness Theory. Porter introduced the terms Valued Relating Style, Borrowed Relating Style, and Mask Relating Style. The terms Motivational Value System and Conflict Sequence were not used by Porter, but were introduced after his death (in 1987) to identify concepts he described. Elias H. Porter, Relationship Awareness Theory, (Carlsbad, CA: Personal Strengths Publishing, 1996); Tim Scudder, ed.

10. Conflict has a specific meaning in Relationship Awareness Theory, as do the terms related to conflict. The terms presented in this section build on Porter's concept and are consistent with those used in recent works about conflict. Porter "On the Development"; Tim Scudder, Michael Patterson, and Kent Mitchell, Have a Nice Conflict, (Jossey Bass: San Francisco, CA, 2012). Other definitions of conflict are similar to Relationship Awareness Theory's definition of opposition; for examples see Roger Fisher, William Ury, and Bruce Patton, Getting to Yes, Negotiating Agreement Without Giving In, Second ed., (New York, NY: Penguin Books, 1991); and Kenneth W. Thomas and Ralph H. Kilmann, "Thomas-Kilmann Conflict Mode Instrument," (Mountain View, CA: Consulting Psychologists Press, 2007).

11. Productivity in a business context generally denotes the degree of output that can be produced from available resources. Personal productivity then if often viewed as the amount of work a person can do. However, there are also philosophical views of productivity based on people achieving their potential and relating with others in a manner that promotes personal development. For examples of this philosophies that are aligned well with the SDI 2.0 see: Carl Rogers, On Becoming a Person (New York, Houghton Mifflin, 1961); and Erich Fromm, Man for Himself: An Inquiry into the Psychology of Ethics, (New York: Henry Holt and Company, 1947).

12. There is no generally accepted academic definition of emotional intelligence. For a comprehensive review of the various models and their views of competencies and traits, consult: Susan E. Rivers, Isaac J. Handley-Miner, John D. Mayer, and David R. Caruso, "Emotional Intelligence," in The Cambridge Handbook of Intelligence, 2nd Ed., ed. Robert J. Sternberg (Cambridge, UK, Cambridge University Press, 2020).

13. Structured SDI-based experiences positively affect self-ratings of emotional intelligence competencies of self-awareness, social awareness, self-management, and relationship management. Tim Scudder, Relationship Intelligence Participant Workbook (Carlsbad, CA, Personal Strengths Publishing, 2005).

14. The five keys to conflict were first presented in: Tim Scudder, Michael Patterson, and Kent Mitchell, Have a Nice Conflict, (Jossey Bass: San Francisco, CA, 2012)

15. Michael Maccoby claims there is only one irrefutable definition of a leader: someone people follow. This implies that leadership is a relationship between leader and follower. Michael Maccoby and Tim Scudder, The Leaders We Need and What Makes Us Follow, 2nd Ed. (Carlsbad, CA, Personal Strengths Publishing, 2018).

16. For a rich consideration of the link between freedom and accountability, see Peter Koestenbaum and Peter Block, Freedom and Accountability at Work (San Francisco, CA: Jossey-Bass/Pfieffer, 2001).

Part 2: Motivational Value Systems

1. The test-retest reliability of the SDI is +/- six points. Porter, *Relationship Awareness Theory,* 68.

2. The term congruent is used here with the same meaning as expressed by Carl Rogers. It is the alignment of experience, awareness, and communication. For a full consideration of this concept see "A Tentative Formulation of a General Law of Interpersonal Relationships" in Rogers, *On Becoming a Person,* 338-346.

3. The first SDI, published in 1971, described three types. The first SDI to feature the charting triangle was published in 1973 and identified six types, but provided interpretive text for only three; there was no circle for the Hub in the center. Instead, the boundaries of the other six types continued into the center. Unpublished versions of the triangle showed two different sets of boundaries, each identifying nine types. Early versions of the *Strength Deployment Inventory - Feedback Edition* and *Strength Deployment Inventory - Expectations Edition* showed as few as six and as many as 10 types on the triangle. The fact that Porter finally arrived at a set of seven types is of historical significance, because these seven types are constructed in exactly the same way as the seven normal personality types described in a little-known article by Sigmund Freud, "Libidinal Types," *Psychoanalytic Quarterly* 1, no. 1 (1932): 3-6.

4. Regarding the Hub, Porter said: "We set the boundary more or less empirically at 11 points above and below the mean (33 ⅓) on each side (approximately 1 standard deviation above and below the mean). We have since learned that this may have been too loose since some studies have indicated statistically discriminable differences between inner-hubs (½ SD above and below) and blue-hubs, red-hubs, and green hubs (from ½ SD out to 1 full SD from the mean). At present, however, we see no reason to press for greater precision in what can at best be an arbitrary boundary setting exercise." Porter, Relationship Awareness Theory, 67.

5. For a full consideration of learning styles see Sharan B. Merriam, Rosemary S. Cafella, and Lisa M. Baumgartner, Learning in Adulthood: a Comprehensive Guide, (San Francisco: Jossey-Bass, 2007).

6. Five-factor models include Openness to Experience, Conscientiousness, Extraversion, Agreeableness, and Neuroticism. Five-factor theory has had a significant effect on personality research and education. For a discussion of this see Robert R. McCrae, "Personality Theories for the 21st Century," Teaching of Psychology 38, no. 3 (2011).

7. Carl Jung believed that each person had a dominant cognitive function, a data collecting function of sensing or intuition, or a decision-making function of thinking or feeling. Carl Gustav Jung, *Psychological Types,* (New York: Harcourt Brace, 1923).

Parts 2 and 3: Motivational Value System and Conflict Sequence

The descriptions for the Motivational Value Systems and Conflict Sequences were assembled from many sources. Chief among them were: Porter, "On the Development"; Porter, Relationship Awareness Theory; and Elias H. Porter, "Strength Deployment Inventory," (Carlsbad, CA: Personal Strengths Publishing, 2005). The authors also referred to descriptions of personality types in Fromm, Man for Himself; and the continued work by Fromm's colleague, Michael Maccoby, Why Work? 2nd ed., (Alexandria, VA: Miles River Press, 1995); Michael Maccoby, Narcissistic Leaders, (Boston, MA: Harvard Business School Press, 2007); and to Personal Strengths Publishing's archival files and several out-of-print training resources written by Porter. The definitions of the words that make up the Motivational Value System names that are provided at the beginning of each MVS section were drawn from the New Oxford American Dictionary. In cases where the exact words were not defined in that dictionary, definitions of similar forms of the words were used to produce the definitions as provided here.

Part 3: Conflict Sequences

1. The descriptions of the Conflict Sequences were not included in the SDI until the 1996 edition, which was also the first edition to delineate the Conflict Sequence regions on the triangle, based on Porter's mathematical definitions. Prior to the 1996 SDI, the conflict information was only available in a facilitator's manual and as "Exercise 4" in a workshop kit called the Basic Course.

2. (see part 2, n. 1).

3. "As a second major premise, Relationship Awareness Theory holds that there are, at the very least, two clear, distinguishably different conditions in the stimulus world that affect patterns of behavior. One of these conditions exists when we are free to pursue the gratifications we seek from others. The second condition exists when we are faced with conflict and opposition so that we are not free to pursue our gratifications but must resort to the preservation of our own integrity and self-esteem. The behavior traits we exhibit under these two conditions truly differ. When we are free to pursue our gratifications, we are more or less uniformly predictable, but in the face of conflict and opposition we undergo changes in motivations that link into different bodies of beliefs and concepts that are, in turn, expressed in yet different behavior traits. We are predictably uniform in our behavior when we are free, and we are predictably variable as we meet with obstructing conditions in our stimulus worlds." Italics in original. Porter, "On the Development," 306.

4. Porter, Relationship Awareness Theory, 25.

Part 4: Strength Deployment

1. For a robust examination of strengths that are not part of a personality typology, refer to Christopher Peterson and Martin Seligman, Character Strengths and Virtues, (New York: Oxford University Press, 2004).

2. For a thorough consideration of other factors that influence the way people perceive each other, refer to David A. Kenny, Interpersonal Perception: a Social Relations Analysis, (New York, Guilford Press, 1994) and Sandr Graham and Valeris S. Folkes, Attribution Theory: Applications to Achievement, Mental Health, and Interpersonal Conflict, (Hilldale, NJ, Lawrence Erlbaum Associates, 1990).

3. The person and situation interact systemically to influence behavior. Refer to the article in Part 5 of this book: The SDI 2.0 View of Personality for an exploration of this concept, which is rooted in Kurt Lewin's theory of personality.

4. The Hub personality and related strengths were not part of the original SDI. See History and Development of the SDI 2.0 in Part 5 of this book.

5. To understand more about the 28 strengths and how they fit within the broader theory of personality, refer to SDI 2.0 Methodology and Meaning in Part 5 of this book.

6. Two excellent sources for the link between choice and accountability are: Edward Deci, Why We Do What We Do, (New York, Penguin, 1995) and Peter Koestenmbaum and Peter Block, Freedom and Accountability at Work, (San Francisco, 2001).

The ability to produce a book like this is dependent upon learning from others. Nothing here would have been possible without the original work of Elias Porter, who introduced the SDI to the world in 1971. And that would not have been possible without foundations built by Erich Fromm, Karen Horney, and Carl Rogers.

I owe a debt of gratitude to all the people who invited me to work with leaders and teams in their organizations, which provided the best possible learning environment for me. I also deeply appreciate partners in dialogue who challenged my thinking and contributed to the content of this book. Chief among them are Gil Brady, Jeff Gaines, Debra LaCroix, Ray Linder, Michael Maccoby, Mike Patterson, Kevin Small, and Steve Wood.

— Tim Scudder